Living In A Fascist Country

Books by Vernon Coleman include:

The Medicine Men (1975)
Paper Doctors (1976)
Stress Control (1978)
The Home Pharmacy (1980)
Aspirin or Ambulance (1980)
Face Values (1981)
The Good Medicine Guide (1982)
Bodypower (1983)
Thomas Winsden's Cricketing Almanack (1983)
Diary of a Cricket Lover (1984)
Bodysense (1984)
Life Without Tranquillisers (1985)
The Story Of Medicine (1985, 1998)
Mindpower (1986)
Addicts and Addictions (1986)
Dr Vernon Coleman's Guide To Alternative Medicine (1988)
Stress Management Techniques (1988)
Know Yourself (1988)
The Health Scandal (1988)
The 20 Minute Health Check (1989)
Sex For Everyone (1989)
Mind Over Body (1989)
Eat Green Lose Weight (1990)
How To Overcome Toxic Stress (1990)
Why Animal Experiments Must Stop (1991)
The Drugs Myth (1992)
Complete Guide To Sex (1993)
How to Conquer Backache (1993)
How to Conquer Pain (1993)
Betrayal of Trust (1994)
Know Your Drugs (1994, 1997)
Food for Thought (1994, revised edition 2000)
The Traditional Home Doctor (1994)
People Watching (1995)
Relief from IBS (1995)
The Parent's Handbook (1995)
Men in Dresses (1996)

Power over Cancer (1996)
Crossdressing (1996)
How to Conquer Arthritis (1996)
High Blood Pressure (1996)
How To Stop Your Doctor Killing You (1996, revised edition 2003)
Fighting For Animals (1996)
Alice and Other Friends (1996)
Spiritpower (1997)
How To Publish Your Own Book (1999)
How To Relax and Overcome Stress (1999)
Animal Rights – Human Wrongs (1999)
Superbody (1999)
Complete Guide to Life (2000)
Strange But True (2000)
Daily Inspirations (2000)
Stomach Problems: Relief At Last (2001)
How To Overcome Guilt (2001)
How To Live Longer (2001)
Sex (2001)
We Love Cats (2002)
England Our England (2002)
Rogue Nation (2003)
People Push Bottles Up Peaceniks (2003)
The Cats' Own Annual (2003)
Confronting The Global Bully (2004)
Saving England (2004)
Why Everything Is Going To Get Worse Before It Gets Better (2004)
The Secret Lives of Cats (2004)
The Cat Basket (2005)
The Truth They Won't Tell You (And Don't Want You To Know)
      About The EU (2005)
Living in a Fascist Country (2006)

novels
The Village Cricket Tour (1990)
The Bilbury Chronicles (1992)
Bilbury Grange (1993)
Mrs Caldicot's Cabbage War (1993)
Bilbury Revels (1994)

Deadline (1994)
The Man Who Inherited a Golf Course (1995)
Bilbury Pie (1995)
Bilbury Country (1996)
Second Innings (1999)
Around the Wicket (2000)
It's Never Too Late (2001)
Paris In My Springtime (2002)
Mrs Caldicot's Knickerbocker Glory (2003)
Too Many Clubs And Not Enough Balls (2005)
Tunnel (1980, 2005)

as Edward Vernon
Practice Makes Perfect (1977)
Practise What You Preach (1978)
Getting Into Practice (1979)
Aphrodisiacs – An Owner's Manual (1983)

with Alice
Alice's Diary (1989)
Alice's Adventures (1992)

with Donna Antoinette Coleman
How To Conquer Health Problems Between Ages 50 and 120 (2003)
Health Secrets Doctors Share With Their Families (2005)

Living In A Fascist Country

Conspiracies, peak oil, greedy politicians, endless religious wars and your disappearing freedom and privacy.

Vernon Coleman

BLUE
BOOKS

Published by Blue Books, Publishing House, Trinity Place, Barnstaple, Devon EX32 9HG, England.

ISBN: 1 899726 36 5

Reprinted 2006

A catalogue record for this book is available from the British Library.

Printed by Antony Rowe Ltd

Dedicated to Donna Antoinette, whose compassion, sensitivity, thoughtfulness and understanding have contributed in so many ways during the researching and writing of this book.

Warning

Don't expect anyone working for an organisation (particularly an organisation associated with the Government) to be on your side. On the contrary you will do well to regard them as your enemy.

Remember that a sense of paranoia is a realistic and effective defence against the oppressive forces of a Government which governs by deceit. Paranoia, not vigilance, is the real price of liberty.

Remember that it is your responsibility to look after yourself. So please do. Your country really does need you. Regard anything said by a politician who is a member of one of the three main parties as a lie until proved otherwise. Post a lookout if you feed birds in the park. Buy newspapers for the crosswords but don't expect to find any news. Take everything you see or hear on television or radio with a very large pinch of salt. And treat everything broadcast by the BBC as fiction.

When you read this book we strongly suggest that you draw the curtains and lock the doors. If you are discovered and questioned by the authorities we suggest you say you picked it up by mistake thinking it to be a railway timetable. Those readers who are particularly nervous might like to take the book with them under the bedclothes and read it by torchlight.

Contents

Preface

We are losing our freedom and our privacy. Everything we hold dear is being threatened by the New Order. The world is changing so fast that it is difficult to keep up. Britain and America are now fascist states. Why? What is going on? Whatever happened to democracy? Who is behind it all? How did we come to find ourselves in what the politicians boast will be an everlasting war?

You will, I hope, find at least some of the answers in this book. The way the Government is clamping down on free speech this may well be your last chance to read the truth.

Vernon Coleman, January 2006

'If you can tremble with indignation every time an injustice is committed in the world, we are comrades.'
CHE GUEVARA

Chapter One

Living In One Of Kafka's Nightmares

1

It is sometimes difficult to realise that what is happening is happening. It's like our world but nothing like it. With increasing frequency I wake up thinking I'm living in one of Kafka's nightmare fantasies.

Then, a little later, when I've caught up with the day's news, I *know* I'm living in one of Kafka's nightmares.

2

'While the State exists, there can be no freedom.
When there is freedom there will be no State.'
LENIN (1919)

3

One day in early September in 2005 I sat listening to the radio. Charles Clarke, British Home Secretary, was appealing to European MEPs (European MEPs not MPs at Westminster you will note) to give him the right to protect the British public's privacy and freedom by allowing him to listen to our telephone calls and to read our e-mails, now, yesterday and for as many tomorrows as you can imagine. The Home Secretary wanted MEPs to force telephone companies to store the details of all the old mobile phone calls we make and to hand over everything they have to the Government. He sounded quite passionate about this. He wanted to protect our privacy by taking it away. He said that only by listening to all our telephone calls and being able to get lists of everyone we'd called in the last year, and when and where we'd been at the time, would he able to protect our privacy. He said he needed to listen to all our conversations and read all our e-mails and faxes because of the suicide bombers who had attacked London. I don't expect Mr Clarke will listen to all our phone calls himself or, indeed, sit and read all our e-mails, though to be honest I wish he would. Firstly, this would keep him busy and stop him doing any more damage. Secondly, he might learn something. However, I suspect he plans to delegate the work to specially hired nosy lackeys.

4

Clarke, and everyone else in the Labour Government, insists that the suicide bombers who are said to have attacked London in July 2005 had nothing whatsoever to do with Britain's illegal war on Iraq. Or the illegal war on Afghanistan. Or any of the other wars we have started recently. They say the bombs have nothing to do with the fact that we are the main allies of the world's most feared terrorist nation and that we are fighting a religious war against oil-rich Muslim countries.

Everyone in the world (except Blair and the members of his crooked gang of thugs) knows that Britain is a terrorist target because our lying Prime Minister is a war criminal who took us into an illegal war.

But Blair, Blunkett, Straw, Clarke, Brown and the other low life bacteria who have taken over our country deny this.

One of the suicide bombers said (in a video message recorded beforehand) that he was blowing himself up because Britain had invaded Iraq. You might think that a man who had decided to blow himself up would know why he was doing it but Blair, Straw and Clarke knew better. Blair, Clarke and Straw decided there was another reason, though they didn't know what it was.

5

'We were the first to assert that the more complicated the forms of civilisation, the more restricted the freedom of the individual must become.'
BENITO MUSSOLINI

6

There isn't a Labour Minister (or, indeed, a senior politician in Britain) who understands and publicly accepts that Britain, America and Israel are, to much of the world, the three worst terrorist nations on the planet. Bush and Blair have made millions of law-abiding citizens feel ashamed of their nationality; under this so-called 'leadership' we are the new Nazis.

7

Listening to Clarke was just too surreal and made me think that perhaps the Government had started putting hallucinogenic drugs into the water supply. So I turned off the radio and turned on the television.

On the television I listened to a TV reporter telling us that the American President's mother (herself a former First Lady and, therefore, no innocent media waif unaware of the significance of her words) had told poor black people who had escaped, at long last, from devastated New Orleans and were sheltering, in a gym somewhere in Texas, that they were better off there than they had been before. They had lost their homes and their possessions and, in many cases, many members of their family, and there was the President's mother telling them how damned lucky they were.

At this point I felt that I had lost all touch with reality. I turned off the television and opened my newspaper.

And there I read that the people of Afghanistan were sending money to America to pay for poor black people who were trapped in Louisiana and Mississippi to be rescued. The troops and helicopters which might have been used to help them were, at the time, busy bombing Afghanistan and killing innocent women and children whose only crime was being born in a foreign country. The dirt-poor Afghans, having had their homes and their businesses destroyed by the Americans, were sending money to America, the rich country which was bombing them, to help its poor people.

As indeed was Iran which America wants to bomb, and Cuba which it has been trying to destroy for longer than most people can remember.

Surreal. Simply too surreal.

And as I turned over the pages of the newspaper, I found a summary of a speech by a Government Minister telling us that we don't bother to vote in elections because we are so content.

So content?

'Life,' said the Minister, 'is better than ever under Labour.'

Here are some of the ways in which life is better than ever before.

♦ NHS patients are forty times as likely to contract an MRSA infection as are patients in other European countries.

♦ If you want a doctor outside office hours your chances of getting one to visit you at home are approximately the same as your chances of winning the lottery. Actually, they are probably worse. If you do the lottery you might win it.

♦ Post offices are closing and old people often have to travel miles to collect their pensions. Many find that the absence of public transport makes this more difficult than it might otherwise be.

♦ In many areas of the country household rubbish is collected every two weeks instead of weekly – although even this service is often unpredictable and unreliable. And it is illegal to have a garden bonfire.

♦ Council rates are rising at a rate well above inflation, and will continue to do for the foreseeable future in order to pay the inflation-proofed pensions promised to former council employees who have retired in their 50s. (Leading many citizens to believe that councils now exist to look after their employees rather than to provide an infrastructure for their rate-paying citizens.)

♦ Many of our villages have no schools or shops. Villagers who do not have cars find life difficult because local bus and train services are rapidly disappearing.

♦ Car owners have a rougher time in Britain than anywhere else in the so-called developed world. Britain's roads are now officially the most overcrowded and worst kept in Europe while fuel taxes are the highest. Motorists pay £126.7 billion a year to the economy through buying and maintaining their vehicles. Over £43 billion a year is collected in taxes from motorists every year. But of that £43 billion, just over £6 billion is re-invested in roads. Much of the rest is presumably spent on orange cones and speed cameras.

- There is a national shortage of dentists. Whenever dentists announce that they are prepared to accept NHS patients long queues form. Providing NHS dentists for all was one of Blair's many forgotten lies. 'If I promise to do something and don't then I've let you down, he said.' If I repeatedly make promises I make no effort to keep then you are right to call me a liar and a cheat and a fraud.' If Blair were running a business he would have been closed down and arrested for dishonesty years ago.

- Seven years after the Labour Government introduced its national literacy strategy almost half the boys and a third of the girls in Britain leave primary school unable to write properly. If older style criteria were used the figures would doubtless be worse – New Labour probably measure a citizen's literacy by their ability to put a cross in the appropriate place on a ballot paper. In my more cynical moments I sometimes wonder whether the high levels of illiteracy are not welcomed by the Government. The illiterate are hardly likely to take much interest in what is going on around them and I doubt if many of their number have spent much time protesting about illegal wars or EU rebates. My fears and suspicions are not allayed by the Government's apparent lack of enthusiasm for traditional teaching methods which work and, the corollary, its seemingly unlimited enthusiasm for new teaching techniques which neither work nor seem likely ever to work.

- Bullying is one of the few growth activities in Britain – hardly surprising since teachers are no longer allowed to admonish children, let alone give them a clip around the ear. Political correctness and American-style no-risk litigation is creating mob rule. There are schools in Britain where English is taught as a second language (if at all).

♦ The Prime Minister insists that he doesn't know how many illegal migrants there are in the UK. He should ask the Home Office. In 2005 the men at the Home Office with index-linked pensions and expensive computers estimated that there could be somewhere between 310,000 and 570,000 illegal immigrants living in the UK. There may be more. There will not be fewer. These are people who managed to get into the country through our anti-terrorist barriers and then stayed here despite the police, the anti-terrorism squads, special branch, MI5, and all the rest of them. Just half a million or so people have successfully avoided the men in cheap uniforms who are so good at confiscating nail clippers from little old ladies.

♦ There is a massive shortage of teachers in British schools today – and the situation is deteriorating. In order to boost the alleged number of staff in our schools, New Labour count trainees and unqualified assistants when they are counting 'teachers'. They probably count dinner ladies and any pedestrians wandering past too.

♦ Queues used to be the trademark of Government offices. There have always been queues at Post Offices and Passport Offices. That's because the people working in these places have a monopoly, don't have to make a profit, don't feel any sense of responsibility towards their customers and don't give a fig about anything other than themselves. Nowadays, there are queues everywhere. If you want to buy a newspaper or a magazine in W.H. Smith or a pair of knickers in Marks and Spencer you have to stand in a queue, edging your way forwards between little barriers as though you're about to see a bed that Henry V slept in. The queues in banks stretch out onto the pavement. The posts and nylon railings make sure we stand neatly in line and wait our turn to get in touch with our own money. All this queuing inspires Orwellian fears that the Government wants to subdue us, as was managed so successfully in the Soviet Union. People who have to spend their time queuing don't have the time or the energy to demonstrate or protest. There's truth enough in that. But in shops and banks the queues are, on a practical level, the result of EU employment laws which have forced companies to cut costs every way they can. Companies

22

now hire fewer people and make us wait to spend our money. There are queues in Government offices despite overmanning but in shops and banks there are queues because of undermanning. As queues get longer customers become irritated. As customers become irritated so the overworked staff become increasingly edgy and bad-tempered.

◆ Our public buildings are deteriorating rapidly. The best railway stations (aesthetically and practically) are decaying Victorian buildings. Many of our sewage systems and water delivery systems are Victorian in origin. Britain was never as well served as it was during Queen Victoria's reign. Since then the public services have declined steadily.

◆ In the former Soviet Union and in East Germany it was official policy to favour the children of working class parents against those from the professional classes when selecting students for university courses. That is what happens in Britain today.

◆ Numerous universities have announced that they will stop teaching boring and unpopular subjects such as mathematics. There has, however, been a rise in the number of students taking brewing, tourism, media and cake decorating courses. Students may not be able to read or add up but their cake decorating and nail painting skills are impressive. A real university education involves learning how to discover facts you didn't know you needed to know about subjects you didn't know existed. Modern education consists of teaching things that students want to learn (because they are intellectually undemanding and fairly glamorous) rather than skills that are in demand. And so we have a constant shortage of dentists and plumbers but a surfeit of unemployed and unemployable television producers and film directors. Employers don't hire graduates because most of them have useless degrees in brewing or surf management, which are neither a measure of knowledge nor of intellectual ability, and because degrees are no longer even an adequate proof of literacy.

◆ Airports and railway stations are routinely patrolled by armed guards with their fingers on their triggers. Our children grow up in a world where no one is sure who is being kept in and who is being kept out. The police shoot innocent travellers. There is no longer a clear dividing line between the good guys and the bad

23

guys. The men in black hats may still be wearing black hats but the white hats are no longer white. They say that they are taking away our freedom and confiscating our civil rights to protect us. This is a lie.

♦ We have to fill in countless forms, and produce reams of confidential paperwork, just to open a bank account. They claim all this helps prevent terrorism and crime. But we know it doesn't. It's another lie.

♦ It is patently obvious to anyone with half a brain that street crime has gone up since policemen stopped patrolling our streets. Only senior policemen (who would have difficulty mustering half a brain between them) deny this obvious truth.

♦ There are 11 million young people between the ages of ten and 25 in Britain. Just under 3 million of them committed a crime last year. One third of all male teenagers and youths commit at least one crime a year. Eight per cent of males in that age group commit six or more crimes a year.

♦ Under the Labour Government of Blair, British manufacturing industry lost one million jobs – in less than eight years. Most of the people who gave up jobs in industry ended up working for the Government as civil servants.

♦ Young women who are or might become pregnant are shunned by sensible employers who know that they can't afford to comply with the absurd legislation brought in to prevent discrimination against young women who are or might become pregnant. (This rapidly growing area of discrimination is said to be despite the legislation. It isn't. It's *because* of the legislation.)

8

'The finest opportunity ever given to the world was thrown away because the passion for equality made vain the hope for freedom.'
LORD ACTON

9

The Government says it doesn't have any money to maintain the nation's infrastructure because it has to spend so much protecting us from terrorists and fighting the endless wars started by Bush and Blair.

I hate to be the one to have to tell you this, but the money and effort they are spending on protecting us will make no difference whatsoever – other than to make our lives increasingly unbearable.

I don't know whether our politicians and anti-terror chiefs are stupid, incompetent or deliberately doing their worst to protect us. Maybe it's a combination of all three.

The fact is that even the Home Office admits that around half a million people have entered Britain illegally in the last year or two. If you're a terrorist you can buy a mobile telephone easily. You don't have to give your name and address. If you're a terrorist (or criminal) you can 'launder' money easily and quickly without ever opening a bank account. If you're a terrorist you can do everything you want to do, and go everywhere you want to go, without using a cheque book or a credit card. You can, if you wish, travel all over Europe without ever once having to give your name.

All the effort and money spent on 'protecting us' simply makes life difficult for those who are honest, and reminds us to be afraid. It's difficult to avoid the conclusion that that is exactly what they want.

10

'Our contemporary Western society, in spite of its material, intellectual and political progress, is increasingly less conducive to mental health, and tends to undermine the inner security, happiness, reason and the capacity for love in the individual; it tends to turn him into an automaton who pays for his human failure with increasing mental sickness, and with despair hidden under a frantic drive for work and so-called pleasure.'
DR ERICH FROMM

11

No one knows exactly how many Iraqi civilians have been killed by American and British troops since the invasion of Iraq. The best estimate is that our joint efforts have killed over 100,000 civilians. Mostly women and children. Most of these have been killed by air strikes. Neither these people nor their Government had threatened us in anyway. Their only crime was to live in a country which had oil needed by fat American motorists who drive big cars and like cheap fuel. Killing all these innocent people, at Blair's behest, has cost the British people billions of pounds.

12

'The socialists believe in two things which are absolutely different and perhaps even contradictory: freedom and organisation.'
ELIE HALEVY

13

Things are going to get worse. A lot worse. In the coming decade, there are going to be more wars (all started by the USA and all supported by Britain), higher taxes (to pay for public employee pensions) and more Government control over our lives. Oil prices will rocket. Illogical opposition to nuclear power will see thousands dying in the cold winters we can expect. Thousands more will die in the heat of ever-hotter summers. (Thanks to global warming – and America – our summers will get hotter and our winters will get colder). There will be riots in the darkness when the oil runs out. It won't be long now.

14

'Something is happening here,
But you don't know what it is,
Do you, Mr Jones?'
BOB DYLAN

15

Most Britons are honest and pay their taxes. The authorities assume the opposite is true and by a combination of incomprehensible legislation and persecution of the innocent they have alienated millions and will eventually create a society which fulfils their low expectations.

16

'For conditions even remotely comparable to those now prevailing we must return to Imperial Rome, where the populace was kept in good humour by frequent, gratuitous doses of many kinds of entertainment – from poetical dramas to gladiatorial fights, from recitations of Virgil to all-out boxing, from concerts to military reviews and public executions. But even in Rome there was nothing like the non-stop distraction now provided by newspapers and magazines, by radio, television and the cinema. In 'Brave New World' non-stop distractions of the most fascinating nature (the feelies, orgy-porgy, centrifugal bumble puppy) are deliberately used as instruments of policy, for the purpose of preventing people from paying too much attention to the realities of the social and political situation.'
ALDOUS HUXLEY

17

Why should you believe me?

You don't have to.

But check out the list of the predictions I have made in recent years. (There is a short list of my medical predictions in my book *How To Stop Your Doctor Killing You.*)

18

'Despots themselves do not deny that freedom is excellent; only they desire it for themselves alone, and they maintain that everyone else is altogether unworthy of it.'
ALEXIS DE TOCQUEVILLE , *L'ANCIEN RÉGIME* 1856

19

So, what is going on? Which came first – the threat from the terrorists or the laws which impinge on our freedom?

It's easy to answer that: in both America and Britain the new, oppressive anti-libertarian laws which have been imposed were planned and prepared long before the terrorist attacks on America in 2001. The terror attacks were, it is clear, a timely and welcomed excuse for the pre-planned new legislation. And that leads to the next question.

Since the terror attacks were so convenient, were they planned or executed by our Governments or did our Governments simply know about them and let them go ahead?

There are many people who believe the first of these explanations and many more who believe the second.

All this is significant because it alters (or should alter) our perception of, and acceptance of, such impositions as identity cards.

20

Why did Bush do it?

The answer is in two words: 'peak oil'.

Think 'oil shortage'.

Not just a modest shortage.

But a major, brain fogging shortage.

The end of oil is in sight.

The fight is on for the final barrels.

21

'What good fortune for governments that the people do not think.'
ADOLF HITLER

22

Why are our traditional freedoms being taken away? Why are we losing our liberty? Why did Blair ignore the wishes of the British public, lie to the House of Commons and the nation and support America's overtly illegal invasions of Afghanistan and Iraq? Why did America invade Afghanistan and Iraq? What is the EU for? How far back does all this go? What's the underlying reason for it all?

I have for years now tried to resist the temptation to believe in a conspiracy theory.

But there has to be something going on.

And here is my theory.

The basic factor is that the world is running out of oil. And without oil the world, as we know it, will change. The future of the USA lies in the balance. China and India will control the 21st century in the way that the USA controlled the 20th century and Britain, France and Spain shared control of previous centuries.

The key to understanding what is happening is the fact that the Americans were secretly aware that the world was approaching peak oil thirty years ago. The American oil and arms industry bosses knew that this would destroy their businesses unless they did something to control the oil. And they also knew that the decline in available oil which would follow peak oil would result in rioting and revolution. They knew they had to bring in laws which they could use to control the people, to ensure that all the available oil was available to be used (at taxpayers' expense) not for heating or for hospitals or for essential industries but for the arms industry.

To do all this they needed an everlasting war. They needed to keep us constantly afraid.

As we descend the slope after peak oil, so oil will become very expensive. But the everlasting war will mean that the armed forces will be able to insist that they buy much, most or all of the oil. Taxpayers will pay for it of course. And the people who own the oil and who sell the arms will get ever richer.

23

George W. Bush is controlled by people who are big in oil and arms. George is a tool. A mouthpiece. A puppet. An actor trying to remember his lines (but not as good at it as Ronald Reagan was).

For thirty years the oil and arms industry bosses have known that their industries are in decline and are threatened by the oncoming problem of 'peak oil'. The oil industry will be threatened with extinction if it runs out of the stuff it sells. The arms industry will be finished if there is no oil to put into armoured vehicles and military aeroplanes. You can't make or transport weapons of mass destruction without oil.

Everything that has happened in the first years of the 21st century can be explained in three words: oil, arms and money. The men who control Bush needed an everlasting war. They needed a war that would give them access to the world's diminishing stocks of oil. They needed a war against the Arabs.

And, as a by-product, the Zionists among the oil and arms hotshots saw a way to do Israel a great big favour while helping to enrich themselves.

24

'Freedom is the freedom to say that two plus two makes four.
If that is granted, all else follows.'
GEORGE ORWELL, *1984*

25

Back in the early 1990s the Americans invaded Iraq for the first time. But the voters, and the world, weren't ready for it. And there was a lot of opposition. The Americans pulled out without killing Saddam Hussein. They needed him alive. A demon for another day.

The Americans knew that they needed to plan things so that we would accept an invasion and occupation of Iraq.

26

'The mass of men serve the state not as men but as machines,
with their bodies. They are the standing army and the jailers and the
constables. In most cases there is no free exercise whatever of the judgement
or of the moral sense; but they put themselves on a level with wood
and earth and stones; and wooden men can perhaps be
manufactured that will serve the purpose as well. Such
command no more respect than men of straw
or a lump of dirt.'
HENRY DAVID THOREAU

27

The people who want to run things knew that they needed to give themselves the power to control us completely. They needed to keep us constantly afraid; so afraid that they would be able to do whatever they wanted to do with us and to us. They needed us to hate (and fear) the Muslims. They needed an everlasting religious war which would give them an excuse to invade oil-rich Middle Eastern countries, and which would also give them an excuse to introduce repressive laws giving them all the power, and taking away from us our freedom to object and to complain.

28

'You are either with us or against us.'
THE AMERICAN GOVERNMENT MOTTO

29

The Americans knew that they couldn't just dive into Iraq (and Iran) and grab the oil without an excuse. September 11th gave them the excuse they needed. (The evidence – which I will tell you about in this book – has convinced me that what happened on September 11th 2001 was either planned or allowed by the American Government.)

The oppressive legislation which was brought in as a result of the September 11th attack was all prepared beforehand. It wasn't produced as a result of the attack. The attack provided the excuse to bring it in.

The Americans blamed the attack on Saddam Hussein (even though they knew very well that it had nothing whatsoever to do with Iraq) because that gave them an excellent excuse to invade Iraq for a second time – but this time with massive public support from the American people.

30

So that's why George did it.

However, I don't believe for a second that Blair, Prescott, Blunkett, Brown, Straw *et al* are part of a global conspiracy.

Do you?

No. Quite. They are too damned dumb, petty and small-minded. And, superficially, they make strange bedfellows for Bush's right wing Republican oil company mogul chums.

But things aren't quite as odd as they seem.

After all, if you go far enough to the right in political terms you become a left-wing communist. And if you go far enough to the left you become a right-wing fascist. Blair and Bush have more in common than most people imagine. Both have created fascist nations.

But that's not why the British and the American Governments of Blair and Bush get on so well together: it just explains why they are able to cooperate.

The simple truth is that the British Government got involved in America's war because Blair is a greedy liar who wants/needs to make loads of money when he stops being Prime Minister. Blair's earning power will be vastly greater if he plays footsie with the Yanks. What's the betting that within twenty-four months of resigning as Prime Minister, Blair becomes a highly paid director of one of the companies close to Bush and Cheney?

And the Labour Party's immediate aim (to stay in power) depends to a large extent upon the support of Rupert Murdoch. Blair knew that Murdoch was essential right from the start and he and the Labour Party have always done everything they can to keep Murdoch happy. Murdoch, after all, controls the editorial policies of four of Britain's most important newspapers (*The Sun*, the *News of the World*, *The Times* and *The Sunday Times*) and the numerous channels of Sky Television. I suspect that Murdoch has made it clear that he is prepared to support Blair as long as Blair supports Bush. (We can however thank Murdoch for keeping us out of the euro. Blair would have happily taken us into the euro if Murdoch had not been opposed.)

31

'Tyranny is always better organised than freedom.'
CHARLES PÉGUY (1943)

32

I believe that Blair took us into an illegal war because he is a vain and greedy man.

First, Blair is now enormously popular in the USA. Whenever he goes there people cheer him. He doesn't get cheered much in Britain. He likes being cheered. So he sucks up to the Americans. And gets cheered.

Second, Blair has bought a large house in London which is well beyond his present means. I suspect that the only way he will be able to pay off the mortgage will be to get good jobs with his American pals. His autobiography won't pay the mortgage. It probably won't even pay for Cherie's frocks. Blair will, I strongly suspect, end up a director of the Carlyle Group (along with John Major).

So is that why we went to war?

Did Blair just want to suck up to Bush and his pals so that he could guarantee himself a wealthy future?

Did our nation get embroiled in an illegal war so that Blair could get rich?

Were Londoners bombed because of Blair's need to pay off his mortgage?

Have the police in England now adopted a shoot to kill (innocent or not) policy because of this?

Yes.

It's all because we have a Prime Minister who wants a house he can't afford.

33

That's why Blair did it.

Blair has huge personal debts. His pal George W. Bush has probably promised Blair a directorship of the Carlyle Group. Blair has sold out his country for a relatively modest mess of potage. The rest of them (Brown, Straw and Prescott et al) are opportunists, small time political crooks who just want to survive in power as long as they can. They like the salaries, the chauffeur driven cars, the bodyguards and the ability to be above the law. They voted for the war because Blair told them to. And because they knew that if they didn't they would have to resign (like Robin Cook) and lose the salaries, the chauffeur driven cars, the bodyguards and the ability to be above the law.

The added laws which are being introduced in response to the instructions from America (sometimes via Brussels but sometimes straight from Washington) are welcomed because they help to make sure that they can stay in power for even longer.

The state of fear in which we now live (thanks to the everlasting war) means that they can bring in countless new laws which will cement their positions in our new fascist world.

Blair and his chums are the ultimately greedy politicians, seduced by the glamour and excitement of their environment, and terrified that it will all be taken away from them. (Remember Blunkett grasping pitifully and pathetically at the remnants of power?)

The New Labour grandees are just pawns in the hands of Bush's 'owners'.

34

The EU has added layer upon layer of its own fascist bureaucracy onto the fascist bureaucracy developed by Blair.

The absence of any conflict between Blair's plans and the EU's dictates is derived from the fact that the EU Commission tends to do what America wants – bringing in oppressive new pan-European laws (such as ID cards) when the Americans demand them, and weakening the strong European countries (France and Germany) so that they are too preoccupied to take much notice of what America is up to.

The Americans created and support the EU and they keep it under control. (It is, after all, much easier to control one superstate than lots of small ones).

35

America has been taken over by a commercial tyranny and we're living in a fascist nation which is, for all practical purposes, little more than an American state.

They dismiss those of us who claim that what happened on September 11th was done by or with the approval of the American Government as conspiracy theorists, but the fact is that those who would have us believe that we are fighting a war against Al Qaeda terrorists are the real conspiracy theorists.

Around the world, more and more people now believe that the American Government was involved in the September 11th attack on its own territory.

More people believe that George W. Bush and his pals were the driving force behind the attacks on the twin towers than believe that Osama bin Laden and Al Qaeda were responsible.

36

If the oleaginous Bush, Cheney, Blair and Co. are in the minority, struggling to persuade us to believe something that isn't true, but that suits their various purposes, doesn't that make them the conspiracy theorists and their version of what happened on September 11th the conspiracy?

37

It is widely believed that the loss of privacy and freedom which has occurred in the first years of the 21st century are a direct result of the September 11th attack on the USA and are essential for our safety and our security.

In the sort of language Labour Ministers would understand, this is bollocks.

In polite parlance it is a lie.

The Government doesn't give a cigar butt about your security. If they did they wouldn't start so many wars, kill so many innocent people and provoke retaliation from terrorists.

38

In America the Government introduced the Homeland Security Act and the Patriot Act. These two bits of cowboy legislation banished many of the rights and freedoms which were guaranteed to American citizens by their Constitution. (America's founding fathers, and the authors of the Constitution, guaranteed inalienable rights to its citizens. Bush and his companions don't seem to understand the meaning of the word 'inalienable'. Actually, there are many words they don't understand. Justice. Peace. Kindness. Caring. Future.)

Bush and his neo-conservative Zionist handlers have introduced face recognition equipment, metal detectors, thumb scanners, retinal scanners, body cavity searches, mass fingerprinting and body scans and other jolly intrusions. These invasions of privacy are now commonplace in the USA. Other countries have introduced similar legislation – often as a direct result of pressure from the USA. In England today our airports and railway stations are routinely patrolled by scary looking police-thugs carrying automatic weapons and wearing flak jackets. They don't much care whether you are innocent or guilty. They have given themselves the right to shoot you anyway.

Our Government of mean and nasty bully boys claim that their hired thugs need to listen to our telephone calls, stick probes up our rear ends and fire dum dum bullets into our brains in order to protect us against terrorists.

And by and large this new legislation has been accepted without protest.

Encouraged by a compliant media, millions have accepted their Government's claims that they must give up freedoms, rights, dignity and privacy because of the war on terror. When the Government says that it must tap all our telephones and listen to all our private calls we accept this invasion of our privacy as essential. Hardly anyone in Parliament or the media dares to question whether or not listening to our telephone calls will actually help stop terrorism (it won't of course, because terrorists and criminals know how to buy telephones which cannot be traced to them).

The argument the Government uses is always the same: 'If you accept our claim that we need to tap your phone then you are with us; if you question our claim then you are clearly against us and for the terrorists.'

This bizarre, indefensible and illogical claim is accepted by millions and, quite disgracefully, by most members of the fourth estate (who would be better off if they were promoted and described as fifth columnists).

The millions who accept this nonsense have, of course, been conned.

39

Think about it carefully.

Having deliberately terrified us (and deliberately exposed us to the constant threat of terrorism) the Government now claims that in order to protect us they need to take away our privacy and our liberty.

Only by taking away our privacy and our liberty, they say, can they protect it.

This is like Casanova seducing a young girl and telling her that the only way for her to save her virginity is to surrender it to him.

40

Politicians make these absurd claims because they are crooks and they need to rob us of our heritage and our rights in order to pay off their own fat mortgages.

Journalists, broadcasters and commentators accept the absurd claims because they are either stupid or bought. (Bought not with money but with a gong in the New Year's Honours List or an invitation to some Downing Street pizza and white wine gala.)

Here are some facts. These are real facts. Not the ersatz variety provided by the Government and the media.

1. The threat from terrorism is no greater now than it was a decade ago. The only difference today is that the September 11th attack was the first significant attack on Americans on American soil. The number of people killed by terrorists in recent years is no greater than the number killed in preceding decades. Our governments have deliberately exaggerated the size of the threat in order to frighten us into accepting their nonsensical new anti-freedom laws. To claim that we are fighting a war on terror is manipulative, populist nonsense.

2. If you take away people's freedoms and rights you are doing the work of the terrorists for them. Bush and Blair claim that the best way we can show the terrorists that they have not won is to continue with our lives as before. But we cannot do this. Bush and Blair have changed our world so dramatically that we cannot possibly 'continue as before'.

3. The new American and British legislation which was introduced after September 11th 2001 was all prepared and ready for introduction well before September 11th 2001. The attack on America may have been an excuse for the introduction of new legislation which limits our freedom but it was most certainly not the cause.

4. Supporters of Bush and Blair defend their policies by saying 'they started it'. By 'they' they mean the Muslims. With monotonous regularity they remind us of what happened (or appeared to happen) on September 11th 2001. But what happened then (or what they want us to think happened then) didn't start anything. It was simply an excuse to rack up the action. The war we are supposed to be fighting was triggered long ago by America's imperialist foreign policies. America started this 'war'. It's a power grab, a money grab, an oil grab and a religious war. The American and British Governments like to pretend that the 'war on terror' which we are supposed to be fighting originated with Muslim extremists wanting to dominate the

world. However, the evidence shows that the Muslim fundamentalists who are said to be behind the recent terror attacks on America and its allies are inspired not by some evil determination to dominate the world but by a not entirely irrational determination to force America out of Arab countries, to put a stop to the Americanisation of Arab states and to stop America stealing their oil. The anger against America has doubtless been helped along by a certain yearning for revenge. Since America and its allies have now killed several million Muslims such a feeling is hardly surprising. (Even saying such a thing is now illegal since any criticism of the Government is counted as support for the enemy. Actually, I know who *my* main enemies are. They are Blair, Brown, Blunkett, Straw, Clarke *et al.*)

5. Much of what is being done in the name of the war on terror is nothing whatsoever to do with the war on terror. Governments, local councils, banks, insurance companies and others who demand that you give them personal and confidential information know very well that they are demanding this information for financial reasons. Governments and local councils want to maximise their tax take and banks and insurance companies want personal information from you so that they can more effectively sell you their products. Both Governmental and private organisations also want your private information so that they can sell it to other organisations.

6. For some time I have believed that it is Blair's personal greed and stupidity which have led him to support America's illegal invasion of Iraq. I thought he wanted to ingratiate himself with Bush's rich and powerful pals so that he could acquire profitable directorships and get onto the lucrative lecture circuit in the USA. And I thought he wanted to please Rupert Murdoch (who supports Bush) to guarantee the support of Murdoch's British papers. I thought he perhaps didn't realise that by taking us to war he would inevitably make us a target for terrorists.

I still think I was right about Blair's motives. But I now think I was wrong about him not realising the consequences. I think Blair deliberately and cold bloodedly took us to war because he knew that in so doing he would increase his powers over us by making us more afraid. Astonishingly, staggeringly, frighteningly, almost unbelievably, I think he deliberately and cold bloodedly increased our susceptibility to terrorist attacks. The corollary to this is, of course, the belief that Blair must accept responsibility for the deaths of the citizens who died in the bombing of London in July 2005. Those innocent travellers were sacrificed by Blair to increase his power over us. (There are many who believe that the Labour Government deliberately arranged or sanctioned the bomb attacks on London. I have no doubt that Labour would have done this if necessary. But in practice I suspect that they didn't need to. The bombings were an inevitable consequence of their policies. Whether the incompetence of MI5 and the police in preventing the bombings was deliberate or merely accidental is open to debate.)

41

I don't want to believe that any of this is happening. I would prefer to draw the curtains, collect together a pile of good books, videos and DVDs and pretend that the outside world doesn't exist.

But the situation is now so bad (and daily getting worse) that we have no choice but to face facts.

Most people don't realise that it has happened, but we now live in a fascist state.

42

In his book *1984*, written in 1948, George Orwell foresaw a world of everlasting war in which the people would be controlled by fear. An invisible enemy would be the reason for the Government to take all the power it wanted. For ever. In *Brave New World*, written in 1931, Aldous Huxley predicted that governments would adopt different solutions. Huxley believed that the people would be soothed and controlled by 'niceness'; by some sort of opiate that would keep them calm and unprotesting whatever might go on around them. The opiate he foresaw, although invented, did not appear then in the form we know it today. Television was merely an oddity, a possibility. Today, television has truly become the opiate of the people. People watch and watch and don't care about anything else. At work and in the streets their chatter is about what happened on television, rather than what is happening in the real world. Reality television (a misnomer since what purports to be reality television is these days about as real as the circus) has taken over from reality. Huxley's vision of a world in which people are controlled by pleasure and Orwell's vision of a world where people are controlled by fear have both come true.

43

Fascism often creeps slowly into a society.

Claiming that there is a need for added security, those who are in power bring in new laws and remove the civil rights of citizens. And that, of course, is what is happening to us.

We can and should pray, hope and work for a better, fairer future. But we shouldn't rely on it. Getting rid of the politicians who run our country won't be easy. There are three basic problems.

First, millions of people still don't understand precisely what is going on. As I have explained extensively in earlier books (such as *Why Everything Is Going To Get Worse Before It Gets Better, England Our England, Saving England, Rogue Nation, Confronting the Global Bully* and *The Truth They Won't Tell You (And Don't Want You To Know) About The EU)*, people's ignorance has been sustained by a dishonest and corrupt media.

Second, the Labour Government has created an army of voters who will support it solely in their own self-interest and who are uninterested in whether or not the motives and actions of the Government are honourable. In the 2005 general election Blair got into Downing Street with a little over 20% of the vote. In other words, he needed the support of only one in five voters. And that, oddly enough, is approximately the same as the number of voters who are entirely dependent on the Government for their weekly income.

Third, ever since Blair and his hideous colleagues took control, hard-working Britons have been leaving the country in droves. Around 300,000 Britons leave the country every year. That figure is rising rapidly. The inevitable result of this exodus is that Blair and company get safer by the year. (The people who leave are the people who will probably never vote Labour). The downside for Labour (and the rest of the country) is that the people who leave are, generally speaking, hard-working and at least moderately well off. These people are taking their work ethic, their money, their pensions and their ideas out of the country. Britain must inevitably head further and deeper into recession. The Government is so committed to spending money on its army of advisers and civil servants (and on voters who receive benefits) that taxes are going to have to rise dramatically. The Labour philosophy of taking from the hard working and giving to the indolent (instead of from the rich to the poor) will continue unchecked.

44

And so our war against our own Government is going to be a long and difficult one. It is not possible to win simply by voting in an alternative Government made up from one of the two main opposition parties. The Conservatives and the Liberals are no better than the Labour Party. The differences between them are superficial and consist of marketing strategies rather than fundamental principles.

We will win only through education; by spreading the truth to our friends and neighbours.

Any advertising guru will tell you that the most powerful way of spreading a message or selling a product is to persuade people to talk about your message or product to their friends. It's called selling by 'word of mouth' and nothing can match it for effectiveness.

Talk to your friends about the things you read in this book. It is the way revolutions start.

45

Meanwhile, as we do what we can to spread the truth about the motives and activities of leaders such as Bush and Blair, we must also do what we can to protect ourselves. We must learn how to read between the lines; we must acquire a scepticism for the sort of propaganda served up by organisations such as the BBC and we must learn to do everything we can to protect our identity and preserve (what is left of) our privacy.

46

We have lost a good deal in the last few years. We have lost our freedom, our liberty and our rights. Our world has changed beyond recognition. Most electors are still unaware of the extent to which they are constantly deceived and manipulated by the people they trust to look after them. What can we do to claim back our freedom and our dignity and to defeat the forces of evil which control our lives?

Read on.

Chapter Two

The State Is Now Our Biggest Enemy And The Biggest Threat To Our Privacy And Freedom

1

You have very few rights left. The police and other state employees can stop your car whenever they like. The police, and a wide variety of others whose salaries you pay, can come into your house when they want to. The Government can put you in prison without a trial and hold you there. You won't be able to defend yourself because they won't say why you're in prison. If the police in Poland, Greece or Italy say they want you then the British police will hand you over. The Polish, Greek or Italian police don't have to provide any evidence of any wrongdoing. If the Americans want you then the British police will hand you over to them. The Americans don't have to provide any evidence showing that you have sinned. Thousands of people you don't know and have never met now have the right to rifle through your underclothes. Your home address, birth date and hip size can all be bought by anyone who wants to buy them. You are not entitled to have secrets. You have no rights. They can spy harder, longer, deeper and more intrusively than ever before. And at a time when your need for your rights to be protected has never been greater your rights have conveniently become non-existent.

You can't have any rights, you see. It might help the terrorists. Or the money launderers. Or the animal rights people. Or the Martians. Or the goblins.

2

It is the Government's job to help keep us safe, healthy and happy. As William Cobbett wrote: 'It is the chief business of a government to take care that one part of the people do not cause the other part to lead miserable lives.'

3

The Government isn't (quite) stupid enough to ban free speech overnight.

But.

But little by little we are losing our freedom of speech every day as countless pieces of oppressive new legislation are pushed through Parliament and brutal assaults are made on our civil rights by one Labour Home Secretary after another.

Our freedom is dying from a thousand small cuts.

4

It is becoming increasingly difficult for any of us to speak out against the Government.

Terrorism is the excuse, of course.

If we criticise the Government we must be supporting the terrorists. Those of us who disapprove of illegal wars are regarded as extremists who must be silenced. The Labour Government has argued that anyone who says that the London bombings were a result of the Iraq war is supporting terrorism.

If we point out that the American and British Governments have been responsible for the deaths of millions of innocent Muslims we are branded as terrorist supporters.

In the new world that Bush and Blair have created we can and must be silenced.

We have freedom to protest, as long as we don't say anything of which the Government disapproves and as long as we say it in a place and at a time which have both been approved by the

Government and by the police. That's what the Labour Party means by democracy, liberty and freedom of speech.

5

'We have not abolished slavery; we have nationalised it.'
HERBERT SPENCER

6

New counter-terrorism legislation will make criticism of the Government's anti-war policies a serious crime (the Government says that even 'understanding terrorists' motives' should be an offence on the grounds that it might encourage or support terrorism) and will allow the Prime Minister or Home Secretary to lock up suspects without trial. No one from the Government will say precisely what this means but legal experts seemed to think that the new counter-terrorism legislation will make it illegal to oppose the Iraq war (or any subsequent war) and, indeed, illegal to criticise the Government in any way.

(Here is yet more proof that the people pulling the Labour Party's strings don't want this war to end. If you don't ever try to understand your enemy how can you ever negotiate your way to a peace?)

7

In November 2005, after failing to persuade Parliament to pass a new law giving the police the authority to lock up suspects for 90 days at a time (without having to offer any evidence to a court) the arrogant Blair announced that Parliament was wrong and had betrayed the country. Blair complained bitterly that MPs who had voted against him were out of touch with the public. This was the same Prime Minister who ignored the will of the people and took the country to war against Iraq. Naturally, there was no evidence to suggest that the country supported Blair, but a good deal of evidence showing that people would like to see him enrolled as Britain's next contribution to the American space programme.

In replying to questions after the humiliating defeat, Blair claimed that the police wanted to be able to lock people up for 90 days. (It had to be explained to him that the police do not – yet – run the country.)

It later transpired that senior police officers had been asked to lobby MPs by the Home Secretary, Charles Clarke. When it seemed likely that the Government was about to be defeated in its plans to detain suspects for 90 days without any evidence or charge, the Home Secretary had asked chief constables for support. The Association of Chief Police Officers urged chief constables to lobby MPs to extend detention without charge from 14 days to 90 days. Allegedly encouraged by the Prime Minister's office, the nation's senior policemen turned themselves into political lobbyists, desperate to take away some of our oldest and most fundamental human rights. Senior policemen had, it appeared, talked to rebel MPs and written newspaper articles urging MPs and the public to support the Government. Chief constables were told to put pressure on their local MPs and were sent a prepared message to send out under their own names. The Government ignored its own Islamic advisers who warned that Blair's anti-terror legislation would alienate law-abiding Muslims and fuel the hatred of fanatics. Even more alarming, perhaps, was the news that, months earlier, some police vehicles had been re-sprayed to carry a message supporting the Labour Party. The police said that the change was made for 'operational reasons'. Always a good excuse.

8

The Echelon system is a multinational eavesdropping system operated by American security officers working in Britain. The system searches phone, fax and e-mail communications for keywords. If you use a keyword your communication will be read or listened to. What are the keywords? Ah, naturally they keep that secret. But there are thousands of keywords and some of them can sound pretty harmless, so perfectly innocent conversations can attract attention. You should assume that every telephone conversation you have, and every fax and e-mail you send will be listened to or read by a Government employee. Naturally, the real terrorists (who probably know all the keywords) don't say or write anything likely to draw attention to themselves. And they undoubtedly use telephones which cannot be traced to them. So apart from being a snoop's charter and infringing your privacy the whole system is a waste of time.

9

An astonishing amount of my reader mail ends: 'Please don't publish my name and address anywhere.' I never do and never will.

10

Beware if you write letters of protest to public figures. There is a danger that your name and address will be passed on to the 'authorities'. It is not unknown for the BBC to pass letters they have received on to the police and even the Queen is not beyond snitching on her subjects. (See my book *The Truth They Won't Tell You (And Don't Want You To Know) About The EU* for the evidence.) Readers who have written to the Queen, asking her to stand up for her country have received replies ending: 'A copy of your letter is being forwarded to the Foreign and Commonwealth Office for the Attention of the Secretary of State for Foreign and Commonwealth Affairs.'

I can imagine that there may be some of the Queen's correspondents who were surprised to know that their letter had been passed on to the very Government they were criticising – a heavy-handed, fascist Government which is not known for its fair-mindedness or tolerance of those who disagree with its views.

11

'Liberalism denied the state in the name of the individual; fascism reasserts the rights of the state as expressing the real essence of the individual.'
MUSSOLINI, THE MAN WHO INVENTED FASCISM, PROVING FROM BEYOND THE GRAVE THAT GEORGE W. BUSH AND TONY BLAIR ARE FASCISTS.

12

A woman who calmly recited the names of British troops killed in Iraq, at a peaceful ceremony held at the Cenotaph in London in 2005, was arrested and convicted under the Serious and Organised Crime and Police Act. She now has a criminal record for reading out the names of soldiers killed in Blair's illegal war. Fourteen policemen, who arrived in two minibuses, were used to arrest this entirely harmless woman.

13

One of the reasons for the Government's existence is to protect our freedom. Our physical freedom and our freedom of thought and ideas.

But I have been physically prevented from speaking in public places by Government agents. And although the Government quickly (and rightly) stamps on animal rights campaigners who threaten the safety of animal abusers I have received no protection from the Government when I have been threatened.

14

'In the case of nutrition and health, just as in the case of education, the gentleman in Whitehall really does know what is better for people than the people know themselves.'
DOUGLAS JAY (FORMER LABOUR MINISTER)

15

Kindly souls who dare to feed the birds in London will now be fined £50 if they are caught. (I claim that I'm a messy eater and that the birds were simply gathered around me to eat up the crumbs. How will 'they' prove otherwise?)

16

'Liberty is the prevention of control by others.'
LORD ACTON

17

A student in Oxford who asked a mounted policeman if he knew that his horse was gay, was arrested and put into jail for the night. He was arrested by six police officers, using a fleet of patrol cars, and was handcuffed before being thrown into the cells. A police spokesman said that the student's homophobic comments were offensive to the policeman and his horse. The spokesman did not say how he knew that the horse had been offended. I wish I were making this up. I am not.

18

When the police arrested five suspects in connection with the murder of a policewoman they took the suspects up the M1 from London to Bradford using seven police vans, eight accompanying cars, 50 policemen, two motorcycle outriders and a helicopter. There is no record of a submarine being involved though I would not have been surprised. The M1 was closed to other traffic, undoubtedly causing great inconvenience (and, doubtless, expense) to taxpayers. The suspects were later all released.

19

Thanks to politicians who lie for a living, and to journalists who merrily repeat those lies (in return perhaps for a mention in the honours list and a few invitations to Chequers for tea and crumpets with the Prime Minister and his loathsome wife) it is commonly believed that the loss of personal freedom which has resulted from the storm of new laws introduced since 11th September 2001 is an acceptable price to pay for security.

You, of course, will know that this is one of the more outrageous myths of modern times.

The truth is that although we have abandoned our privacy and handed over our individual human rights we have gained nothing whatsoever.

The changes which have taken place in our society (many of which have been described as 'temporary' but which will doubtless be permanent unless we fight them) have contributed nothing whatsoever to our security.

Indeed, on the contrary, our security has been severely compromised by Tony Blair's apparently inexplicable (and thoroughly indefensible) insistence on supporting George W. Bush's illegal and immoral war on Muslims.

The laws which have led to a loss of privacy, dignity and freedom throughout the western world were introduced to oppress and suppress rather than to defend. The evidence shows quite clearly that these laws were planned long before the attack on America which allegedly triggered their introduction.

20

Everywhere you look our rights are disappearing. The Government's constant determination to make us afraid and keep us afraid is changing every aspect of our lives. For example, I often put bags full of unwanted books and clothes in the doorway of a local charity shop. It's easier to park at night when the shop is closed (the alternative is to lug heavy bags of donations through the town). I know there is a risk that some passing itinerant will steal from the bags but to be honest I'm happy about that. The goods are there to help poor people. If someone is so poor that they need to steal from a bag outside a charity shop then that's fine by me. Now, however, the shop has put a large notice on its door. The notice informs me that the police have given instructions that bags are not to be left in the doorway. Why could this possibly be? Are the police worried that roaming itinerants may steal unfashionable cardigans or old paperbacks and use them to cause mayhem in the streets? No. The police say that bags are not to be left out at night because of the 'risk of terrorism'. Are they serious? Do the police really think that Osama bin Laden and his chums are sitting in their cave in the furthest corner of Afghanistan planning to bring down the imperialistic, oil stealing western world by blowing up charity shops? Does the local chief constable really lie awake worrying that Al Qaeda plans to bring us to our knees by blowing up empty Cats Protection League shops? All those old skirts and blouses blown to smithereens. Do they envisage the British electorate devastated at the loss of countless tiny china figurines, an assortment of previously owned handbags and a few handfuls of freshly laundered second-hand lingerie? Not even the police could be that stupid. This is just another part of the plan to keep us scared, oppressed and under control.

21

The Government actually brought in a new piece of legislation so that they could get rid of a sole anti-war demonstrator in Parliament Square. The demonstrator, Brian Haw, who has been protesting about the invasion of Iraq since it started and is a modern day hero far worthier of a Nobel Peace Prize than most of the recent recipients, had upset some members of the Government. As fascist totalitarian war criminals they presumably, found it embarrassing to have to face *Peace* placards when they went to work to plan more wars. And so, in an attempt to evict Mr Haw, the Serious Organised Crime and Police Act contained a clause outlawing unauthorised demonstrations in Whitehall and Parliament Square. Ironically, and with commendable ineptitude, the Government made a mistake and failed to make the legislation retrospective. They ended up with legislation which stopped everyone protesting in Parliament Square – everyone, that is, except the man who was already protesting.

Sometimes you just have to laugh at the sad, inept morons whose only skill lies in destroying everything that is good, honourable and decent.

22

They tried hard to get him, of course. The police arrested Brian Haw just before Christmas 2005. According to one report he had been arrested for sleeping within a kilometre of the Prime Minister. According to another he was arrested for a breach of the peace. Allegedly the police arrested someone who was sitting nearby while he was sleeping and Haw, having protested at this, was duly arrested too. (The law the Labour Government passed to get rid of Haw actually protects him while making it illegal for anyone else to protest outside Parliament.)

No one in the police or the Government seemed aware of the irony of arresting a man who was campaigning for peace, and an end to an illegal war, for an alleged breach of the peace. If anyone in Britain deserves to be arrested for a breach of the peace it is warmonger Tony Blair.

23

In this morning's mail I had a letter from a reader who told me that the entire print run of the latest edition of a newspaper called 'Freedom' had been confiscated on its way from the printers. And two readers sent me newspaper cuttings.

The first cutting reported that a teenager had been fined £100 for saying 'miaow' to a police dog. The teenager was charged with using threatening and abusive words and behaviour.

The second cutting reported that a woman had been arrested

for wearing a shirt critical of Tony Blair. The woman had worn a shirt with the words 'Bollocks to Blair' printed on it. She was later released after agreeing to cover up the anti-Blair slogan by putting on a jacket.

During the General Election in 2005, police cars drove around the English countryside festooned with advertisements telling the world to vote Labour.

24

A woman author who dared to say, on the wireless, that she did not believe homosexuals should be allowed to adopt children, was telephoned by the police who told her that a 'homophobic incident' had been reported against her and that it was police policy to investigate homophobic incidents as they are a 'priority crime'. Here is another example of the police state. Now it is not our actions which will get us into trouble – but also what we say (and presumably what we think – if only they can catch us at it).

25

Here's another example of practical fascism in action.

When the Chinese leader last visited Britain, a few people who were concerned about China's record on human rights protested. Their protest was entirely peaceful though they waved a few placards and one or two of them probably shouted at the official motorcade.

The police dragged the protesters away to avoid embarrassing Blair or the Chinese leader.

26

Blair *et al* seem determined to stamp out all protesting and campaigning.

The Government is stopping peaceful protests by branding anyone it doesn't like as a terrorist. For example, animal rights campaigners have for some years now been officially branded as terrorists. People who protest about green issues, human rights or the Government's record on anything are now likely to be described as terrorists. It's an easy way for the Government to excuse its high handed attitude.

27

An animal rights campaigner, peacefully inviting passers-by to look at his leaflets about vivisection, was reported by the police for a breach of the 1824 Vagrancy Act because he 'attempted to obtain or gather alms by exposing wounds or deformities'. (I didn't see them but I can guess that his leaflets contained pictures of animals who had been subjected to obscene procedures).

It took three policemen and two community support officers to invoke the 1824 Act (which was originally designed to stop soldiers who had returned from the Napoleonic Wars displaying their tattered limbs in the street in an attempt to beg money for food) and to take away the campaigner's animal rights material.

On another occasion protestors who were carrying placards showing pictures of distressed animals in an abattoir were threatened with arrest if they did not cover up their placards. The police claimed that the photographs might distress passers-by. The protestors pointed out that there was a butcher's shop across the road. The police deemed this irrelevant.

28

A group of excited schoolchildren, visiting London for the day to take photographs in aid of charity, were marched away when they tried to take photographs of Trafalgar Square.

I have tried hard to think of a sensible reason for this high handed nonsense but it's a struggle.

The best I can come up with is that they were banned from taking pictures in case the photographs fell into the hands of terrorists who then used them to plan an attack on Nelson's column.

But unless the authorities blindfold visitors to central London, and ban the sale of postcards, it's not a well thought out anti-terrorist move.

29

A heckler who dared shout out 'Nonsense' during a speech by the hideous Jack Straw at the 2005 Labour Party Conference was manhandled and forcibly ejected from the building by two stewards (one of them allegedly a professional bouncer). The heckler had his security pass confiscated. The 82-year-old Jewish refugee of Nazi Germany, mildly diabetic and hard of hearing, was detained under the Terrorism Act when he tried to re-enter the hall. Pictures in the press showed one of the stewards grabbing the man by the collar to drag him from the hall – even though he was clearly not defending himself. Had Labour Party bosses not realised that their thuggish actions were attracting some criticism the man would have probably been dragged into a Tube station and shot by police marksmen at close range. No one from the Labour Government stopped the man being evicted. Afterwards the Prime Minister refused to meet the man face-to-face to apologise.

30

Two pensioners who protested against massive rises in council taxes were imprisoned. A male protestor was sent to prison for 28 days while a female protestor got just seven days. (I did think about complaining about this to the Equal Rights Commission but since the ERC doesn't have much of a history of being interested in equality, I decided that I could find better uses for the stamp.)

This protest was triggered in part at least by means testing. Pensioners who have not managed to save anything for their old age, or who have simply spent their money on wine, song and whatever goes with them, will find that their council tax burden is shared by taxpayers. But those pensioners who were silly enough to save for their autumnal years, and who believed that their virtue would be rewarded, are learning the error of their ways. Under the Labour Government thrift is a sin, to be punished not praised.

31

Six students at Lancaster University were prosecuted for demonstrating on their own campus. The students were charged with 'aggravated trespass' after they heckled at a corporate conference held in one of the University's buildings and attended by representatives of an arms dealer, an oil company and a drug company. The protestors, who were accused of interrupting a speech by Lord Sainsbury of Turville (the Labour Government's Science Minister) said that they were concerned about the commercialisation of research. One of the students was arrested immediately after the protest, the other five were summonsed five months later. The University was asked to drop the prosecutions on the grounds that it threatened free speech. The University did not drop the prosecutions and all the campaigners were found guilty. They were given two-year conditional discharges and fined £300 each for being so stupid to think they were living in a democracy and entitled to express their views.

32

Free speech is now no more than a memory in Britain. Five men who published a right wing magazine were sent to prison because their magazine praised Adolf Hitler and Rudolph Hess. Well, a lot of people have said nice things about Hess though not so many have said nice things about Hitler, though I do remember a respectable colleague of mine once stunning a dinner party by insisting that the man with the silly moustache had provided Germany with some excellent roads. I don't know the contents cf the magazine which put the five defendants in prison (bizarrely for widely differing sentences of five years, four years, two and half years, twelve months and a suspended nine months) and I don't much care. I suspect that I would have found the magazine pretty repulsive. But surely the whole point of a free society and a free press is that people are allowed to think what they like, say what they like and write what they like. Those, in fact, are rights that the Human Rights Act promises us. But the Human Rights Act doesn't count when the Government and the judiciary decide it doesn't count. Animal rights campaigners have been arrested merely for publishing leaflets advocating an end to vivisection. There are all sorts of things I would like see banned and all sorts of authors and publishers I would like to see behind bars. I have no doubt that some people would like to see me banged up for some of the things I've written. But once you start locking people up because you don't like what they've written you are admitting that you no longer believe in free speech. In fact you are *proving* that you don't have free speech.

33

A defendant's previous convictions can now be read out in court during a trial.

34

The Government is setting up a Criminal Assets Recovery Agency. This will have the power to seize assets from suspected criminals without trial and to tax suspected criminal proceeds. Please note the word 'suspected.'

35

A new Data Sharing and Privacy Act entitles Government departments to share information on tax records, benefits and so on. In other words any information which one Government has about you can be passed to any other Government department which wants it. In addition to having much better pensions than anyone else, people who work for the Government can now snoop on their neighbours.

36

If you are a member of a 'subversive' group then the Government will almost certainly be keeping a close eye on your mail. Subversive groups include those which campaign for animals, against the wrongful imprisonment of political prisoners, against war and for the environment. Anyone who joins such a group or attends a march or has their name on a mailing list is, these days, likely to be branded a terrorist. You don't need to have been arrested. The police photograph and video protestors and make lists of the number plates of cars parked near marches and demonstrations. And they also use credit card companies and CCTV cameras to check up on who has visited protest scenes. The Government keeps lists of anybody who has ever protested against anything and they keep lists of people who have written letters to their MP or the media complaining about the Government.

37

Since they came to power in 1997, the Labour Government has produced an average of two major criminal-justice bills every year, many of them drafted hastily and then patched and re-patched more often than sloppy software.

38

It is now illegal to wear a fake Rolex watch – even if, when you bought it, you just thought you were getting a bit of a bargain. A man in Belgium was sent to prison for six months just for wearing a fake. The judge decreed that he must have known that it was fake when he bought it. Since what is law in Belgium is now (thanks to the EU) also law in Britain, holidaymakers who return home with a few iffy watches could soon find themselves and their friends doing time.

39

British citizens can now be extradited to many countries without there being any evidence that would convict them in a British court.

All other countries within the EU can extradite British citizens without having to go through the arduous task of producing any evidence to show that they have done anything wrong.

Similarly, thanks to Blair, Blunkett and the Labour Government, British citizens can be extradited to the USA without having done anything that a British court would regard as illegal. The American authorities don't even have to be able to prove that the British citizen has done anything that an American court would regard as illegal.

New laws give the FBI the right to obtain secret warrants and break into homes and offices without consent or knowledge.

It is an interesting thought that if the innocent Brazilian whom the police in London executed for no reason had been an American, the police involved in the shooting would have probably been extradited to the USA and tried for murder.

40

You might not have noticed (the new laws pour in faster than even the lawyers can keep up with them) but it is illegal now to carry a penknife. The Government has imposed a five-year minimum jail sentence on adults who carry knives in public. And you can be sure that the police will not be looking for gangs of dangerous youths (they might turn nasty) but for middle-aged men peeling apples and sharpening pencils. You can go to prison for five years for carrying a pocket knife in a public place even though you might only intend to use it for sharpening your pencil, peeling an orange, opening letters, or performing a tracheotomy.

It is, presumably, still legal to carry picnic knives and forks, ice axes, hammers, screwdrivers and pitchforks.

41

Did you think that your home was your castle and that you could do what you liked with it and be invaded only by members of the police carrying warrants?

Wrong.

The Labour Party has introduced legislation requiring home-owners to pay extra council tax if they have made any improvements to their home. A loft conversion, a conservatory, a summerhouse or a garden shed will all mean more taxes. As will converting your front garden so that you have somewhere to park your car.

Traditionally, governments have encouraged homeowners to improve their property and haven't penalised people who do so. But the Labour Government, in its constant search for more of your money, has changed that.

Why and how does this affect your right to privacy? Simple.

The Labour Government is introducing new legislation which will entitle council tax inspectors to enter your home and take photographs. The army of inspectors appointed by the Government (at great expense) will have the right to demand entry to your home to examine any improvements you have made. You have no rights.

The tax inspectors, from the Valuation Office Agency (an arm of the Inland Revenue) will, if they wish, even be entitled to take photographs of your bedroom. This is all being done as part of the re-evaluation of 22 million properties in England.

The re-evaluation will be done to enable local authorities to raise tax revenues by charging higher rates for better kept homes. The visits will mean that taxpayers will pay more if they have a patio, a greenhouse, a pleasant view or somewhere to park their car away from vandals. The inspectors (whose salaries, pensions and expenses will, of course, be paid for by taxpayers) will have the authority to measure the size of patios, greenhouses and other additions. They have been equipped with 2,126 digital cameras for which we the taxpayers have paid the rather hefty sum of £438,749. (I have a suspicion that if the Valuation Office Agency, an arm of the Inland Revenue, had bought them on a television-shopping channel it would have probably got a better price.) The Government claims that the Human Rights Act will not protect citizens from these intrusions. (It seems that the Human Rights Act only works when the Government finds it convenient for it to work.) The tax inspectors will be told that it is 'good practice' to ask for permission before marching into an Englishman's castle. But they will also be told that they don't have to ask permission and can, if they wish, just walk in without consent. If the householder won't open the door the inspectors can, presumably, break it down with their hob-nailed boots. (Though one wonders if the damaged house might then perhaps be worth a lower rating.) Anyone who refuses to let the inspectors in will be fined £500 and will end up with a criminal record. So there you are: defend your property and you are now a criminal.

Personally, I have no intention of letting the inspectors into my home. I intend to make them use the law, against my permission, to enter my house. That way I may be able to fight them using the Human Rights Act. And I will have struck a vital blow for freedom and privacy.

42

There are around four million surveillance cameras in Britain. That is more than six per square mile. Only Monaco (where every square inch of the principality is under 24-hour Government video surveillance) has more cameras. It won't be long before Britain catches up since our Government is having more cameras installed every day.

The evidence shows that these cameras don't help the police catch criminals and they don't prevent crime. CCTV cameras are the main reason why so many city-centre thugs now wander around wearing hooded jackets. When we really need them (as, for example, when the police shoot an innocent man) it turns out that either the cameras weren't working or the tape has been accidentally erased. And courts are wary of pictures from CCTV cameras because they tend to be fuzzy and unclear.

Who watches all these cameras? What are they really for? Who watches all the video tapes and where do they keep them? These cameras remove our privacy (CCTV cameras have been used to point at a woman's flat so that taxpayer financed peeping Toms could watch her) but add nothing of value to our lives.

Why do they have cameras all over the country recording car number plates? Has anyone ever been caught this way? Has any stolen car ever been tracked? Or is some sad civil servant crouched over a hundred thousand monitors collecting car numbers?

Why?

43

If you use a computer the Government can demand that you hand over your passwords and encryption keys on demand. If you refuse to do this they can, and will, send you to prison.

44

The Criminal Justice Police Act entitles police to keep DNA samples and fingerprints taken from suspects. Forever. Even if the suspect has not been charged with anything, let alone convicted, the police can still keep fingerprints and DNA samples indefinitely. It is, of course, easy to use this material to frame suspects who might otherwise not be convicted. And, if offered the right amount of money, the police and the Government will undoubtedly sell DNA samples and fingerprints to outside, commercial agencies.

45

Government departments can put cookies onto your hard drive so that they can, if they wish, spy on you, get access to your Internet movements and passwords and read the private files on your computer.

46

When new laws about house arrest were being debated in the House of Commons (arguably the most important piece of legislation in British parliamentary history) a large chunk of opposition MPs didn't even bother to turn up to vote – thereby allowing the Labour Party to push through their legislation without difficulty.

47

In 2003 the Home office gave permission for 39,564 bugging operations. (I can guess the identity of one of the buggees. I wonder who the other 39,563 were?) The excuses given for all this bugging were: organised crime, drug smuggling, money laundering, animal rights and Al Qaeda. This number of operations doesn't include covert surveillance carried out by MI5, MI6 and the listening post at GCHQ. A spokesman for the Conservatives (their shadow homeland security minister) said: 'it is precisely because of this sort of intelligence operation that we have not been attacked so far in this country'.

48

Here are just some of the people who will snitch on you – and who could get you into a great deal of trouble (without your ever having done anything wrong):

1. The European Commission has ruled that information about all fixed and mobile telephone traffic must be stored for one year. The Government has access to telephone records which tell them whom you called, when and for how long, and where you were when you made the call. Data about communications using the Internet must be stored for six months. This means that telephone and Internet operators must store detailed information about all your telephone calls and all the websites you visit, including location data (matching cell phone identification to the geographical location of the caller). The

European Commission (an unelected group which includes such luminaries as Peter Mandelson) has given itself the right to know everything about you. (If you communicate with America by e-mail the USA Government will certainly take a close interest in what you write. The USA Government has instructed universities, online communication companies and whole cities to make it easier for law enforcement agencies to monitor their Internet computer networks. The action is said to be aimed at 'catching terrorists'. Universities alone claim that the new regulations will cost them at least £5 billion while doing little or nothing to apprehend law-breakers.)

2. The European Union has passed regulations meaning that every one of the 450 million people with passports in the EU will have to queue up in processing centres and compulsorily have their fingerprints taken and have a facial scan when their passport needs renewing. The biometric data gathered will be stored on a chip embedded in new passports. Personal data and the biometric data will be held on national databases and on an EU wide European Register which will be accessible to the authorities. Regulations will be binding on all member states of the EU. Debates in the House of Commons about all this are irrelevant. Mass fingerprinting is coming whether you like it or not and whatever the House of Commons has to say about it. (The gas chambers will come later and will be decorated by a team of well-known designers.) The processing of individual citizens will probably continue on a 'voluntary basis' until 80% of the population have one of the new approved passports (which will, of course, also serve as identity cards). The processing will be voluntary in that if you don't want to have a passport/ID card you won't have to have one. (Of course, you won't be able to leave the country, open a bank account, receive state benefits or obtain health care without one). When 80% of the population have the new ID cards they will become compulsory for everyone else. None of this is the EU's idea. It was an instruction from George W. Bush and the neo-conservatives. The EU Commission slavishly and gutlessly agreed to obey the instruction. (Numerous other EU laws are also a result of demands from the USA. It is the USA which has demanded that the EU introduce tax harmonization, a lack of privacy of

bank account information and iris scans. The USA wants the rest of the world to conform to American laws. And the EU constantly supports and helps this aim.)

3. Since May 2004 the EU has kindly provided the American Government with information on all airline passengers heading for the USA (even if they are just passing through). They have given the American Government the names, addresses, credit card details and telephone numbers of everyone travelling across the Atlantic. The Americans are even entitled to information about the religion of travellers. The deal was opposed by the European Parliament but approved by the unelected European Commission. The American Government warned that if the EC didn't comply airlines wouldn't be allowed to land in the USA. More than ten million passengers fly from Britain to the USA every year and the American Government knows everything it wants to know about them all. If there were any dishonest people working for the American Government it would be easy for them to arrange for travelling Britons to be burgled. They do, after all, have the names and addresses (and the dates of travel) of everyone travelling. Many in Europe believe that handing over information in this way violates European human rights legislation. Naturally, the Americans say they need all this information for their global war on terrorism.

4. Everyone must report cash transactions to the police. If you buy a car with cash, pay for a holiday with cash, buy furniture with cash then you will be considered a possible money launderer and reported to the authorities. They must report you or they will face prison.

5. Banks cooperate with the authorities. If they think any of your transactions are suspicious (and that's a very subjective thing) they will tell the Government. If you sell your car for more than £3,000 and pay in the proceeds as cash you will be reported to the authorities as a possible criminal.

   America has introduced regulations (which are, of course, now slavishly followed by the British authorities and by British banks) which are said to be designed to catch money launderers, criminals and terrorists. (They aren't, of course, but that's what they say they are for.)

If a bank thinks you might be guilty of something they must send either a Suspicious Transaction Report or a Suspicious Activity Report to the authorities. They will not tell you that they have submitted one of these reports. Even if the bank manager is your best friend he will not tell you. He is not allowed to.

What counts?

a) A refusal to provide identification. A bank can ask you for as much identification as it wants. If you decline to give information you will instantly be branded as either a terrorist or a money launderer.

b) Refusing to offer an explanation. If a snotty, spotty bank employee asks you why you want money or where money has come from you are obliged to tell them. Otherwise they will probably file a Suspicious Activity Report or a Suspicious Transaction Report.

c) Running a bank account with a third party – particularly one who is absent. So, for example, if you run a bank account for an aged relative who can't get to the bank then there is a good chance that the bank will regard you both as potential terrorists or financial criminals.

d) If you put more money into your bank account than you would normally earn then your bank may well snitch on you. So, if you win money at the dog track or sell an old painting for a tidy sum, and are then silly enough to put the money into your account, you will attract attention.

e) Not knowing or being ignorant of charges, rates or taxes will brand you as a financial criminal. (Yes, I know it's stupid. I know that no one – not even bank employees – can keep up with all the charges. On the other hand, I know that financial criminals are likely to be completely *au fait* with all the rules.)

f) If you buy lots of gold coins you will automatically be reported. As I write, the limit is £5,000 worth in a single transaction or £10,000 during the space of a year.

g) If you have money but no apparent income you will arouse suspicions. So, if you are living on income which goes into another bank account or you are living on your savings then you will be regarded as a terrorist, criminal or money launderer.

h) Something called 'structuring transactions' gets bank

employees and Government snoops very excited. You are structuring a transaction if you divide it into smaller pieces. The authorities will assume that you are doing this to avoid attention. So if you and your wife or husband go into the bank together and both order some foreign currency for your holidays then you will trigger a secret investigation. If you and your wife or husband or a friend go into the bank together and then go to separate tellers to conduct your business separately the transactions may be suspect.

i) If you ask a bank clerk about the bank's policy on record keeping, disclosures or reporting then you will be suspected of wanting to do something illegal.

j) Don't talk about politics to a banker, broker, financial advisor or accountant. Don't complain about taxes. Don't discuss financial privacy either. All these things could lead to a secret investigation.

6. The courts now sell the names and addresses of people accused of crimes (such as debt). So, if you are taken to court for non-payment of a debt your name and address may be sold to debt collecting agencies. You don't have to be convicted for the court to sell your details. The courts sell the names and addresses of people who have been accused – before they are found guilty of anything. If you have a county court judgement against you the Government will sell your name and address to loan sharks and other companies. They sell names and addresses through a private company which works for the Lord Chancellor's Office.

7. Local authorities now make money by selling the names and addresses on the electoral register. Some councils keep two lists. The first list contains everyone's name and address. This list is only sold 'for the prevention and detection of crime and checking your identity when you have applied for credit'. The second list excludes the names and addresses of voters who have asked that their names be excluded from the full register. This second list is sold to anyone who wants it and it can be used for any purpose.

8. Some local authorities now fit microchips into wheelie bins to monitor the amount of rubbish a household produces. Residents who are considered to be generating too much rubbish will

receive advice from specially hired council officials who will 'get in touch'. The microchips will be read by technology fitted to refuse vehicles. Councils do not seem to have realised that burglars would only have to hack into the computer to see which households were producing less rubbish than usual to find out who was on holiday. (Nor does it seem to have occurred to councils that they might be better occupied trying to persuade large companies to wrap their products a little less impenetrably in rather fewer layers of plastic and that they themselves might be well advised to produce rather fewer of the self-congratulatory glossy newsletters which many now seem to produce on a regular basis boasting of their success in reducing the number of rubbish collections.)

9. When you make a copy of a document there is a good chance that the copy you have made will contain a hidden marking identifying the machine which made the copy. Since retailers keep track of who bought which machine this hidden mark will enable the authorities to identify the person responsible for the creation of a document. Some (but not all) laser printers copiers and multifunction workstations put a serial number of each machine coded in little yellow dots in every print out. Although invisible to the naked eye the tiny dots are printed all over each page. The American Government has for some time used the hidden markings to identify the machine with which a copy was made. And the British Government now sometimes does this too.

10. The authorities now check out which books you have taken out of the public library. If you take out a number of books on politics then they will know and take note. Information about your reading habits will be mixed in with all the other information about you.

11. The DVLA sells information about cars (and who owns them) to commercial companies. I know this because when I needed to ring the RAC one of their representatives told me that my car is a BMW 3 series diesel estate. When I asked how he knew this the man from the RAC told me that they got the information from the Government's DVLA computer. I pointed out to him that every single piece of information he had about my car was

wrong. He sighed but was not surprised. 'Their computer gets it wrong a lot of the time,' he said.

12. If you go to the Government's Land Registry website you will be able to find out all sorts of information about your neighbours. You can find out the names of your neighbours, how much they paid for their house and from whom they bought it.

And finally, if you buy a television set the retail store may tell the television licensing authority. I have a letter on my desk (addressed to a reader) which says: 'We have recently been advised that you purchased television receiving equipment in October 2004 from Comet Group plc.'

I wonder on what authority the Comet Group hands out personal information of this type.

49

Privacy is like virginity. You either have it or you don't.

50

Radio frequency identification tags (RFID) are already fitted in millions of consumer items. The RFID tags work like bar codes but without needing physical or line of sight contact. They will soon be in or on individual items ranging from bus tickets to underwear. The radio tags identify each item and enable trackers operated by the Government, and large businesses, to know where every bra and pair of knickers are at any one moment.

If you buy items with a credit card there will be a record linking you to the item.

(It should now become clear why the authorities are bringing in rules making it harder for citizens to use cash.)

The tags are as small as a grain of salt and cannot be removed without destroying the item to which they are attached. They can be read from a distance, and read through your clothes without your knowledge or your consent. Someone with a tag reader can aim their device at you and tell how much you paid for your shoes, your clothes and your underwear. They can find out where you live, how old you are, how much you earn and where you bank.

Tag readers will enable criminals, perverts and stalkers to find out as much as they want to know about their targets. Complete strangers will, thanks to the Government, be able to identify who you are, where you live, what you are wearing and where you bought it.

There is no evidence that I am aware of proving that RFID tags and scanners are safe to use. I doubt if anyone has done long-term studies to measure the health effects of chronic exposure to the electro-magnetic energy emitted by these devices or the scanners.

Many major stores already put RFID tags into the items they sell and the Government wants to put RFID tags into ID cards and onto car number plate chips.

I believe these tags will mean that crime rates will rocket since crooks armed with tag readers will be able to identify pedestrians and motorists who are away from their homes.

51

In America, children obtain their school lunch by putting a finger or a thumb into a scanner.

52

A new camera called a SenseCam is now available. It is so small that it can be hung around your neck or hidden in jewellery. The camera takes a digital picture whenever it detects a change in light, motion or temperature. It takes up to 2,000 pictures. Scientists intend to add face recognition technology and broadband connectivity. People wearing one of the cameras will be able to identify everyone they meet. They will also be able to determine their names, addresses, shoe sizes and so on.

53

In case you haven't already noticed, while you weren't looking things changed. A lot. Your doctor, lawyer, accountant and bank manager can no longer be trusted with confidential information. Doctors, lawyers and the rest no longer have the legal right to keep your secrets. You should give as little information as possible to your doctor, for example. And ask him not to put your private information into any sort of computer. Your accountant and solicitor and financial adviser and banker all now have a statutory duty to inform the authorities if they suspect that you might have been doing anything illegal – however minor the possible infraction might be. So, for example, if you send out personal Christmas cards using the office franking machine and your accountant, solicitor, financial advisor or banker finds out about it, they must inform the authorities because you have cheated the Inland Revenue. It doesn't matter that the infraction adds up to an extra 50 pence of tax. The offence is just as serious as it would be if you had defrauded the revenue of a million or two. And, in case you are thinking that this couldn't possibly happen to you because your accountant, solicitor, financial advisor and banker are all good and true friends you should be aware that if they tell you that they will have to inform on you then they will be committing a serious offence for which they can be sent to prison for a long time. And if you think, well, I'm safe because my accountant, solicitor, financial advisor and banker are all really good friends of mine and they would rather go to prison for twelve years than inform on me you should also be aware that every employee who works for or with your accountant, solicitor, financial advisor and banker is also bound by the same laws. If they even suspect that you might have done something improper and they don't blow the whistle on you (and the authorities find out) then they too could go to prison for a long time. And if they warn you then they could go to prison for that. The moral is that, however much you like them and enjoy their company, you probably shouldn't tell your accountant, solicitor, financial advisor and banker anything more than you absolutely have to tell them.

54

'Subjects must be deprived of their liberties by the courts, not politicians.'
TONY BLAIR (SPEAKING IN 1994, WHEN PROTESTING AGAINST THE
CONSERVATIVE GOVERNMENT'S LAW-AND-ORDER POLICIES AND
DECLARING HIS SUPPORT FOR 'OUR TRADITIONAL RULE OF LAW AND
THE PRINCIPLES THAT MUST GO WITH IT'.)

55

Political correctness, means testing and multiculturalism aren't the only great evils of our time. Absurd health and safety regulations are making life miserable (and no safer) for many. A church in Suffolk was recently forced to pay £1,315.66 to have four light bulbs changed because the man changing the bulbs had to do it from scaffolding rather than an old-fashioned ladder.

56

With the USA, the UK and the EU taking the lead, numerous countries now regard anyone who has an account abroad as either a terrorist or a criminal. Every country in the world is now forced to keep a list of countries which are regarded as pandering to money launderers or terrorists. (The real irony is that the two countries whose banking systems are most amenable to, and most popular with money launders and terrorists are the USA and the UK.)

The level of competence shown by the authorities can be shown by the fact that Venezuela once managed to blacklist itself as being an unacceptable tax haven. Mexico has blacklisted Patau since 1996 – despite the fact that there is no such country anywhere in the world. Portugal, Argentina, Mexico and Venezuela have also blacklisted the UK territories of St Helena and Ascension Island although neither had a bank until the spring of 2004.

To describe the way these lists are drawn up as arbitrary, subjective and discriminatory would be generous. The result of all this is that you may be as honest as a judge (OK, I could have chosen a better example, but you know what I mean) but if you have a holiday home abroad and need to open a local bank account in order to pay electricity, gas and telephone bills you could easily find yourself classified as a tax-evading, money-laundering terrorist.

57

The Government announced towards the end of 2004 that schools would in future be searched regularly by the police looking for weapons. It is difficult to avoid the feeling that this is to get children used to the idea of police searches so that they will be more pliable and less likely to complain when they are searched when they are older.

58

If you have a mobile telephone in your name the authorities can pin point your location now, yesterday, last week and going backwards for – well, a long time. If they decide that someone they want to arrest was in the same location as you were, on a particular date, then you could become a suspect. Indeed, with a shoot to kill policy, your life could be in danger.

59

The Government is abolishing the principle of double jeopardy. In future the courts will be able to keep trying an individual who is found not guilty until the 'correct' verdict is obtained.

60

Although they didn't remember to do it in the case of Brian Haw, the Labour Government is the first ever to enact retrospective legislation. In 2005, the Government announced new retrospective tax legislation designed to affect legitimate tax schemes set up as long ago as 1986.

Under this Government (and, presumably, future Governments) nothing – and no one is safe. If the Government is prepared to enact retrospective legislation which of yesterday's actions will prove, in future, to be illegal?

It has always been the case that ignorance of the law provides no defence. Constantly increasing legislation has made this stricture absurd. By introducing the concept of retrospective legislation the Government has turned every innocent, law-abiding citizen into an unwitting potential criminal. Nothing you do, and nothing you have done in the past, is now safe from recriminations. Every financial decision you make, every sensible tax-planning move you take, could turn out to be a terrible mistake because the Government can, and will, change the rules retrospectively.

61

Theoretically, the truth shall set you free. In practice it will get you into a lot of trouble.

62

The presumption of innocence has gone. The burden of proof has changed from them to us. More and more often we are being told we have to prove that we didn't do something. If a fraudulent debit appears on your credit card statement you have to prove that you didn't use your credit card. You have to prove you didn't plot against the Government. And if you are picked up by the Germans or the Americans and taken to Hamburg or Chicago for questioning you will have to prove that you didn't do whatever it was they eventually claim you did. If they say you are a terrorist you will have to prove that you are not.

It is, of course, difficult (verging on impossible) to prove that you didn't do something.

63

When they tried to set up a direct debit to pay for a utility bill relating to their new house a couple were told that they couldn't. The problem was that their name was different to the name that the electricity company had for their address. The couple's entreaties fell on stony ground. There was much talk of the need to protect the country from terrorists and money launderers.

The name the electricity company had in their computer?

The occupier.

64

Red tape has got out of control and is slowly strangling us all.

Thanks to the EU, bureaucracy has become a way of life. According to a poll of members by the Forum of Private Business, an employers' body for small and medium sized companies, British companies now spend more than 10 hours a week on form filling. The poll found that more than a fifth of respondents were not confident that they knew how to deal with regulations. The same number said that red tape was preventing them from expanding their business or adding staff.

It is small companies which suffer most. (And, indeed, there is good reason to believe that much of the red tape produced by the EU is created with the enthusiastic support of large companies which want to protect their territory by making it impossible for small companies to survive, grow and threaten their position. Many new regulations are introduced due to encouragement from well-established industries who want new regulations to limit competition.) Other regulations are introduced in order to enable struggling industries to gouge more money out of customers.

Industries use all sorts of regulations to protect themselves. It is quite common now for existing industry leaders to lobby for more legislation not less because they know that as large, established 'players' they will be in a much better position to cope with new legislation than newcomers.

When MOTs were first introduced they seemed a good idea. The aim was to take dangerous cars off the road and so help reduce accidents. It sounded as though it was being done for the benefit of individuals rather than companies. But, even if that was ever the intention, the MOT examination has gone way beyond that and is today simply a way for garages to make extra money, both by performing entirely unnecessary 'repairs' and 'improvements' and by encouraging buyers to dump their old cars and buy new ones. The MOT scheme has had a dramatic effect on the value of second-hand cars. The British car industry isn't the only one to have spotted the value of this sort of scam. In Japan, it is cheaper for motorists to buy a new car every three years than to try and keep their existing cars on the road. These artificial 'standards' are designed to ensure that the automobile industry prospers, but they lead to an enormous amount of waste. (Actually, British and Japanese cars are often so cheap to buy and so expensive to own in Britain and Japan that they are bought up in huge quantities and exported to countries where the automobile industry isn't yet powerful enough to have made old cars impractical. Many African countries are now well supplied with second-hand cars which are perfectly acceptable and quite safe.)

65

*'The Home Office practice now is to bring forward new legislation
which is absolutely abhorrent and totally disgraceful
in its abuse of civil liberties and then, when
there is uproar, replace it with something only
slightly less abhorrent and tell us a major
concession has been made.'*
BARONESS KENNEDY, HUMAN RIGHTS BARRISTER

66

In the eight years since the Labour Government first came into power
in Britain in 1997, around 12,000 new pieces of EU legislation have
been introduced into British law. (There were 10,000 new EU laws
during the 40 years from 1957 to 1997). The Labour Government
has constantly promised to cut red tape and reduce the number of
new laws being introduced. They have, of course, done exactly the
opposite.

67

The amount of red tape produced by the EU and by the Government
has resulted in employees being increasingly unwilling to employ
people on the traditional terms. The proportion of employers hiring
workers on fixed term contracts went up from 25% to 46% in the
eighteen months prior to September 2005, and the proportion
employing people as temporary workers rose from 26% to 46%.
Since in both these cases the workers are deprived of the normal
security associated with employment, both the EU and the
Government have actually succeeded in making things considerably
worse for a growing number of people.

68

The average small business spends five hours a week on VAT and
income tax administration and another four hours a week on health
and safety rules. In practice all this means that the average British
entrepreneur now spends a quarter of his working week on official
red tape. And that, of course, doesn't include other form filling and

the red tape engendered by banks, insurance companies and other large companies and institutions. The cost of all this red tape is now estimated to be around £40 billion a year.

69

Thanks to new employment rules, bureaucracy and government interference, every shop has now become like a post office; daunting, depressingly long queues of sad, blank-faced customers have given up hope; they stand, patiently, uncomplainingly waiting to be ignored and treated with summary disdain by bored, disinterested, discourteous clerks.

I have conducted whole transactions in shops without a member of staff looking at me or addressing one word to me. Often the assistant will moan to a friend while accepting money and operating their till. Sometimes they just stare into something fascinating hanging in the air about five foot behind me and two feet above my left shoulder.

70

'Civil litigation is still something any sensible person should look at with horror at the possibility of being involved in.'
LORD PHILLIPS, BRITAIN'S MOST SENIOR JUDGE, RATHER CLUMSILY POINTING OUT THAT THE BRITISH LEGAL SYSTEM NO LONGER OFFERS MUCH IN THE WAY OF JUSTICE.

71

The Labour Government's response to the constant barrage of red tape from the EU has been to set up two new teams of bureaucrats – the Better Regulation Executive and the Better Regulation Commission. These will be added to the other 674 different sets of regulators commissioned by the Labour Party to wrap red tape around British businesses. These 674 (now 676 and rising) regulators employ 61,000 bureaucrats and cost the taxpayer £4 billion in salaries and expenses. There are, of course, many thousands of additional bureaucrats employed to ensure that the dictates of these regulators are obeyed.

72

A reader wrote and told me that a boiler maintenance company hired to service his boiler had reported him to the authorities because he was in breach of some minor regulation he didn't know about. The regulation had been introduced just a few months earlier and, like most new regulations, had not been publicised.

73

The Freedom of Information legislation, introduced by the Labour Government, has been at best a shambles and at worst a piece of political propaganda. The Labour Government has failed dismally to produce documents which relate to things done by Labour Ministers but it has successfully managed to produce masses of documents relating to things that might humiliate previous Governments. They have used technicalities, privilege and the catch all excuse of national security to refuse to reveal information. Where these excuses haven't worked they have simply used the shredder.

You think I'm being cynical?

Not a bit of it.

Prior to the introduction of the Freedom of Information Act on 1st January 2005, the British Government instructed civil servants to shred all documents which (although of immense historical importance) might prove to be embarrassing or incriminating. We will probably never know just how many illegal and immoral things Blair's Ministers did.

Civil servants were also instructed to destroy e-mails (though they should know that this is pretty well impossible to do).

74

'You know how it is...give a bureaucrat a clapboard doghouse to look after and you end up with a luxury zoo complete with an administration office block.'
LEN DEIGHTON, WRITING IN *SPY LINE*

75

Dame Eliza Manningham-Buller, director general of MI5 has warned the British electorate that an erosion of civil liberties might be necessary to stop more British citizens being killed by terrorists. Her comments were expected to make it easier for the Labour Government to defeat the courts and to bring in tougher rules enabling them to arrest people without charges and to get rid of what is left of our civil rights. Dame Eliza didn't bother to specify which human rights needed to be compromised to help the police. She also said that MI5 would not be coerced into sharing intelligence with friendly agencies. So, presumably, she regards her agency as being above the law and above Parliament (since the only people who are likely to try to coerce MI5 would be Parliament and the courts).

Can the head of MI5 really be so naive, stupid and incompetent that she thinks that, for example, forcing mobile phone companies to store records of every call made will help the 'fight' against terrorism? Terrorists will simply use stolen phones, or phones that are unregistered to them. The best way to stop terrorism threatening the British public is to arrest Tony Blair, throw him in the Tower of London and bury the key in a silo full of nuclear waste.

I was appalled that the head of MI5 should dare to warn us that we might have to lose our civil liberties in order to fight the so-called war on terrorism. MI5 is no more entitled to tell us what liberties we are or are not entitled to, than traffic policemen are entitled to tell us what make of car we may or may not drive.

76

Blair's Government kept sixteen foreigners in British prisons, (mainly Belmarsh high security prison) for up to three years without trial.

The Labour Government seemed to believe that when the evidence against a terror suspect wouldn't stand up in a court of law (or had been gathered in a way – such as torture – that made it inadmissible) – they should have the right to just lock up the suspect anyway, ignoring any rights he might claim to have. (Actually, the Government wanted evidence obtained through torture to be admissible in court.)

In December 2004, the Law Lords rather meanly ruled that locking up people without trial was illegal, partly because it was disproportionate to the supposed threat (in other words the Government was exaggerating the threat for political purposes) and partly because it discriminated against foreigners.

After the Law Lords ruling the Government proudly and delightedly announced that they had found a way round the illegality of their actions. They said that they would introduce a type of 'house arrest' for suspects (on the grounds that 'house arrest' doesn't involve putting people in prison) and to get round the accusation of discriminating against foreigners they would lock up Britons as well. This would have the added advantage of bringing animal rights campaigners (mostly British) within the new tough law.

When there was some opposition to this the Government said that we just had to trust them to do the right thing.

'I just want to make the world a better place,' said Blair, who has, like his neo-conservative chums in the USA, undermined the values he purports to uphold and made the world, our world, a distinctly nastier place.

When the Labour Government's plans were questioned by other politicians Blair span his way out of it (as usual) by saying that 'nothing must stand in the way of protecting the security of our people'. Without even a giggle Blair told MPs: 'What we are desperate to do is to avoid a situation where, at a later point, people turn round and say: if you had only been as vigilant as you should have been, we could have averted a terrorist attack.'

It didn't seem to occur to him that if he could only stop himself starting wars we would all be a lot safer.

A retired law lord, Lord Ackner, condemned the proposals for house arrest as unlawful.

'This is a species of internment,' he said. 'There is no difference between prison and house arrest; it is the same thing, but in a different environment. It is replacing one bad law with another and is still a breach of human rights.'

But, as usual, no one in the Labour Government was listening.

77

Tony Blair dismissed the cold-blooded execution of an innocent Brazilian electrician on the London Underground as an unfortunate accident. But it wasn't; it was a symptom of something far more sinister.

This awful, tragic incident left those of us who care about what is left of our liberty and democracy asking a number of questions.

First, who decided that the police should have a 'shoot to kill' policy? Until the Brazilian electrician was executed hardly anyone in Britain (and probably no one outside the Home Office and a few police stations) knew that there even was such a policy. In a supposedly democratic country shouldn't such crucial decisions be at least debated in Parliament? Is this a secret EU policy which was imposed upon the UK? Is it true (as has been suggested) that the policy was based on advice given by Israel's security forces? (If so, wouldn't we have done better to take advice from a country which isn't constantly at war with just about everyone?) Or did a policeman take it upon himself to turn Britain into a country ruled by the gun? (This was not, it should be remembered, the first time that policemen in Britain have shot an innocent man). Many weeks after what was an incompetent state execution it appeared that the authority to shoot to kill innocent people might have been rubber-stamped by Blair and Blunkett (before he resigned in disgrace from the position of Home Secretary). If he did approve the shoot to kill policy, Blunkett, with the characteristic disinterest in any of the basic principles of democracy which was a hallmark of his years in power, didn't bother to make a statement to Parliament. A spokesman for Blair, when questioned about having approved of the shoot to kill policy claimed that he 'couldn't recall if it had crossed his desk'.

One of the reasons we don't have capital punishment in this country is because of the risk of the State killing an innocent man. But the police have now acquired the right to kill without either judge or jury. This surely poses a greater long-term threat to our freedom and safety than that posed by terrorists.

(The killing of innocent members of the public is becoming an increasingly popular pastime among police officers. Several readers have sent me local newspaper cuttings showing that previously healthy prisoners have died in police custody – some of the prisoners were surprisingly young and, presumably, quite healthy before being incarcerated. It is almost unheard of for policemen to be arrested or charged with any offence when this happens. Disciplinary action is hardly ever taken. Reports of these killings are often confined to local newspapers, with the result that most of us aren't aware just how often this is happening. Police brutality has become endemic and it is, perhaps, hardly surprising that the police should appear to have no qualms about having moved on to shooting innocent travellers. A solicitor, reporting yet another unlawful killing in a police station, wrote to me and explained that no one would be prosecuted for the murder because 'one policeman will not give evidence against another'. Furthermore, he also pointed out that unlike ordinary members of the public, the police can refuse to answer questions put to them. The same solicitor told me that 70% of the police in one area now take early retirement on the grounds of 'ill health' and receive large pensions paid for by taxpayers.)

Whenever a policeman is killed in the line of the duty there are stern cries for the police to be armed and for the death penalty to be re-introduced for the killing of a policeman. The police already kill far more members of the public than people kill policemen (and women) and it is much easier to make the argument that policemen should be hung for killing innocent citizens than that people should be hung for killing policemen. (The police are, after all, being paid to risk their lives protecting the public. It's part of why they get paid so generously. It has recently been revealed that police constables – the sort of policemen who used to patrol our streets but who now usually spend their time sitting in expensive cars on motorway bridges – can earn £100,000 a year).

Second, it has been claimed that the police have decided that suspects whom they decide to kill should be shot five times in the head. Who decided that it is necessary to shoot someone five times in the head in order to incapacitate him or her?

Third, is it true that the police gunman (or gunmen) who executed the innocent Brazilian used modern versions of the notorious dum dum bullets? These hollow point bullets are designed to expand on impact and are banned under the rules of international warfare. They were banned by the first International Peace Conference in 1899 and armies are not allowed to use them. But the British police do use them, though just who authorised their use is unclear.

Fourth, what happened to the CCTV film of the incident? It seems that none of the cameras on the tube station platform were working that day. Or the tapes went missing. One or the other. It's always the same, isn't it?

Fifth, why was there so much confusion and misinformation after the execution? The role of the media has been a disgrace. The day after the shooting of the Brazilian *The Sun* ran the headline 'One down – three to go'. They ran this even though the man who had been shot was not a terrorist. At least one national newspaper described the executed man as having worn a 'bomber' jacket. There were reports at the time of him having vaulted over the ticket barrier after ignoring police requests to stop. Where did this misinformation come from? It turned out later that the victim had wandered quite normally into the station, bought a newspaper, got on a train, sat down and then been shot in the head seven times. Possibly with dum dum bullets.

The police claim that the man was under observation. How many suicide bombers stop to buy a newspaper before they blow themselves up?

The gold medal for the crassest, most ignorant comment must go to a national newspaper columnist. 'Jean Charles was a casualty of war,' he wrote. 'And we are all very sorry about that. But it was a war that we did not start.'

'It was a war that we did not start.'

When national newspaper columnists are allowed to exhibit such staggering ignorance it is difficult to have hope for the future. Just as startling as the ignorance of the columnist is the fact that there apparently wasn't an editor or a sub-editor on the newspaper who is aware that for a century America and the UK have been waging an oil inspired war on Muslim countries throughout the Middle East. That columnist may be ignorant of Middle Eastern history and the fact that we and the Americans have been killing innocent Arabs to satisfy the needs of the oil industry for the best part of a century but one might reasonably have expected him to know that we invaded Iraq in 1991 and did it again in 2003; that 90% of the casualties in Iraq and Afghanistan are civilians (so much for 'surgical' precision bombing) and that independent observers claim that the Americans and the British in Iraq had, within the first two years of their illegal invasion, managed to kill over 100,000 Iraqi women and children.

Sixth, why did the police try to stop the Independent Police Complaints Commission from investigating this murder? The police are supposed to cooperate with the Commission whenever a prisoner dies in their custody. In this case the police deliberately killed a man who was not even their prisoner. The Metropolitan Police Commissioner suspended the Police Reform Act (passed by

Parliament) which requires the police to give information to the Independent Police Complaints Commission. He allegedly did this because he claimed that Britain was in what he rather dramatically called 'a fast-moving multi-site terrorist situation'. Once again, terrorism was used as an excuse to ignore the law and our rights.

Seventh, if the police are now permitted to carry guns, and to shoot perfectly innocent members of the public, would it not be reasonable to allow members of the public to carry firearms with which to defend themselves?

78

Once the police have power they never give it up. They're like the Government. A power gained is a power retained. The police in England now have the power to shoot to kill. And they will keep that power. A society in which the police carry guns and shoot before asking questions can reasonably be described as fascist. The companion policy to 'shoot to kill' is 'shoot on sight'.

But the shoot to kill policy is fatally flawed for one reason only: it is flawed because the people who shoot first are the bad guys.

In adopting this aggressive 'shoot first and then you won't have to waste time asking questions' policy the British police have merely followed the example of the British Government which now bases its international policies on exactly the same underlying philosophy.

79

According to the authorities, a racist or homophobic incident is any incident which is perceived to be racist or homophobic by the victim or any other person. So, if I think that Tony Blair is a racist because he signed the new EU constitution then he is.

80

In the 1980s, when travelling on a busy book promotion tour, I forgot my passport. I flew to Northern Ireland, took the train down to Dublin and then flew back to Birmingham with nothing more than a credit card as identification. The customs officers at Birmingham airport didn't blink an eye.

I wouldn't like to try it now. It's difficult to remember that at the beginning of the 21st century it was perfectly possible to wander in and out of Britain without showing a passport at all.

Forget all the nonsense about our living in a small world. If you want to travel then I suggest you do as much as you can as quickly as you can. Within a decade the process of travelling will be unbearable for two reasons.

First, the new laws, allegedly introduced to stop terrorists, money launderers and bird flu, will make air travel in particular time consuming, exhausting and tiresome.

Second, travel will be too dangerous (particularly for Britons and Americans.) When pirates attacked a cruise ship off Somalia in November 2005 the incident was widely reported because some of the tourists on the ship had filmed part of the attack. But what had not been reported was that the attack in November was the 28th similar attack of the year.

81

Travel used to be fun. All you needed was a wallet, a passport and a carpet bag. Customs officials weren't exactly friendly but they weren't downright rude, either. Today's traveller is assumed to be a bomb-carrying terrorist until proved otherwise and is, consequently, subjected to constant harassment at airports, ports and railway stations.

Ministers say the security precautions are there to protect us and to make us feel safe. If you believe that then you probably believe that Saddam Hussein had weapons of mass destruction stored in his garage. The truth is that the guards are there to make us feel frightened – not safe. The flak jacketed policemen and soldiers who patrol our airports, with their fingers on the triggers of their guns, are there to remind us that we are at war and that our Government is fighting a permanent war on terrorism. In reality the danger to our safety comes not from terrorists (who can remember when a group of terrorists last attacked a British airport?) but from trigger-happy security guards.

82

Visitors to the USA will now automatically be fingerprinted and photographed whether they like it or not. Immigration officials will take a digital photograph of every visitor and take prints of both index fingers. (It is because of demands from the USA that the EU has introduced new biometric ID card style passports for all European citizens.)

83

'Her Britannic Majesty's Secretary of State Requests and requires in the Name of Her Majesty all those whom it may concern to allow the bearer to pass freely without let or hindrance, and to afford the bearer such assistance and protection as may be necessary.'

Those are the words inside a British passport. Quaint.

84

Today every traveller can tell absurd stories of over-zealous guards. My eighty-something-year-old mother was berated when the half-witted thugs fingering their way through her handbag found a nail file. Full alert! Danger! Crisis! Men with guns came running. A full search uncovered a tiny pair of nail clippers too. Both nail file and nail clippers were confiscated. (What do they do with all these harmless toiletries? Are the nail file manufacturers responsible for these confiscations?) My mother who had seen considerably more real bombs than the entire security contingent at the airport wearily accepted that she had to re-purchase such harmless bits and pieces every time she travelled. (Just how could anyone hijack an aeroplane with nail clippers?)

I have fired off alarms by carrying too many paperclips in my jacket pocket, a notebook with a metal clip and a belt with a buckle. On each occasion adult guards have stood discussing these discoveries as though seriously concerned that I might hijack the aeroplane or train with them.

At one airport I (predictably) had my Swiss Army Penknife taken from me. There were a lot of British men on my flight and nearly half were walking around suffering from withdrawal symptoms. (An Englishman without a penknife is like a Frenchman without a packet of cigarettes.) The joke was that as soon as I got onto the plane the waitress handed me a much larger metal knife. The Swiss Army Penknife would have enabled me to take a cork out of a bottle or a boy scout out of a horse's hoof. I could have possibly done a tracheotomy with it. On the other hand, the knife they gave me was plenty big enough to stick between someone's ribs. The airline had presumably decided that since I had been given the knife so that I could use it to eat my plastic airline meal I would not dream of using it for any other purpose.

(And you can, of course, buy as many sharp objects as you like in the airside shops after going through security.)

I've lost count of the number of times I've 'pinged' when going through gates at airports and been roughly and incompetently searched by a half wit who has failed even to ask me to lift my hat (let alone examine it) before waving me on.

A friend of mine who is a professional photographer, and who was being thoroughly searched by policemen who correctly suspected him of having photographs of an event likely to embarrass the Government, successfully brought a roll of film into the country under his hat.

On one occasion, after I had gone through a metal detector and pinged (I always ping) a pleasant Japanese policeman asked me to open my shoulder bag. There was a book lying on top of the usual mixture of electronic gadgets. The guard peeked inside (seeing only the book), nodded and sent me back through the metal detector. Naturally, I pinged again as I went through the metal detector.

'Do you have a phone?' he asked.

'Yes.' I said.

'OK.' he said, nodding me through. 'That's OK then.'

85

Most people accept these pointless intrusions into their privacy because they believe the official line that these intrusions will protect us from wild-eyed fanatical terrorists committed to the destruction of our way of life.

It's all nonsense, of course.

Countless millions of ordinary decent law abiding travellers have now been searched, embarrassed, humiliated and delayed by brusque and arrogant guards at departure points all around Britain.

Do you know how many terrorists and money launderers have been arrested as a result of these rude intrusions?

Guess.

100,000?

10,000?

1,000?

Try again.

Try nil. Zero. None. Not one.

The arrogant and half-witted gropers employed to search travellers and their baggage have no chance of finding and stopping genuine terrorists and anyone who really believes that putting minimum wage half-wits in police style uniforms is likely to stop terrorists is certifiably insane.

Allowing slobbering, sweaty-fingered men to spend twenty minutes searching through the lingerie in a female traveller's case is unlikely to defend anyone. I don't suppose the security men ever think they're likely to find anything exciting; to them the chance to search through a fistful of panties and bras is just a perk of a dull and poorly paid job. They know that no traveller dare protest or object to a search. (To protest at their excesses is to invite immediate arrest as a potential terrorist or terrorist supporter.) On more than one occasion I have seen a guard who is conducting a search hold up items of clothing, wave them to a colleague and exchange a snigger or two.

(These days women can hide rocket launchers in their cleavage if they are sufficiently well endowed. After endless complaints guards are no longer allowed to check there.)

No Government Minister or security expert really believes that confiscating nail clippers from 80-year-old ladies does anything whatsoever to stop hijackers or other terrorists. They know that if terrorists want to smuggle weapons or bombs onto a plane they will do so. (Some of the most potent explosives are invisible to X-rays and it is, of course, possible to make a variety of weapons out of plastic.) Humiliating body searches conducted in public are never going to stop terrorists getting through.

But then the politicians must know that.

The searches are done to keep us afraid.

86

Recently a guard searched me (one of his moronic colleagues had placed my shoulder bag on top of my jacket and the man studying the X-ray screen had been confused by the resulting montage).

The guard methodically searched my jacket but when he handed it back to me he had completely missed two zipped pockets, one of which contained quite a large palm top computer.

On other occasions guards have examined bags but failed to find zipped compartments which weren't intended to be hidden.

The general incompetence of these searches (and the over-zealous enthusiasm with which the searchers pounce on and confiscate utterly harmless objects) is yet more evidence that these searches are conducted not for any practical purpose but merely to remind travellers of the terrorist threat. These are the day-to-day equivalent of Blunkett sending tanks to Heathrow airport.

The Government, which insists that travellers are harassed in this way, gives absurd powers of search, delay and confiscation to unregulated, commercial gangs of cheap hoodlums and backs the wretches with laws which make it an offence even to question their authority.

Why?

Simple.

The Government needs us to remain frightened. The Government wants us to be constantly reminded of the terrorist threat. They need to keep us cowed so that they can continue to introduce new laws which take away freedoms which have been ours for centuries. Fear is the Government's most potent weapon and they know how to use it.

Sending tanks to Heathrow airport was clearly absurd. But pictures of tanks at an airport on the evening television do two things: they make it look as though the threat is real and they make it look as though the Government is doing everything it can to protect us.

Forcing airports and railway companies to hire teams of thugs to harass travellers is equally absurd and pointless but, like the tanks, the uniformed guards who search our bags and pat us down are serving an underlying political purpose: they are there to remind us that we are under threat, that we must abandon our rights and dignity and that we must obey orders unquestioningly.

The guards and the searches are essential because they help to keep us subdued, guilty and frightened. Everyone with a functioning brain knows that they serve no practical purpose whatsoever.

87

The irrelevance and stupidity of all this so-called security is illustrated by the fact that security on the entrances to the Channel Tunnel is appallingly poor.

A 38-year-old man, wearing flip-flops and carrying no equipment of any kind recently walked through the Tunnel from England to France. He got through completely undetected. He was eventually spotted by French security cameras and arrested by the French. He was, they said, mentally ill.

Hardly reassuring.

If a nutter can do it, asylum seekers can clearly do it too. Not to mention people with bombs.

This was, by the way, the second time someone had walked from England to France through the Channel Tunnel. (No one has yet walked through in the other direction).

88

It's going to get worse.

Some new machines now being used at airports invade personal privacy to an alarming degree and may well expose travellers to physical danger.

For investigating baggage they are planning to use devices which employ low level radio waves to scan for explosives residues, and a scatter X-ray device which creates a three dimensional image of a bag's contents.

Far more alarming are the devices now being used to examine travellers themselves rather than just their luggage. There are, for example, X-ray scanners now available which penetrate clothing and provide airport security personnel with a real image of your naked body. So, those drooling security guards will now be able to gather round and leer at the breasts and sexual organs of all the travellers who pass through their gate. These are mass market strip searches.

Transsexuals and transvestites aren't the only people who are worried by this new invasion of our privacy. Complainants and protestors are firmly told that the equipment is vital for the war on terrorism. As usual, anyone who complains or protests is likely to be accused of being a terrorist or a terrorist supporter.

Just how dangerous all these X-rays are, is something we will have to wait to find out.

If plans to instal X-ray machines at railway stations go ahead then most commuters will probably die of cancer long before terrorists can get them.

89

The Americans have claimed sovereignty over all airspace and now rule the sky. Everything that flies, anywhere in the world, is in their jurisdiction. They have also claimed sovereignty over the sea. All of it. It's all theirs. Who says? They do.

90

A German traveller who was told that he couldn't leave his seat called the stewardess and, in halting English told her that if she didn't allow him to get up he would burst. The stewardess told the pilot who diverted the plane. The German was arrested and spent several months in an American prison before finally appearing before a judge who spoke German and who realised that the unfortunate man had had a full bladder and was merely trying to tell the stewardess that he needed to use the toilet.

91

I sometimes find myself welcoming the latest absurdity; the latest piece of legislation which takes away another small, remaining piece of our freedom. I live in hope that every new removal of our rights, every new piece of pointless red tape, will make a few more people realise that things are out of control. Every absurdity, every extra yard of red tape, takes us closer to the peaceful revolution which will free us from our chains.

92

How long will it be before our other rights disappear? How long will it be before we have to ask for permission to hold a perfectly peaceful demonstration? (Oh, sorry. Too late. We already have to do that.) How long before we have to ask for permission and buy a licence to sing Happy Birthday in the local pub? (Oh, dear. They've already got us with that one). How long before we have to get permission if we want to collect stamps? How long before we need permission to celebrate St George's Day? (No, sorry. Can't do that. Banned.) How long before we need permission to hold a carnival? (Ah. They got us on that one too.) Still, the stamp collecting is OK. For the time being.

93

The New Labour Government has criminalised protest, compassion, mental illness and homelessness. Hypocrisy is their only guiding force. They did the impossible and united lawyers and doctors in horror and astonishment when they planned new mental legislation which meant that mentally ill patients could be locked up, against their will and with no treatment, for up to 100 days. To the Labour Government the Human Rights Act is a piece of fluff; window dressing which they use when it is convenient and ignore when it is not. They hate the hard working English middle classes with a wholly politically incorrect venom.

When you hear politicians threatening to take 'measures needed to protect the public' you know things are getting worse. Every move they make, every new law they pass, is designed to make us more afraid and more willing to accept the loss of our liberty.

And, if you ever get tempted to think that you live in a civilised country, just remember that we have a Government which approves of torturing prisoners.

94

Every time our privacy and our freedom are taken away the politicians and the television commentators reassure us by saying : 'If you have nothing to worry about then you have nothing to fear.' They will tell you that all these new laws are being introduced to make your life safer, and to help protect you from dangerous people. Some people are actually taken in by these lies. They seem to welcome the new laws. They are frightened and they believe that sacrificing their freedom is the only way to be safe.

Actually, all I want is for someone to stop the vandals and the petty thieves and the muggers and the hooded yobs and thugs who make our towns too dangerous to enter after dark.

None of the new legislation will do anything to stop that.

But the new freedom crunching legislation that the Blairs, the Blunketts, the Clarkes, the Straws et al are introducing is destroying our way of life and exposing us ever more to the power of the bureaucrats and the politicians and the shadowy backers behind them.

None of this new legislation will ever be revoked (unless we force a major change in the way our country is run). New legislation never is withdrawn. Politicians never give up power.

Even if all the so-called terrorism threats disappeared overnight (and don't forget that Bush and Blair have warned us that the war on terrorism will go on for ever) the laws that have taken away our privacy and our freedom will not be revoked.

95

The Government's distaste for trial by jury and such old-fashioned concepts as 'innocent until proved guilty' may have been acquired from the EU, and some of their more fascist notions are undoubtedly imported directly from the USA, but some of the Labour Government's attempts to take away our freedom are all their own work. For example, it has even been suggested (quite seriously) that individuals merely accused of sex offences should be jailed and put on the sex offenders register. Merely accused, you note. So, if you have a row over parking with your neighbour and, out of spite, he accuses you of a sex offence you will be jailed. No defence. No trial. No chance.

Nothing it seems, is too outlandish or too great an insult to justice.

And always, when challenged, the Government resorts to its catch-all defence: 'Our laws are designed to stop terrorists, money launderers and paedophiles. If you oppose our laws you must either be a terrorist, a money launderer or a paedophile.'

Those who oppose new, fascist legislation are described as appeasers, at best encouraging the terrorists by opposing plans to combat them and at worst endangering the lives of innocent babies and old ladies by comforting the enemy. Critics are threatened with ignominy and (if they persist) with ruin and indefinite imprisonment.

96

Writing about our fascist leaders is becoming an increasingly hazardous activity.

In 2004 a total of 129 journalists and other media workers were killed in strange, mysterious, undefined or violent circumstances. It was the deadliest year since records began for writers and photographers.

When journalists and authors die mysteriously there are rarely, if ever any investigations.

For example, in the 129 deaths which occurred in 2004 there were very few investigations. No findings were released and all members of the military or police who were thought to have been involved were exonerated.

Chapter Three

How We Stopped Being A Democratic Country And Became A Fascist State. Who Are The People Who Are Wrecking Our Lives? What Sort Of People Are They? What Drives Them?

1

A democratic country is one which is run by the people. To avoid the practical problems of having 60 million people voting on every conceivable issue (and all having their say) we use a system in which groups of citizens delegate their authority to elected representatives. The theory is that our elected representatives speak on our behalf and ensure that our wishes are followed. This is what is known as a parliamentary democracy. It's what we are supposed to have. (And it's what we used to have.)

The primary requirement for a real parliamentary democracy is an assembly of honest, dedicated men and women who treat the electorate (who are, after all, their employers) with respect, and who uphold the honour of the authority they are loaned with a real sense of public responsibility.

Sadly, instead of this, we are cursed with a bunch of greedy, self-serving liars and cheats who have, on the whole, chosen politics as a career because they are neither competent enough nor honest enough to follow careers in any other sphere.

Most of the people going into full-time politics these days are professional politicians in their 20s and 30s who have never had proper jobs. They join a party while at university and choose politics as a career in the same way that other students might choose to become insurance salesmen or orthodontic specialists. Most have little or no interest in 'improving the world' but are interested primarily in carving out a good and profitable career for themselves. Their energy is spent defending their own interests and that, invariably, means defending the interests of the party and the establishment. Because they have no real skills or talents and no experience outside politics they are terrified that they will lose what they have suddenly, undeservedly (and, probably to their own surprise) found themselves enjoying. So they lie and cheat, do what they are told and vote for bills for which neither they nor their constituents have any enthusiasm.

And they don't listen. They don't listen. They never listen. In the bad old days of Macmillan and Wilson it was possible occasionally to get through to the people running the country. Even with Thatcher you now and then felt that what you were saying made a difference. Up until then politicians occasionally had the sense and the inclination to take notice of the electors. But with the arrival of Blair, self-serving whore and weapons dealer extraordinaire, that feeling ended. Blair and company never listen. They don't give a damn what the people think. They're in this to pay the mortgage. So bugger truth, bugger honesty, bugger integrity and bugger the people.

Modern professional politicians in the Labour Party are driven so much by personal greed that all their reforms are built on performance-related pay and bonuses. It never occurs to them that people might work better – and harder – if encouraged to do the right thing, or to care about what they do and the people they do it for. It never occurs to them because they themselves are not driven by these things.

2

Today, in Britain we have no democracy.

Instead, we have an electoral lottery every few years; a lottery which results in the leader of the party which gains most parliamentary seats claiming absolute power. We have a Prime Minister who does many things – including taking the country into war – against the wishes of the electorate.

In our version of a parliamentary democracy the only people whose votes count for anything are the ones who live in marginal constituencies where there is some doubt about the electoral outcome.

Most electors live in constituencies where their vote is pointless. Many will never vote for a winning candidate because the party they support is too weak in their area to have a chance of victory. There are only about 100 seats which change hands on a regular basis. So only about 15% of British electors have any real influence on the nation's Government. The other 85% have no influence whatsoever.

Moreover, our bizarre and utterly unfair 'first past the post' system means that there are many MPs who represent constituencies where a huge majority of electors voted for someone else.

Is it any wonder that the number of people who bother to vote has been falling steadily for years? The Labour Government claims that people don't vote because they are happy with the way things are and don't feel any need to make their voices heard. But, as always, the Labour Party is woefully out of touch; it isn't apathy which explains why people do nothing, it is the knowledge (not a feeling, the knowledge) that whatever they do, nothing will change. The knowledge that things have got out of our control.

3

Britons who want to live in an area with good hospitals, decent roads and a moderately efficient infrastructure, should choose to live in marginal constituencies. Generally speaking the standard of living will remain higher in those constituencies where a Government is frightened of losing a valuable parliamentary seat than it will be in those where the Government either takes victory for granted or has abandoned all hope of gaining the seat. Governments will be slow to close hospitals and allow schools to run down in marginal constituencies.

4

*'Democracy and socialism have nothing in common but one word:
equality. But notice the difference: while democracy seeks
equality in liberty, socialism seeks equality in
restraint and servitude.'*
D'ALEXIS DE TOCQUEVILLE

5

Our version of democratic politics means that one party wins because the other party loses. And even at his long-ago height of popularity, before the electors realised just how much of a liar and confidence trickster he is, Blair never got to run the country by having a majority of the people vote for him. I suspect that many of the people who voted for Blair didn't really vote for him; they voted against the Welsh Transylvanian 'with something of the night about him', the funny little chap with the bald head and the double barrelled name, and the rather pleasant but naive chap who wore a baseball cap and boasted of drinking 15 pints of beer a night. People voted for Edward Heath because they couldn't stand Harold Wilson and suspected that he was a crook. (They didn't know at the time that Heath was – even worse – a traitor.) They voted for Thatcher because they didn't like James Callaghan and they voted for Blair in '97 not because they were taken in by the grin and the hype but because they were thoroughly fed up with John Major's incompetent and rat infested Tory party.

6

A voting system only works – and does what it is supposed to do – if it reasonably reflects the balance of public opinion. Britain's system clearly fails since we have, since 1997, had a Prime Minister, elected with a minority of votes, who treats the House of Commons and the Cabinet as an inconvenience and rules the country as a dictator. Occasionally, when his Government's activities become too much (starting wars, killing witnesses, re-nationalising private companies) there are legal enquiries. Everyone knows the result of the enquiry before the hearings start. Today's Government enquiries invariably deliver the hoped for result.

Blair has governed as though he has a massive popular majority – pushing through unpopular measures and starting unwanted wars – with the excuse that his mandate gives him this authority. But even in 2001, when he won a second massive parliamentary majority, Blair gained only 40% of the popular vote. I suspect that as long as he has the power Blair doesn't give a fig. To him, and to all modern professional politicians, democracy is an outrageous inconvenience which they do their best to ignore.

Our voting system is grotesquely unfair and has been for decades. In some parts of the country MPs are sent to Parliament by 20,000 voters. In other areas there are 100,000 voters for each MP. In 1983 the Liberal/SDP Alliance won over a quarter of the popular vote and ended up with 3.5% of parliamentary seats. As each party gets into power it fine-tunes the voting system, and the constituency boundaries, in order to improve its own chances of winning. The Labour Party introduced postal voting not because they thought it would improve democracy but because they thought it would improve their chances of winning. Despite the fact that the evidence showed the postal voting system to be heavily flawed (not to mention crooked) the Labour Party resolutely stuck to it.

It is perhaps hardly surprising that so many people believe that the saying 'if voting changed anything they would abolish it' isn't much of a joke.

7

'Both parties will merchandise their candidates and issues by the same methods that business has developed to sell goods. These include scientific selection of appeals and planned repetition. Radio spot announcements and advertisements will repeat phrases with a planned intensity. Billboards will push slogans of proven power. Candidates need, in addition to rich voices and good diction, to be able to look 'sincerely' at the TV camera.'
An editor of a leading business journal writing in 1956 about how political parties would in future choose their candidates.

8

'All that is now needed is money and a candidate who can be coached to look 'sincere'. Under the new dispensation, political principles and plans for specific action have come to lose most of their importance. The personality of the candidate and the way he is projected by the advertising experts are the things that really matter...The methods now being used to merchandise the political candidate as though he were a deodorant, positively guarantee the electorate against ever hearing the truth about anything.'
ALDOUS HUXLEY (WRITING IN 1959)

9

Two centuries ago journalist and publisher William Cobbett wrote about Pocket Boroughs and Rotten Boroughs. He complained at the way that parliamentary seats could be bought and at corruption and bribery affecting the decisions of MPs. He raged about the 'sinecurists, placemen and taxeaters' who took from the country but never gave anything back in return.

Nothing has changed.

Today, parliamentary seats are effectively in the gift of the political party. Instead of local noblemen and landowners handing out seats, it is now the party leaders who choose new MPs. Their assistants, researchers and dogsbodies are rewarded with parliamentary seats because they have proved their faithfulness to the party and to the leader, not because they have proved their integrity or their ability to serve the public. The House of Lords is stuffed with Blair's chums and former flat mates. The nation is run by quangos peopled almost exclusively by hangers on. Dishonest non-entities are rewarded for loyalty and small services with hefty salaries and positions of power. Two hundred years later everything is just as corrupt as it was in Cobbett's day.

10

Our bizarre system means that, on the whole, the major political parties have far too much power.

Most people vote not for individuals but for parties. And once a party has won an election its leadership will have dictatorship-like powers. Through a mixture of carrot and stick (handing out jobs to

MPs who behave themselves and threatening to withdraw the party's backing from MPs who don't) Blair (and any other leader) can control Parliament with ease.

For several decades British Prime Ministers have been steadily losing touch with the electorate – and taking more and more power to themselves. Blair has taken this to a new level. He talks of 'debate' and 'dialogue' and 'The Big Conversation' with the electorate. What deceit this is.

11

*'As I would not be a slave, so I would not be a master.
This expresses my idea of democracy.'*
ABRAHAM LINCOLN

12

We loan our power to the people we elect as leaders but as soon as they are given the keys to the grace and favour mansions and allocated the chauffeur driven limousines which go with the power, they ignore the needs and wishes of the people who lent them that power. They forget all the 'promises' they made when trying to persuade the electors to vote for them.

We need politicians who think long-term but we get politicians who think short-term. Blair's only concession to long-term planning was to start planning his second general election the moment he had won the first one.

Our form of democracy favours dishonest political entrepreneurs. The liar who promises most and does so most effectively, and with a winning telegenic smile will now always beat the honest, practical politician who genuinely wants to do good.

We have created a system which requires the skills of the salesman and the actor rather than the skills of an intellectual or a statesman.

The Labour Party picked Tony Blair as their leader because they had cold-bloodedly recognised his grotesquely Clintonesque qualities.

13

We are living in a country which is controlled by a unique mixture of dictatorship, communism and totalitarianism. The only accurate word to describe it is 'fascism'.

We don't have a Prime Minister (in the sense that Winston Churchill was a Prime Minister). Instead we have a malevolent dictator, a man for whom most of us never voted in any election, a man whose primary motive seems to be self-aggrandisement and self-enrichment rather than any sense of public service.

14

When the invasion of Iraq took place there was no doubt that an overwhelming majority of the British people disapproved of the war and didn't want it to go ahead. (The American people, who had been misled into believing that Saddam Hussein was responsible for the attack on the twin towers in New York, supported the war on a tit for tat basis.) In any sort of democracy Britain would not have supported the war.

15

'Security is no justification for the breach of the fundamental principles which underpin our democratic system. No deprivation of liberty by ministerial say so, no midnight secret knock on the door, no gulags whether in Siberia or in Guantanamo.'
LORD THOMAS, FORMER HIGH COURT JUDGE

16

Our democratic rights have been eroded to the point of non-existence. Despite the fact that the French and the Dutch people voted against the EU's new planned constitution much of the constitution has, nevertheless been put into action. The European Commission, and the bureaucrats, have simply ignored the will of the people and have carried on as they wanted. The bureaucrats claim that since the 25 member governments and the European Parliament have endorsed the EU constitution the public vote simply doesn't matter. The Labour Government supports this blatantly fascist attitude.

Here are just a few of the parts of the EU constitution (the one which was rejected by the people of Europe) which had been put into practice by the autumn of 2005 (just a couple of months after the European Constitution had allegedly been abandoned):

- The EU criminal code
- The European Space Programme
- The European Defence Agency
- The Mutual Defence Clause
- The External Border Agency
- The Fundament Rights Agency (the monitoring centre for racism and xenophobia)
- Autonomous politico-military command structures
- The European External Action Service (the EU diplomatic corps)
- The EU Prosecuting Magistracy
- The EU Foreign Minister
- The Charter of Fundamental Rights

By the time you read this I doubt if there will be much of the Constitution left which hasn't been made law.

Meanwhile, there is a remarkably anarchic flavour to much of the EU's activities.

Five out of the 12 euro-zone members were, by October 2005, in breach of the stability and growth pact (the EU's fiscal rules) and the EU had given up trying to show that it cared. Only three of the 15 pre-enlargement member states (Ireland, Sweden and, wouldn't you just know it, the UK) are applying the principle of free movement of people to the 10 states that joined the EU on May 1st. France and Germany (which regularly meet together to decide what the EU will and will not do) take virtually no notice at all of EU decisions and make it clear that they regard themselves as above such things.

17

The EU wants a single taxation system for the whole of the new European superstate. They are working remorselessly towards that end.

But that end is merely a beginning.

What *they* really want is a global tax. A world tax.

And that is coming too.

Just wait for it.

Wait for the politicians to start talking of the need for world taxes to pay for saving Africa, dealing with global warming, helping children, fighting poverty, defeating cancer or overcoming terrorism.

And with a global tax will come a global currency.

One single currency, shared by people around the world.

That, I now suspect, was one of the reasons for the development of the euro.

A well placed friend of mine, with contacts in the right places, tells me that as the American dollar crashes (as it is bound to do since America's debt to the rest of the world is so huge) so the Americans will replace it with a new currency – abandoning all the fiscal responsibilities associated with the dollar as it exists today.

The new American dollar (whatever it is called) will be merged with the euro.

And that will be the start of a new global currency.

18

Petitions taken to No 10 Downing Street are simply stored for a while and then shredded. No one looks at them or cares what message they carry. The signing and delivering of petitions is a hollow process which is regarded with mild contempt by politicians. As taxpayers we carry the moral stains of the crimes committed in our names, but we have no way of protesting about them. Our duties and responsibilities are constantly extended but our rights and freedoms are constantly diminished.

19

It is fairly widely accepted that political viewpoints can be illustrated by a circle. At the top of the circle, just to the right of the centre point, where a clock would show twelve o'clock, sit the ultra-right-wing fascists. The sort who usually wear shiny boots and favour small moustaches. Move further down the circle, going clockwise, and you come first to the extreme right wing conservatives, and then to the more moderate right wingers. At the bottom of the circle, roughly in the middle of the traditional political spectrum, are the liberals: the fence sitters, people who are neither right-wing nor left-wing but who describe themselves as 'middle-of-the-roaders'. Moving on round the circle, we come to the more left-wing orientated. Depending on their country of origin and what they had for breakfast they may describe themselves as 'socialists' or 'social democrats' or, in Britain, old-fashioned Labour supporters. And then, at about 11 o'clock on the circle, are the communists. The far left hammer and sickle socialists: the Marxists, the Trotskyists and so on.

You will have noticed that by now we are pretty well back where we started: at the top of the circle. And the hard-line, hard-left communists are mixed up with the hard-line, hard-right fascists.

That's exactly how it is in the real world of politics.

In practical terms there is no discernible difference between the political fanatics on the far left and the political fanatics on the far right.

In the past this curious similarity between communists and fascists has been largely of theoretical interest.

But now, suddenly, it has become quite real.

George W. Bush and his right-wing Republican neo-conservatives have now teamed up with Britain's far left Labour party.

20

Blair, who based his political style on Bill Clinton (minus the disappearing cigar and the accommodating young assistant) originally sold himself and his party to the electorate as a moderate middle-of-the-road politician. But, in the first eight years of the Labour Party in power it became increasingly clear that this was a facade: a piece of spin designed to win votes from middle England; a device to deflect criticism and to encourage right wing newspaper proprietors to provide the support the Labour Party needed to win elections. Gordon Brown's obsession with means testing and Stephen Byers's re-nationalisation of Railtrack were just two examples showing precisely how far to the left Blair and Co. really are. The ruthless, freedom crushing laws introduced by David Blunkett at the Home Office provided a vivid and quite shocking illustration of just how little difference there is between communism and fascism. (The word 'statism' is an attractive one, describing a political system in which the state has substantial central control over social and economic affairs, and accurately summarises the sort of policy favoured by New Labour. But it doesn't go quite far enough.)

In practice, the American Republicans under Bush and the British Labour Party under Blair, have both introduced practical fascism into their respective nations.

21

The official Oxford English Dictionary definition of a fascist is: 'One of a body of Italian nationalists organised in 1919 under Benito Mussolini to oppose Bolshevism.'

Now, this, admittedly, doesn't take us much further forward so the next step is to see how Mussolini, the 'inventor' of this political philosophy defined fascism. And this is where it gets interesting.

Here is Mussolini's definition: 'Liberalism denied the state in the name of the individual; fascism re-asserts the rights of the state as expressing the real essence of the individual.'

Read that and remember that Mussolini invented practical fascism. His definition is, by definition, unarguably correct. Mussolini's views on most things may well be best brushed under the carpet. But his views on fascism are the very best you can get. Fascism was, after all, a topic on which the man was an expert. If Mussolini had gone in for Mastermind his chosen subject would have been fascism and he would have scored top marks.

And you don't need to think about Mussolini's definition for long to realise that both America and Britain are now being run as fascist states. Bush and his oily-fingered comrades got there from one direction; Blair and his slimy comrades got there from the other; but they both ended up in exactly the same place. Both America and Britain have fascist governments. And fascism reduces our freedom and privacy because only the state really matters and the state (and those who work for it and control it) takes precedence over everyone and everything else.

22

Practical fascism means that the state comes first and the people come a long way second. The state's employees exist to defend the state (rather than to care for the people) and that is why their loyalties are to the state. That's the fundamental difference between a fascist state and any sort of democracy.

23

The state used to provide leadership, representing the people in the nation's relations with other countries and making decisions designed to protect the safety of the citizens, and to manage the infrastructure without which no country can survive.

The state's original purpose was to provide services which could not properly be provided by individuals within communities. These requirements are more limited than they might now appear to be and the original, expected role of the state was considerably smaller than the role which politicians have adopted.

The primary purpose of a proper democratic government is to protect the lives, liberty and property of its citizens. Any time a government does anything that isn't protecting the lives, liberty and property of its citizens it is exceeding its authority. Running an army is an essential government activity. Providing a decent transport infrastructure (roads and railways) is an essential government activity. Starting wars for no good reason is not within the remit of a proper government.

Today the state has taken on a management role, and politicians who were hired to protect individual citizens have adopted policies designed to exploit the citizens and to take advantage of them. Politicians who were elected to look after the voters now expose the people they are paid to look after to increased danger.

Worse still this micro-management style (practised by governments for several decades but dramatically exacerbated by Blair) has resulted in the creation of a fascist government which exists to protect its own survival rather than to protect the interests of the electorate. The people didn't want to go to war with Iraq. Parliament didn't want to go to war with Iraq. It was always clear that going to war with Iraq would dramatically increase – not reduce – the danger to individual citizens. (Decent countries don't start wars unless they are necessary for the defence of the realm.) In the end Britain went to war with Iraq because it suited Blair's personal agenda. We went to war with Iraq so that Blair could ingratiate himself with Bush and other powerful Americans and, therefore, ensure for himself a more than ample income on his retirement.

The micro management fascist style of government favoured by the British Labour party has led to another dramatic change in the way people behave. The Government's programme of welfare support, and its blind enthusiasm for means testing, mean that increasing numbers of people are now content to lie back and let their nation look after them. They demand and expect free care. Instead of encouraging and rewarding self-sufficiency we are encouraging dependence. This is not going to be easy to cure and is almost certain to get considerably worse before it gets better. There are millions of citizens in Britain today who genuinely believe that the state owes them a living. They seem to assume that the state has a duty to provide them with money and services and they never seem to question the origin of either. Their dependence on the state is the reason for their loyalty to the state. Blair and Brown and company exploit this loyalty to strengthen and maintain their power.

24

When running for office, politicians aim to avoid annoying people. Once they've got the chauffeur driven car, the free house, the expense allowance, the fat salary, the guaranteed index-linked pension scheme, the perks, the party invitations, the free travel and the power, they tend to be less cautious and less restrained about upsetting the voters. Before an election the voters are treated as wise and discerning. They are much respected. After an election the voters are dross – to be ignored and reviled. The aim of winning an election is simply to win. The power is everything. As soon as one election is won the next objective is (as a Labour spokesman admitted) to win the next one. There are no real passions or policies. The only 'p' word that matters is 'power'.

Modern Labour politicians want to destroy our freedom, privacy and independence so that we do not question the power of the state, so that we put up with whatever happens, so that we allow the state to take ever more power over us and so that we continue voting for Labour. If the Conservatives ever claw their way back into power (and if they do it will be because of disillusionment with Labour rather than anything else) they will doubtless behave in exactly the same way.

Today's politicians are in business to get their noses into the trough. Think Labour. Think greed. Think Blair. Think greed and vanity. The freebies, the petty thieving, the deceit.

If you think the duty of politicians is to protect their country and their responsibility is to the people who voted for them, then the vast majority of MPs (and all of those who are unquestioningly loyal to any one of the three main political parties in Britain) are traitors and betrayers. They are traitors to their country and they have betrayed their constituents.

25

The New Labour Government has made sleaze an art form. Tory sleaze usually involved a few quid in a brown envelope. Or sex. Labour sleaze is far, far worse than anything the Tories ever thought of. Within days of taking power the Labour Government was taking what looked suspiciously like bribe money. Remember the million pounds they accepted from the motor racing people? And the decision to allow racing cars to carry tobacco advertising? In the weeks and months prior to their first election the Labour Party promised animal lovers everything they wanted: an end to abuse and animal cruelty. Immediately after taking power these promises were forgotten, ignored and denied and the Labour Party switched its allegiance to the international pharmaceutical industry. By 2005 the number of entirely pointless animal experiments being conducted in the United Kingdom had soared.

26

The entire Labour Government shows how people fail when they are promoted above their capabilities. There is not one member of the Labour Government whom I would trust to handle the unwanted ornaments counter in a local charity shop. These are seriously inadequate bozos who have been raised to positions of power despite (or, perhaps, because of) their possessing no human qualities other than greed, ego and self-interest.

27

The electors used to be swayed by policies, hopes, dreams and aspirations. Today, people vote for the party which lies best and the leader who has the most engaging TV smile and the best make-up artist. Depressing, isn't it?

28

Politicians survive because we tend to assume that there must be at least some truth in what they say. This is our weakness and it is their strength. These days politicians don't even bother to get facts straight before distorting them. The Blair-faced liar is a relatively new phenomenon in English politics. But it is, it seems, a phenomenon which is here to stay.

29

We need a leader of insight and integrity more than ever. Instead we have an unappetising selection of greedy, self-serving opportunists.

Blair has abused the words 'trust me'. How many would trust him, liar, war criminal and general all round self-serving fascist, to do anything? How many would trust Brown to run the household accounts? (It was, let us not forget, Gordon Brown who, to the astonishment and puzzlement of everyone who knows anything about investment, insisted on selling 60% of the Bank of England's gold at rock bottom prices – losing over £1.6 billion through his stupidity.) How many would trust that pathetic Lothario, Blunkett with their wives or daughters? How many would trust Straw or Prescott to go to the corner shop and buy a newspaper?

30

When I turned up at University to start my six years as a medical student I was told that I had to be member of the National Union of Students. I've never liked people telling me what I have to do or join. My refusal to join the NUS led to all sorts of problems. I used the United Nations Charter to force the University to let me stay out of the union. Eventually the University changed its rules. Students no longer had to be members of the NUS.

I remember the name of the President of the NUS.

Jack Straw.

I thought he was a loathsome piece of detritus.

But my opinion of him has gone steadily downhill ever since.

31

Name one thing John Prescott has done to improve the quality of life in Britain. OK. That's perhaps a bit mean. I'll make it easier. Name one good thing done by any Labour Minister.

Still got you, didn't I?

New Labour Ministers like to masquerade as right wing liberal humanists; social democrats; socialists who have seen the light and moved a little to the right. But in reality they are the meanest sort of rabid left-wing fascists. It is impossible to think of leaders who have done less for their country than Labour Party Ministers have done for Britain.

32

The Labour Government can't resist interfering in everything. Their obsessions with multiculturalism, means-testing and political correctness have ensured that the country's problems have got worse more speedily than they might otherwise have done. The Labour Party's gang of incompetent thugs now control almost every aspect of our lives. The old Roman emperors ruled by bread and circuses. Modern Labour politicians rule with the aid of child allowances and Big Brother.

33

'...millions of abnormally normal people, living without fuss in a society to which, if they were fully human beings, they ought not to be adjusted, still cherish 'the illusion of individuality', but in fact they have been to a great extent de-individualised. Their conformity is developing into something like uniformity. But uniformity and freedom are incompatible. Uniformity and mental health are incompatible too...Man is not made to be an automaton, and if he becomes one, the basis for mental health is destroyed.'
ALDOUS HUXLEY

34

The Labour Party has used both the tax system and its own appallingly unfair means-testing system to help strengthen the power of the State by destroying the institution of marriage.

The Labour Government doesn't want people marrying and being secure. People who feel secure and safe are likely to be independent. And independent individuals are an anathema to a fascist state. So Blair, Brown and the rest of the Labour Party have done their best to make marriage economically unattractive. For example, property gains tax reliefs are much better if a couple stay single – both can claim a property as their home and pay no capital gains tax. The Inland Revenue has targeted couples who have set up small companies together. This has been done in such a blatant way that independent observers have described it as a tax inspired attack on marriage as an institution. Two people who aren't married are allowed to share dividends without the Inland Revenue getting interested. If two people who are married do it then it is regarded as tax evasion. If half of a married couple needs institutional care the other must pay for it. If half of an unmarried couple needs institutional care the state will pay. The state gives and gives and gives to unmarried couples, to encourage them, and takes and takes and takes from married couples. Unmarried couples are given all the rights previously bestowed on the married. But they have none of the fiscal responsibilities. It is difficult to argue that homosexuals who commit themselves to long-term relationships should not be allowed the same rights as heterosexual couples. But why should heterosexuals who refuse to marry be given those rights too? The only possible point of that is to devalue marriage and stability. The whole outrageous attack on marriage has become so potent that Labour's benefit system is totally destroying marriage by rewarding couples if they live apart. Tax credits which were introduced by the Britain's worst ever Chancellor, Gordon Brown, in 1998, favour single parents and discriminate against two-parent families. Evidence produced by the Government's own Office for National Statistics (never published, but leaked) shows that 1.2 million couples in Britain now choose to live apart together. They lie and pretend to be single because the Government's absurd anti-marriage tax credit system means that they will be hugely better off if they do so. The average couple who split up will be £58 a week better off in handouts. Some couples are more than £200 a week better off if they aren't married. From an economic point of view the system is stupid and indefensible. There is no sound economic reason for it. The Government's system means that it loses tax revenue and has to pay out extra tax benefits and credits. Why would a Government which is desperately short of cash to pay for wars and civil servant pensions behave so stupidly? The only possible explanation is that the Government has a hidden agenda. And the only possible hidden agenda is the destruction of marriage as an institution. And the only possible explanation is that the Government knows that if they destroy marriage they will strengthen the state. Practical fascism in action. Pure, unadulterated fascism.

35

Why is the Government so desperately keen for everyone to become computer literate? Could it possibly have anything to do with the fact that if we all communicate via computers they can spy on us – and control us – more easily?

36

Polls show that people distrust their political leaders more than ever before.

A global poll conducted in 2005 showed that:

- ◆ 63% of electors view politicians as dishonest
- ◆ 52% of electors say that politicians are unethical
- ◆ 50% of electors say the world is less safe because of the invasion of Iraq
- ◆ 73% of electors in Britain say that Blair and the Labour Government gave in to pressure from the American Government
- ◆ 90% of British electors say they would not trust Tony Blair to look after their savings

37

We have Government by crony. Judges are appointed to key posts if they are friends of Blair or Blair's wife or Blair's cronies. The Labour Government has become more of a family business than the Royal Family. And the family in control is called Blair. Ever shared a flat with Blair? Help yourself to a peerage and a well paid job.

38

The greed of Blair's wife seems well documented. She is the first Prime Minister's wife to seek to make a fortune out of her position. (Though, thanks to her own lack of talent and charm and some vestigial sense of public good taste, she has been gloriously unsuccessful in this.) She went to Australia and took huge fees from a charity for making speeches to plug her book on Downing Street spouses. Fortunately, the book was not a great success. The wretched woman wears flashy watches given to her by an Italian Prime Minister who is constantly defending himself against charges of corruption.

By declaring his wife's earnings in the official register of MPs interests, Blair has effectively admitted that his wife Cherie Blair (a woman who could and probably would whinge for the EU at the next Olympics) has cashed in on her husband's infamy in a big way. More than 1,000 people paid £50 a head for 'a conversation with the wife of Tony Blair' in which the loathsome grinning witch talked about her life as a prime ministerial consort. Cherie was promoted as 'The First Lady of Downing Street' in advertising material. Why anyone on the planet would pay money to spend time in the same room as this thoroughly obnoxious woman is a mystery to me. Anyone willing to pay to be within a mile of the Blair witch requires urgent medical attention.

39

Bush and Blair are the 21st century's most notable modern war criminals. Compared to these two cheap crooks, the much despised Milosovic seems positively avuncular and should be in line for the Nobel Peace prize. We can't do anything about Bush. He is President of another country. But Blair is our responsibility and our disgrace. Blair, who will surely be remembered as the least trustworthy and most disgraceful of all British Prime Ministers, has lead Britain into more wars than any leader in modern times. Kosovo, Sierra Leone, Bosnia, Afghanistan and the Gulf. It's difficult to keep track of his war crimes. None of Blair's wars have advanced our national interests; all have gravely damaged national security and exposed us to further risks.

40

Bush can at least claim that the wars he has started were going to make money for some of his fellow countrymen. To that extent he can claim justification. And the invasion of Afghanistan was (misguided) revenge.

What is Blair's excuse for taking us into America's wars?

Personal aggrandisement and wealth.

Bush wants to make big money for himself and his pals. Blair is content to help Bush in return for the crumbs.

41

Blair is a reality television Prime Minister; constantly searching for photo opportunities, living for the latest sheaf of press cuttings and the next TV appearance just as much as any Big Brother contestant or minor pop star passing through the lower reaches of the pop firmament.

42

Blair has only two skills: smiling and lying (though, to be fair, I must admit that he does seem perfectly capable of doing these two things at the same time). He is a political manager (and a bad one at that) who has used fear to give himself and his party a fake purpose.

43

'Do not underestimate the significance of a doubled membership,' said Tony Blair to the Labour Party in 1997. 'It puts us in touch with real people, real communities. This is a party of the people, not pressure groups.'

Since then the membership of the Labour Party has halved.

So it is presumably fair to infer that the Labour Party is out of touch with real people and real communities and is a party of pressure groups, not the people.

44

Blair doesn't call his invasion of Iraq a war. He calls it a conflict.

This is a typically slimy, slippery piece of verbal spin which denies even the honour of death in war to the Britons he sent to a pointless death. Everyone who voted for the Labour Party in 2005 has blood on their hands and should be tried as an accessory to war crimes.

45

The civil servants who helped New Labour prepare the 'dodgy dossier' on Iraq (which provided false support for Blair's War) were rewarded in the honours list. That is symptomatic of what is wrong in Britain today. There is no sense of right or wrong. No one takes responsibility for their actions. No one apologises or resigns. Neither politicians nor civil servants have principles. Modern politicians (as exemplified by Blair and Brown) have only one golden rule: 'Never apologise.'

46

The Labour Government gets on very well with totalitarian oppressive fascist regimes – such as China. Maybe this is because Labour Ministers feel comfortable with such regimes.

47

The sort of people who go into politics these days are the sort of people who can't possibly get a real job. They wouldn't even be honest enough to work as estate agents. They are too crafty, deceitful and two-faced to get work selling second-hand cars. Today's politicians seem to regard honesty and truth in the same way that Dracula regards sunlight and wooden stakes. The Labour Party is led by small-minded rather pathetic creeps like Blunkett (the ex-Minister who fiddled his House of Commons train tickets so that he could take another man's wife away for a dirty weekend) and Byers who shocked the world by actually apologising to Parliament for telling 'an untruth' to a House of Commons select committee. (Most newspapers and broadcasters were happy to report Byers as having 'told an untruth' rather than having 'lied'.)

Modern politicians live in ostentatious splendour, at our expense of course. They travel in chauffeur driven cars or by private jet (at our expense). They take their holidays abroad, in villas borrowed from wealthy businessmen (we end up paying the bill when the favour is called in). They entertain lavishly, with vast numbers of servants and flunkeys (at our expense). They eat and drink in expensive restaurants (at our expense). Everything is luxurious. Everything is paid for by us. They are guarded constantly by armed policemen and secret servicemen. They consider themselves to be, and in practise are, immune to the laws which so restrict the lives of the people who put them in power. They quickly get accustomed to all this high living and cling desperately to power when it seems that their sins have been spotted. (Remember the increasingly pathetic Blunkett before his two resignations). It is all horribly reminiscent of the way important committee members lived in the final days of the Soviet Union. This is what the men and women of the Labour Government get out of power. This is why they will do anything – anything – to ensure that they stay in power. They are not members of any conspiracy. They don't want to take over the world. They just want vintage champagne, a limousine with leather seats and free holidays in the sun.

It is hard to think of words to describe people like Blair, Blunkett, Prescott and company, though 'greedy', 'self-serving' and 'incompetent' will do to be going on with. These are brutal and ruthless individuals, with their own agendas. It is their self-serving idiocy which has resulted in them exposing us to the worst of American life (the litigation) and the worst of European Union (the endless red tape). Blair et al are followers not leaders. They have no passions and no original ideas: their sole aim is to use the electorate to improve their own positions; it is the ultimate betrayal.

48

'He knows nothing and he thinks he knows everything.
That points clearly to a political career.'
George Bernard Shaw (*Major Barbara*)

49

Few, if any, modern politicians have ever held down proper jobs. Very few have ever built up a company or would, indeed, know how to start one. Very few have any real talents. Most would be hard pressed to manage a proper job with any degree of success. Can you imagine anyone employing Blair, Prescott, Clarke, Blunkett or Straw to do real jobs? Blair's acting skills might get him a job as fourth spear carrier in a fifth rate touring company and a few years ago Prescott might have been hired as a bouncer outside a third rate night club but the others probably couldn't even get airport jobs confiscating nail files from old ladies.

You can judge Blair's business acumen by the success of his ventures in the world of property speculation. The Blairs seem to be one of the few propertied families in Britain to have actually managed to lose money in one of the nation's biggest ever property booms.

50

British politics is now dominated by stupid, greedy people who have no passion or purpose other than their own advancement. In 2004/5 the average MP in the House of Commons claimed £122,677 in tax free expenses – in addition to her salary.

51

The movie industry claims that buying pirated videos funds terrorism. That may or may not be true (though I suspect it is more of a marketing ploy than a serious accusation). But, and here is the irony, what is certainly true is that buying a non-pirated video will definitely fund terrorism because the taxes the company pays will be used for terrorist attacks on countries such as Afghanistan and Iraq.

It is paying taxes that funds terrorism.

The slightly surprising truth is that the best way for us to end terrorism would be for us all to stop paying taxes.

52

David Blunkett is the one man who for many people characterises the Labour Government. It is worth examining his career as a Minister in some detail.

Blunkett was such a disaster as a Minister (his policies as Home Secretary made Attila the Hun look like a charity worker) that I can't help suspecting that he was given high office because of his blindness, rather than despite it.

When the Labour Party decided to introduce horrendously fascist legislation into Britain, Blair and his aides knew that such legislation would be opposed by every thinking citizen. Giving the job of introducing this legislation to a blind man made things much easier. Very few people dared to criticise a blind man. The real issues were ignored, and the Labour Government's fascist proposals were passed, because no one dared point out the truth about the blind man's policies. It would have been as politically incorrect to criticise the policies proposed by the blind man as it would have been to criticise the blind man himself.

Blunkett was, I believe, given the job of Home Secretary not *despite* his blindness but *because* of it. Blunkett is a monument both to political correctness and to the ruthless exploitation of our fears of being seen to be politically incorrect.

Sadly, before he was destroyed by his own greed and stupidity, Blunkett did a good deal of permanent damage to the country he was paid to serve.

53

I cheered when Blunkett resigned as Home Secretary because it was Blunkett who introduced into Britain the concept of 'guilty without trial'. It was Blunkett who introduced the principles of the Spanish Inquisition into British life. It was under Blunkett that innocent citizens were imprisoned without trial and it was Blunkett who introduced the idea of detaining suspects indefinitely.

It was under Blunkett as Home Secretary that the United Nations Committee on Torture asked the British Government to review its policies on dealing with prisoners. It was under Blunkett that the Law Lords in Britain ruled that the Government's policy was unlawful. Blunkett did not, of course, resign because of that – though he should have done.

It was Blunkett who wanted to ban civil servants from membership of the British National Party (one of Britain's biggest political parties) because he didn't like the party's policies. (Would he, I wonder, have dared to suggest banning Scottish Nationalists or Welsh Nationalists from posts in the civil service?) It was Blunkett's

Home Office which came up with the idea of criminals being let off if they apologised.

Blunkett seems to me to behave like a thug, seemingly uninterested in justice, freedom or the other basic ingredients of a good society, and constantly threatening, and bullying everyone he thinks he can threaten and bully. He also seems to have little respect for the law. When a football hooligan escaped punishment through a department cock-up Blunkett said: 'We'll get him.' My immediate thought was that Blunkett was planning to send Prescott round in the night. When he didn't like a chief constable he simply got rid of him – overruling the relevant police authority. As Home Secretary he may have been legally entitled to do this but it was hardly in the spirit of democracy. Blunkett didn't seem to realise that just because you have the power you don't have to use it. It was Blunkett who ended the centuries old double jeopardy rule that stopped people being tried twice for the same offence. It was Blunkett who changed the law to allow juries to hear evidence of bad character (though New Labour, it seems, wants to do away with juries completely – particularly when they prove inconveniently impartial.)

One senior Law Lord suggested that one of Blunkett's laws (the Anti-Terrorism, Crime and Security Act) was a bigger threat to the nation than terrorism itself. Lord Hoffman has said about Blunkett's law: 'It calls into question the very existence of an ancient liberty of which this country has until now been very proud: freedom from arbitrary arrest and detention. The real threat to the life of the nation, in the sense of a people living in accordance with its traditional laws and political values, comes not from terrorism but from laws such as these.'

That is Blunkett's true legacy: to be more of a threat to Britain and Britons than terrorists.

It was the snivelling, whingeing Blunkett, the one who shed buckets of tears when he lost his chauffeur driven car and the perks and privileges which enabled him to impress his mistress, who helped create a world safer for criminals and more dangerous for honest citizens. It was Blunkett who introduced the idea of forcing every citizen to carry an ID card. It was Blunkett who introduced secret files into Britain. It was Blunkett who introduced repressive, oppressive policies into Britain. It was Blunkett (a man who likes people to think of him as a caring, sensitive human being) who muttered about opening a bottle of champagne when he heard that Dr Harold Shipman had hung himself so that his wife could get an enhanced NHS pension. Shipman was obviously as mad as a hatter and Blunkett had ultimate responsibility for his care but that didn't stop Blunkett sniggering rather than apologising. (Shipman's innocent widow, incidentally, found out about her husband's suicide after her son heard the news on the radio. Blunkett's prison service didn't even bother to give her a call and the Home Secretary himself was too busy sniggering about opening his champagne to celebrate the death of a man in his care to make the effort.)

It was the almost infinitely nasty Blunkett who reportedly planned to add a bully-boy clause to his 'serious crime bill' to outlaw 'continuous demonstrations', 'encampments' and 'the use of megaphones'.

Fascists don't like free speech. It frightens them. And this example of Blunkett's practical fascism in action was designed to help the Government suppress all remaining dissent, to outlaw animal lovers (protesting about vivisection and hunting) and to get rid of a campaigner called Brian Haw (the best example of real democracy in Westminster) who had, since the onset of the Iraq war, held a vigil outside Parliament. Blunkett, like Blair, found any reference to the fact that we have a Government comprised of war criminals to be embarrassing. And so he wanted Mr Haw silenced. When history is written Mr Haw will be remembered as a real patriot and a man of principle. Blunkett, whose policies have doubtless had Adolf Hitler looking up from hell and nodding and smiling approval, will be remembered as an utterly abominable little man who has completely misread the needs and mood of the people who pay his salary. The words 'Blunkett' and 'fascism' go together like 'Blair' and 'war'.

And, of course, it was Blunkett who sent tanks to Heathrow when the Government felt our fear levels needed topping up.

It was not, however, any of this which led to Blunkett's first resignation from high public office.

His first resignation came as a result of a much publicised and very messy affair with a married woman.

54

Inevitably, Blunkett's defenders claimed that his private life had nothing to do with his public responsibilities. But Blunkett's private life says a great deal about his sense of justice, his understanding of the word 'morality' and his New Labour sense of self-importance and unrelieved arrogance.

After his first resignation, the shamed Blunkett left office claiming that he was going for his child's sake. As he abandoned his chauffeur driven car and the power to get visas for nannies he cried. I found it difficult to avoid the feeling that here was a man so shameless and so manipulative that he was simply turning on the tears to get more sympathy. When he resigned he talked about public duty and serving the country. The Blunkett who had moralised to the nation about the sanctity of marriage not only had an affair with another man's wife but then seemed to do his best to break up their marriage. Blunkett showed himself to be a real 21st century politician; a man with all the self-serving thick skin of a professional politician but with none of the qualities required by someone capable of serving his country.

Within weeks he was reported to have taken a lucrative consultancy with a firm of management consultants said to have many contracts with government departments and public bodies. The words 'snout', 'trough' and 'greedy' sprang to mind.

Prisoners appearing before prison parole boards are expected to show some sense of understanding their crime, and some genuine remorse. The swaggering Blunkett would surely not satisfy these requirements. Blunkett, like other Labour ministers, escaped prosecution for offences which might, I suspect, have led others into court.

55

Blunkett's resignation tears were, I suspect, not shed for the nation he betrayed, nor for the family he attempted to destroy, but for himself.

When Blunkett finally threw in the towel and resigned, Blair, unconvicted but serial war criminal and the nation's best known liar, told the former Home Secretary that he had left Government 'with your integrity intact and your achievements acknowledged by all'.

Only an unregistered, unconvicted war criminal and serial liar could have come up with anything quite so obscenely false and genuinely seem to expect anyone other than *The Guardian* journalists to accept it as truth.

In the end Blunkett, who had picked his own judge and jury, resigned when the man conducting the enquiry tipped him off that he had found a 'killer' e-mail which showed that someone at the Home Office had brought improper influence to bear and had arranged for Blunkett's mistress's nanny's visa to be fast tracked.

And what a trial! Twenty two allegedly responsible and intelligent witnesses at the enquiry all pleaded amnesia. Not since Ernest Saunders developed (and then miraculously recovered from) Alzheimer's disease has a medical disorder been so useful. Had they all been over-using their mobile phones, perhaps? Civil servants who might have known what happened either kept silent or conveniently forgot the relevant facts. Key correspondence disappeared. The long running fiasco involving Blunkett's mistress, her nanny, a pair of visas, one child, one unborn baby and some train tickets would have made a good Whitehall farce. It did, indeed, provide the raw material for a play and a television comedy. At the end we were left with yards of unanswered questions.

Why did Blunkett intervene and ask the police to investigate when two schoolboys knocked on the door of his mistress's home and then ran away? Why did Blunkett give a railway ticket issued for an MP's spouse to his mistress? Why was Blunkett not investigated by the police for what was surely a misuse of public funds?

Is it true that Blunkett revealed sensitive security information to his mistress? At a time when we are losing our freedom in the so-called war on terrorism it was alleged that the Home Secretary might have leaked secrets all over his mistress's pillow. Did he? Shouldn't someone bother to find out? The married woman who was his mistress turned out to have several other lovers too. No one in Government seemed to think that this might make him a security risk. Blunkett had already been shown to be a man of appallingly poor judgement, capable, it seemed, of using his office to personal advantage. No one seemed to think that he might be a security risk, susceptible to blackmail or likely to share secrets with his mistress that she might share with one or more of her other lovers. Is it true that Blunkett used his official ministerial car and driver to take his mistress away for dirty weekends? Is it true that Blunkett's former principal private secretary at the Home Office and his Home Office PR adviser were sent to his mistress's solicitor when she ended the relationship with him?

Blunkett and his chums escaped serious censure by the enquiry Blunkett himself instigated because no one could be criticised because everyone claimed that they could not remember what had happened. The Home Office was, it seemed, the Ministry of Amnesia. Essential faxes went missing and it seemed that the civil service had failed to keep any record of what happened at meetings. Civil servants are usually expected to keep copious amounts of paperwork (they demand that of the rest of us) and they are paid to know what is going on and to remember a good deal of it. In this case it seemed that no one could remember anything.

The Blunkett affair made the Profumo affair look simple, but whereas Profumo apologised and left public life Blunkett subsequently crawled back into office, apparently without shame or embarrassment. Blunkett's memory about this whole affair is so bad that it is impossible to conceive of him attempting to run a stall at the village fete, let alone run a Government department. He changed his story so often that it was, in the end, impossible to believe a word he said.

Blunkett simply kept saying that he was an honest man, presumably in the hope that if he said it often enough somebody would believe him.

56

Blunkett will be remembered not just for a rather grubby affair but for the way he removed our freedom and our rights. As part of Blair's New Labour Government he did more to help turn Britain into a fascist, totalitarian state than any man in history. Blunkett's oppressive policies had less to do with squashing terrorism than with taking power over the people he was supposed to represent. Has there ever been a Home Secretary who has done more to help criminals and less to help honest, hardworking citizens? Has there ever been a Home Secretary who has done more to remove our liberty?

57

Blunkett was, I believe, the worst Home Secretary Britain has ever had. But, actually, I don't think any of Blunkett's policies actually originated with him. His policies came, via Britain's home-grown unconvicted war criminal, from the EU and America. While he was busy showing off by getting visas for his mistress's nanny we were losing our freedom.

58

Politics today is not a question of right or left. It is, rather, simply a question of right or wrong.

59

Everything that national and local government does (some of it in the name of progress and some of it in the name of protecting us) seems designed to make the world a less pleasant place.

60

In a way, it was Blunkett's blindness (the quality which I believe got him the job) which made him the worst and most dangerous Home Secretary Britain has ever had; perhaps incapable of seeing that he had become part of a fascist Government; a Government oppressing, ignoring and betraying the people he was elected to serve. Did he want to be what he became? Was it forced upon him? Did it happen by accident? Or was he, perhaps, unaware of precisely what he was doing?

Some of Blunkett's defenders seemed to want him to be judged as a blind man, making a creditable attempt to do the job. But the reality is that if he is judged as anyone else would have been judged he was a disaster as Home Secretary. Surely the whole point of success over a disability is that you can be judged alongside your peers who are not disabled?

It is politically correct to assume (and indeed insist) that everyone (regardless of natural aptitude or any disability) should be given the opportunity to do any job they want to try their hand at. This, as Blunkett has proved very ably, is arrant nonsense.

The (to some unpalatable) truth is we aren't all capable of doing everything. Skills and abilities vary and some disabilities make it difficult to do some jobs properly. People who need to move about in wheelchairs simply do not make the best fire fighters. Even though they may love animals, and might be wonderful at the job, people who are allergic to fur don't make the best vets or veterinary nurses. The politically correct argue that there is no reason why blindness does not make a man (or woman) unsuitable for high political office. This is dangerous nonsense. A blind Home Secretary can only read or see what other people want him to read or see. Most publications aren't available in Braille or on audio tape. Books produced by small publishers and newsletters written, edited and distributed by publishers not working for the media giants must, of necessity, remain unread. Pamphlets and letters sent in by members of the public will only be read if those around the Home Secretary decided to pass them on to him and make them available in Braille. Inevitably, this means that the people who make these sort of decisions are the people with the real power. The nature of the job means that a blind Home Secretary will, on the whole, only go where he is led and will, to a large extent, only know what those around him want him to know. This is particularly true of someone who has been blind since birth.

The politically correct who claim that anyone should be entitled to do any job might like to ask themselves these simple questions:

1. Would you sit in a plane piloted by a blind man?
2. Would you allow a blind surgeon to operate on your brain?
3. Would you allow your children to travel to school on a bus driven by a blind man?
4. Would you give David Blunkett a job as a lollipop man, controlling your local school crossing?

There are dozens of other jobs Blunkett could not have done. Would you hire him as a mountain guide, juggler, war reporter, sentry, steeplejack, fireman, tank commander, sniper or trapeze artist?

We all have limitations. There are things we just cannot do because of our physical weaknesses, our mental weaknesses or our lack of suitable skills. Just wanting to do something simply isn't enough.

61

To say that Blunkett was a disaster as Home Secretary is like saying that Cherie Blair isn't the most popular person in Britain; it's an understatement of Himalayan proportions. The citizens of Britain are now much more at risk of terrorist attack than they were before he took office. (Blunkett supported the illegal invasion of Iraq and so must share the responsibility for that criminal act.) His daft proposals mean that the streets of Britain are more dangerous than ever before. Criminals, crooks and thugs have prospered under Blunkett. Law abiding citizens have suffered badly. Blair would have been better off digging up Hitler and giving him the job. (Come to think of it, and with that antecedent in mind, Blunkett is a good reason to believe in reincarnation.)

I believe Blunkett has probably done more lasting damage to Britain than any other individual in history – British or foreign. Any New Labour minister who wanted to keep his job would have brought in dangerous totalitarian policies. But I suspect that Blunkett went further than most of Blair's Babes would have gone. Some of his proposals would have had the Nazis drooling.

62

After Blunkett had resigned as Home Secretary I wrote that I really didn't think he realised just how much damage he had done to the country he had been paid to serve.

'In a fair and decent world,' I wrote, 'Blunkett's career would now be over. But given the example of the equally loathsome Mandelson (now an EU Commissioner in charge of Trade and Industry) the chances are good that Blunkett will be back. I suspect that, unless Blair can find a suitable blind, deaf mute to use as a pawn, Blunkett will be back in office after the next election.'

I was right.

63

Blunkett's second incarnation as a Minister didn't last quite so long. Blunkett, now yet another ex-Labour Minister suspected of being a less than punctilious custodian of the truth, exhibited extraordinary arrogance and a series of alarming misjudgements.

In October 2005, it was revealed that Blunkett had broken strict parliamentary rules by sending (on House of Commons notepaper) an objection to a building development near a house he owned and signing the letter as a Government Minister and an MP. Cash from the sale of the development was earmarked to redevelop a school for the blind and partially-sighted but Blunkett, following the NIMBY principles espoused by other Labour Ministers, opposed the development because of its proximity to a house he owned and rented out for around £15,000 a year. (It's sometimes difficult to keep up with the property portfolios of Labour Ministers. Blunkett lived in a £3 million a year grace-and-favour official residence which had been one of his main homes since 1997. He also had a home in Sheffield and rented a cottage on the estate of the Duchess of Devonshire. In 2004, the seemingly unembarrassable Blunkett claimed a tax free allowance of £20,608 to cover the cost of running his home in Sheffield. Just what sort of house requires that sort of expenditure I cannot imagine. Nor is it easy to understand why Blunkett needed taxpayers' money to cover the running costs of a house which would, presumably, become his sole responsibility when he sells it and takes the capital gain.)

And then there were the well-paid jobs he accepted, the investments he made and the accusations of 'conflict of interest'. Even among Labour Party politicians Blunkett stood out alone for greed, incompetence and poor judgement. An extra large piece of excrement floating in a sea of political sewage.

64

I cheered until I was hoarse the night the utterly loathsome and contemptible Blunkett finally agreed to resign the second time. What joy to see one of the most self-righteous and sanctimonious members of the New Labour gang whining and whingeing. What a joy to see an arrogant New Labour Time Lord brought to his knees by his own hubris. What joy to see the Blairites reminded that they do not (yet) totally own Britain.

65

Politicians and Government employees now seem to feel that they are entitled to make any number of mistakes without apologising or resigning.

If someone in the private sector makes a serious mistake he is likely to be pilloried. If a doctor makes a serious error he may well be struck off the medical register. His ability to earn a living will disappear. His entire career may well be wrecked. It will be no excuse to argue that he was under tremendous pressure or that he was overworked. Numerous doctors have been ruined by errors resulting from long working hours.

However, if a Minister, civil servant or senior police officer makes a string of errors he is extremely unlikely to suffer any serious consequences. Politicians may be subjected to some bad publicity (which I suspect some of them might even enjoy – on the dubious grounds that no publicity is bad publicity) but civil servants, bureaucrats and policemen will expect, and will be given, anonymity and complete protection (unless, for some specific reason, it is in the best interests of politicians or other employees for their identity to be 'leaked'). Their mistakes may be crass and deadly and may be evidence of great incompetence but the guilty will remain in their posts with little or no punishment. Their salaries, status and pensions will remain unaffected. Resignations are as rare as mare's nests.

When this sort of special status is added to the fact that state employees are the only people in the country to have pensions which are protected from the vagaries of the stock market and the economic climate, it becomes clear that the divide between the way citizens who work in and for the Government are treated and the way that citizens who earn their living in the private sector are treated is growing constantly wider.

This is another symptom of practical fascism in action.

Oh how things have changed.

Lord Carrington misread the signals from the South Atlantic that led to the Falklands conflict. Because of that he resigned as foreign secretary.

When a fellow called Michael Fagan found his way into the Queen's bedroom at Buckingham Palace, the then Home Secretary Willie Whitelaw quickly offered his resignation.

Today's politicians are too enamoured of the champagne lifestyle even to contemplate an honourable resignation. Men like Blunkett, who seem to know neither shame nor honour, cling on to power until their position becomes utterly untenable.

66

It is important to remember that the people running the Labour party may be crafty and sneaky, in an insurance company sort of way rather than a barrow boy sort of way, but they are not bright people. Who but morons would threaten to have successful suicide bombers arrested, and apparently mean it?

The Labour Party seem to be blissfully unaware of the way our country is changing demographically – and the effect this is likely to have on us in the future.

There will be many more MPs in Muslim dominated seats soon. Some of the new Muslim MPs will probably be quite militant. They will have learned to hate the people who have voted for politicians who have bent over backwards, sideways and forwards to support the USA and to protect and support Israel's illegal activities.

Remember too that the EU will soon be controlled by Muslims. Holland and France both have huge Muslim populations and Turkey, when it is 'allowed' to join the club (the Americans say it has to be allowed to join and so it will be) will be the largest country in the EU.

Blair has deliberately allowed Muslims into the country in vast numbers *and* at the same time annoyed them.

How unbelievably reckless and stupid.

There are, of course, relatively few Muslims living in the USA.

67

The British Government has joined itself at one hip to America. The other hip has (under instructions from the USA) been joined to Europe. Not surprisingly this has produced a nation which is, to say the least, in an uncomfortable position. Thanks to our politicians, we have the worst of America and the worst of Europe.

The trend throughout the world is for large countries to break up into smaller ones. Only fans of the EU want the trend to go in the opposite direction. The former Soviet Union is now fifteen countries. What was Yugoslavia is now six countries. Czechoslovakia has become two countries as has Ethiopia. There are four separatist movements in Spain where people living in Catalonia, Castilla and Navarre are, like the Basques, seeking independence. The chances of the European Union ever becoming the superstate its proponents dream of are slim.

The EU was an American idea and has been strongly supported by America since its inception and through its various growth phases. The Americans like the idea of the EU because they think it will be easier to negotiate with one big country than with lots of independent minded, troublesome countries. (The Americans are so arrogant that they have never thought of the United States of Europe as being a threat to their global superiority.)

68

The politicians who support the bombing of Iraq and other Muslim countries are frequently politically very correct on minor issues.

So, for example, the same politicians who are quite happy for our troops to have killed over 100,000 Iraqi women and children since we invaded Iraq (remember: the precise numbers aren't known because no one has bothered to keep count) get very worked up about Christmas fairy lights and insist that they are called 'winter lights' so as not to offend Muslims.

Why do the people who worry about Muslims being offended by Christian children having piggy banks not think that Muslims might be *more* offended by the fact that we keep bombing their home countries?

The Muslims themselves don't care about Christmas lights or piggy banks. Time after time puzzled Muslim leaders stand up and say that neither they nor anyone they know is offended by Christians celebrating Christmas. And why should they be?

Can our politicians really be this stupid?

I really don't think so.

Because there is another explanation.

Could the politically correct nonsense about not celebrating Christmas, and about not using piggy banks because they might offend Muslims, be proposed to make us resent Muslims – and to drive a wider rift between Christian and Muslim so that Christian populations of America and Europe will welcome the continuing religious wars which are a consequence of peak oil? Do the people who propose all this politically correct nonsense realise just what they are doing?

Many undoubtedly do. I suspect that many who claim to be 'politically correct' are, in truth, manipulative racists.

The rest are just stupid.

69

It is the EU bureaucracy which is largely responsible for the increasing damage being done to all sorts of interpersonal relationships in Britain. The nastiness, the lack of respect, the shoddy service (and shoddy goods), the impatience – all these are a direct consequence of the fact that EU bureaucracy has resulted in costs being cut, staff numbers being reduced and corners having to be cut in order to make a profit. Manufacturers have to make products which are at the bottom edge of functionality in order to make a profit. Naturally, this means that new products break down a good deal, don't do their jobs very well and don't last very long. It is the EU which can, quite specifically, be blamed for the breakdown in the quality of the relationships between doctors and patients, parents and teachers, shop assistants and customers and so on. Everyone suffers. Doctors, teachers and shop assistants find their work becoming harder, more threatening and less satisfying. Patients, parents and customers find the quality of their lives deteriorating. Everything, for everyone, becomes less satisfying, less satisfactory and more stressful.

70

During the court martial of British soldiers in Osnabruck (they had been charged with abusing Iraqi prisoners) Blair (who should have been on trial for abusing the entire Iraqi nation) commented on the case in the House of Commons. He was not charged with contempt even though his own attorney general has repeatedly used the contempt laws to stop editors commenting on (for example) the arrest, torture and holding (without trial) of terrorism 'suspects'.

So, once again a Labour politician rode merrily and without consequence, over contempt laws which other mortals would ignore at their peril.

In the truly fascist state there is one law for us and one law for the state's functionaries.

71

After trenchant criticism of his illegal invasion of Iraq had adversely affected his popularity among British citizens, Blair said that his relationship with the British public was a like a relationship between two people when they have a bit of a row and one throws some crockery.

Only Blair could compare a war crime to a mild domestic tiff.

72

The Government claims that it is introducing new laws restricting what is left of our freedom because it wants to stop innocent people being killed for political purposes. But for several years now the British Government's primary mission has been to kill vast numbers of innocent people for political purposes.

73

It is easy to regard Blair as a buffoon. But, despite the politician's glued on grin and the stupid, greedy wife with her own sickly grin, it is important not to forget that Blair, although crass and pathetic, is by any stretch of anyone's imagination, an evil man.

74

Milosovic should have joined the Labour Party. They would have made him Minister of Ethnic Cleansing and told him to get rid of the English.

75

Blair, who has expensive tastes far beyond his skills and who has a wife with expensive tastes, needs and expects to make £20 million out of being Prime Minister. His main talent (apart from being able to smile and lie simultaneously) is in gouging freebies out of rich people.

76

Why isn't Blair considered to be a security risk? He owes millions of pounds that he has no reasonable way of paying back without obtaining highly paid jobs in the future? Don't his vast personal debts make him vulnerable to outside pressure and influence?

77

If New Labour Ministers, who like to think of themselves as being of the people and for the people, find it difficult to understand why they are unloved, they should remember that when Che Guevara was a Minister in the Cuban Government in the early 1960s he worked at weekends as a manual worker so that he could keep in touch with the people he was serving. He loaded sacks of sugar at Havana port and helped build schools. He didn't get his press office to arrange photographers and TV crews to film his £300,000 a year wife giving a few unwanted cuddly toys to a charity shop.

And it was Che who tried to unite the world's underdeveloped nations and to present a coherent front against American imperialism.

Here, in contrast, are Tony Blair's Achievements

1. Thanks to Tony's War a newborn baby in Afghanistan now has a one in four chance of dying before the age of five.

2. Since Labour came to power the number of bankruptcies in Britain has gone up dramatically.

3. Since Labour came to power the number of seriously mentally ill people has increased.

4. And the number of people committing suicide has risen too.

Blair will probably take great comfort from the fact that bankruptcies, suicides and the incidence of mental illness have also risen dramatically in George W. Bush's America.

78

I recently saw a newspaper headline: 'My Father Is A Murderer.' My first thought was that it must have been written by one of Blair's children.

79

'Our mission is to rebuild trust between government and people.'
NEW LABOUR PARTY MANIFESTO 1997

80

I used the word 'craven' about Blair in a pre-war column which was banned from *The People* newspaper but the editor, who really didn't seem to me to understand the significance of what was going on and who could do little but mutter about standing by our boys and girls in the desert, insisted that the word was utterly inappropriate. And yet I thought then and think now the word 'craven' was totally appropriate. I believe Blair was frightened to upset Bush because he didn't want to damage his chances of making big money through American directorships, speaking tours and book contracts after quitting politics. Blair wouldn't be so bad if he was just craven. But he is self-centred, vain and greedy too.

81

It has always seemed to me that the Blairs and the Beckhams have a great deal in common and are pretty much interchangeable. They all seem to be publicity seeking and self-centred. None of them seem to me to be particularly talented. All seem hugely greedy and vain. Would anyone notice if they all swapped places?

82

This isn't the first time England has had a Government so scared of criticism that it has given itself the power to lock up its critics. In 1817 the Government suspended the Habeas Corpus Act so that it could imprison, without trial, anyone whom it regarded as undesirable. The suspension of the Habeas Corpus Act was done to get at author (and self-publisher) William Cobbett who had complained of corrupt politicians and 'rotten boroughs', sinecures and fiat money. To escape, Cobbett fled the country and went to France for a while.

83

The secret of Blair's success (apart from the ability to smile and lie at the same time) is the fact that he learned one thing from Clinton: he learned that to achieve success in politics you must find out what people want. Whatever it is, and however impossible you know it is, you must then promise to do it. When you are elected you can forget the promise.

84

The Nuremberg trials established that we all remain responsible for our own actions, whoever employs us and whoever's orders we are following. As many Germans discovered after World War II, it is no defence to say: 'I was following orders' when charged with a war crime.

85

In olden times (i.e. before I was born) kings and other leaders were given nicknames. One Welsh king was known as Howell the Good. Richard was known as the Lionheart.

So what will Blair and his chums be remembered as?

Blair the Lying Warmonger. Prescott the Fat Slugger. Mandelson the Mendacious. Byers the Untruther. Blunkett the Simply Terrible.

Vermin all of them.

86

A Government Minister, Patricia Hewitt, has admitted that she sexually discriminated against a man and gave a job to a less well-qualified woman. When she was Trade and Industry Secretary, Hewitt overruled an interview panel's decision when trying to fill a development agency post. She awarded the job to the panel's third choice – a woman. The Secretary of State (Hewitt), was found guilty of a breach of sexual discrimination legislation and was ordered by the High Court to pay the man who had been discriminated against £18,000 in costs.

The woman who was illegally given the job kept it. And Hewitt didn't resign from her job as Health Secretary. It seems not unreasonable to assume that the £18,000 was paid by taxpayers.

So, in the end, the man who was discriminated against didn't get the job he should have got, the woman who got the job she shouldn't have been given kept it and the woman who was responsible for breaking the law kept her job too. The only people who won were the lawyers and the only people who lost were the taxpayers and the man who won the lawsuit.

87

Between 1996-7 and 2005 poverty in Britain remained unchanged among adults of working age. Despite all its bluster and promises the Labour Government has done nothing to deal with the real poverty in Britain: the poverty among working couples on low wages.

88

The dishonest and ignorance of Labour party politicians was well illustrated after the July 7th bombings in London in 2005.

Jack Straw, masquerading as a politician, said that the fact that the attack on America's twin towers occurred before we invaded Iraq proved that the London bombings were not related to the invasion of Iraq.

Can anyone really be that stupid?

Is our Foreign Secretary really not aware that we invaded Iraq ten years before the attack on America?

When asked whether he thought the recent invasion of Iraq might be the reason for the bombings in London in July 2005, Blair answered with his usual slimy spin. He said that the invasion of Iraq is no excuse for a suicide bombing. Of course it isn't. No one ever said it was. But it is the reason.

89

When the Government deliberately discriminates against certain members of our society (by, for example, giving women and black candidates preferential treatment) it is practising institutional sexism and racism. This is a great cause of resentment and is an example of the blinkered, evil way in which practical fascism damages society.

Chapter Four

The Truth About Peak Oil, The Coming Fuel Shortage And America's Oil Wars

1

Our life style depends on oil. Oil keeps our cars on the road and our aeroplanes in the air. Without oil we would sit in the dark and the cold. Oil enables us to move stuff around the world and keeps factories and offices going. Oil is the lubricant without which our society would grind to a halt. As the global warming caused by fossil fuels results in dramatic changes to our climate so the demand for heating and for air-conditioning will continue to rise.

For well over half a century oil has been vital to the Western way of life. We have taken a plentiful supply of moderately priced oil for granted. Oil has helped to spread the Western lifestyle. Those who cannot afford oil have, generally speaking, aspired to the sort of lifestyle that oil makes possible.

2

The demand for oil is rising fast – faster than at any time in history. Back in 1945 the world managed very happily on around seven million barrels of oil a day. By the year 2000 the world demand was running at ten times that – just under 70 million barrels a day. The demand is now heading inexorably towards 100 million barrels a day. As rapidly developing countries such as China and India grow ever more thirsty for oil so the global demand continues to rise. India has 16% of the world's population and just 0.4% of oil reserves. One in six people in the world lives in China. Billions of people who have never used oil are now adopting and enjoying the lifestyles of affluent nations where oil is the most fundamental and ubiquitous fuel.

3

But just as the world's need for oil has started to rocket we have reached the moment in our history when the amount of oil available for us to extract from the ground has reached a peak, and is about to start falling.

For twenty years the world has been finding less oil than it has been using. Demand has been soaring but the dribs and drabs of new oil that have been discovered have been found in out of the way, difficult to reach places. There have been no world-class oil discoveries since the finds in Alaska and the North Sea in the 1970s. Despite the huge amounts of money spent on drilling and exploration no major new oil fields have been discovered for twenty years. In not much over a century we have used up oil reserves which took millennia to form.

The discovery of what oil experts now still regard as the 'supergiant' fields began in the 1930s. The al-Burgan field in Kuwait (currently still the world's second largest oil field) was discovered in 1938 and has been in constant service ever since. The Saudi al-Ghawar field (still the world's largest oil field) has been slowly emptied since 1948. There are only 14 oil basins in the world which are capable of producing half a million barrels a day. All were discovered in the 1940s or earlier.

The days of sticking a well into the ground and then standing back as the oil gushes out are long gone. Today, the oil that is discovered tends to be the type of stuff that takes a good deal of (expensive) work to refine.

According to oil company Chevron 'the world consumes two barrels of oil for every barrel discovered'. And that's worrying. Oil is about to get scarce and, like all things that are scarce, it is going to get considerably more expensive. Our behaviour is going to have to change. Things we accept as normal – and as a right – are about to alter dramatically.

4

Part of the problem is undoubtedly due to the fact that the USA (the main cause of global warming) has a seemingly unquenchable thirst for oil. And American citizens expect to pay very little for their oil. In 2005 it cost £8.50 to fill up the tank of a family sized car in the USA – a fraction of the cost of fuel in other countries. And by paying the environmental costs for their oil habit the rest of the world subsidises America's addiction.

5

You don't have to be a genius to work out that we're heading for trouble, though neither governments nor journalists seem ready to acknowledge the problem. Many commentators still seem to believe that anyone warning about the coming oil shortage is some sort of scaremonger trying to push up the price of oil. 'What is not in doubt,' wrote Andrew Alexander in the *Daily Mail* on 16th September 2005, 'is that there is lashings of the stuff around, consume it as we may....'. Mr Alexander didn't say where this oil was to be found.

In the spring of 1999 The Economist (which, in my view, has an unparalleled knack for getting big stories wrong and for misinterpreting the evidence on issues as varied as investing, currencies, genetic engineering and animal experimentation) produced a cover story called 'Drowning in Oil' which suggested that Saudi Arabia had decided to flood the world with enough extra oil to take oil prices down to five dollars a barrel, and to keep oil at this low price for at least five years. Just a few days after the publication of this story the Saudi Arabians, together with other countries, cut their production of oil. The price of a barrel of oil went up threefold in 18 months.

Gordon Brown has limited himself to complaining about the rising price of oil and, with the sort of breathtaking hypocrisy which is now widely associated with the Labour Party has claimed that the high cost of oil is a tremendous burden on poorer people. He has ignored the fact that 80% of the cost of a gallon of petrol goes direct to the Chancellor of the Exchequer as tax. Britain has the most expensive petrol in the world because the British people pay more fuel tax than anyone else.

In his Budget statement in December 2005, Brown yet again did the stupid thing and took action designed to produce short-term relief for his Government and long-term problems for the British people. Taking advantage of the high oil price, and good oil company profits, Brown followed the lead of Venezuela and decided to grab more of the money that was being made. Although there are tax reliefs for exploration costs I suspect that the 10% surcharge he put on oil company profits will mean that oil companies will have less money to invest in finding more oil and less incentive to do so. The end result of Brown's typically inept intervention will be less oil and higher oil prices. But then Brown is, of course, the idiot who sold much of Britain's gold store at rock bottom prices soon after taking office.

6

People in the oil industry have a phrase to describe the problem we are facing. The phrase they use is 'peak oil'. We may have got there already. Or it may be a few years away. No one really knows. The one thing that the experts agree on is that when we reach 'peak oil' we will be in big trouble; we will have reached the point where the amount of oil being taken of the ground has reached a peak. From that point on the amount of oil being produced will shrink each year.

And that matters.

It matters for two reasons.

First, our society is heavily dependent on the constant supply of oil.

Second, other countries, which were previously not dependent on oil, have recently discovered the sort of lifestyle that oil can provide. And they like it. These other countries aren't small and inconsequential. They are big and very consequential. China and India are big enough to start building up relationships with oil producing countries so that they can secure supplies of oil for the future. China and India are the world's most populous nations and they have the world's fastest growing economies. They will, within the lifetimes of most of us, be the largest national economies on the planet.

(I recently bought a toy in a shop in Paris which is run as a showpiece for Japanese culture. The tag on the toy carried the three most famous words in the world: 'Made in China'.)

While China has become the world's factory, India has concentrated on the service sector. Out-sourcing is going to take in all sorts of areas we haven't expected. Patients are travelling to India for surgery. Many British hospitals send dictated letters to India for typing. Television and radio broadcasting can be done from India. Very few British jobs are safe. China and India will grow for decades to come. And their demand for oil will grow too.

7

Iran wants to build nuclear power stations of its own. When one of the world's richest oil producing nations wants to start building nuclear power stations it is surely time for the rest of the world to take the concept of peak oil seriously. My guess is that the Iranians, knowing better than most of us that oil is running out and will soon become very expensive, want to equip themselves with a cheaper form of sustainable energy so that they can sell what oil they've got left to the Chinese.

8

China and India need huge amounts of oil and their leaders are already doing everything they can to secure long-term oil supplies. They are using diplomacy, trade, direct investment, technological assistance, military support, bilateral agreements – and all the other tricks previously used by Britain and America. China, for example, has recently done deals with such vital oil producing countries as Iran, Nigeria, Saudi Arabia and Venezuela. China has secured, or is in negotiations for, free-trade pacts with 25 countries. Two years ago China had no such trade agreements.

China already has excellent relationships with North and South Korea, Iran, Pakistan and India and good relationships with the EU and with Australia and Canada. Many countries now regard

China as a better future ally than the USA and regard a relationship with China as a good defence against American hegemony. The Chinese are in discussion with Canada about a joint effort to develop a number of energy-related projects, including developing the huge oil sands of Alberta. China is positioning itself as a world leader in trade and investment and is beating the USA at all its own games.

9

The oil sands of Canada are said by those who sneer at the concept of peak oil to be the answer to the world's coming oil shortage. But getting the oil out of these sands is difficult. The sand has to be 'cooked' to get the oil out. And it takes a fifth of a barrel of oil to get one barrel of oil out of the sands. Using natural gas is one option but there doesn't seem much point in using vast quantities of natural gas to release oil. However, Canada has some of the world's biggest deposits of uranium and it seems likely that Canada will use some of its uranium to get the oil out.

Theoretically, there is enough oil in Canada's oil sands to provide up to half of America's oil use. But the Americans have so annoyed the Canadians that it seems very likely that any surplus oil will go not to the USA but to China.

This, of course, is assuming that the Canadians are happy to put up with the vast amount of permanent environmental damage that will be done by extracting oil from the sands. It's a dirty, really nasty business and toxic by-products from the extraction process are already being dumped into ponds that can stretch for miles and will probably last for ever. Or at least until hell freezes over.

Oh, and there is another problem: Canada can't extract oil from the sand and stick to the Kyoto Protocol which it has signed. Canada is committed to reducing its greenhouse-gas emissions to 6% below its 1990 level of 560 million metric tons by 2012 but things are not looking too good. In 2003 Canada's emissions rose to 740 million metric tons. And the oil-from-the-sand industry is going to add around 82 million metric tons a year to that total. 'How do we stick to 1990 emissions levels when our population is greater and our opportunity is many times greater?' asks the Alberta energy minister Greg Melchin, who has obviously learned a thing or two about global responsibility from his neighbours to the south.

10

The Chinese have a well deserved reputation for foresight. They always take the long view. (It was, it is worth remembering, Chairman Mao's deputy, who, when asked for his assessment of the impact of the French Revolution replied: 'It is too early to tell.') The result of Chinese foresight is that the Americans (and the British) have been out-manoeuvred.

America has upset so many oil producing nations that it and its satellite, Britain have been forced to resort to force. China, Russia, the Arab states and the USA are all scrambling for the world's diminishing oil.

Knowing this it is now not difficult to see why it was so desperately important for the Americans to invade Iraq and grab the Iraqi oil fields. The whole project was a crude, but effective, plan to convert public (taxpayers') money into private money. The American and British taxpayers paid the cost of the war. The private arms and oil companies run by the friends of Bush and Cheney made the profits out of selling bombs and tanks *and* out of the oil the Americans grabbed.

Since the disaster of the first invasion of Iraq in 1991 the Americans had been trying to get control of the Iraqi oil. They had to invade when the Chinese, the Russians and the French did oil deals that would have clicked into place when the sanctions ended. (Despite the fact that hundreds of thousands of Iraqi women and children died, the Americans and the Britons kept the sanctions going while trying to get their own deals done. The sanctions, which prevented the Iraqis having clean water, food supplies or medicine were responsible for over a million deaths.)

11

The Americans, not the British, will get the Iraqi oil. Britons will get nothing (except huge bills and an exposure to terrorism) out of the war, though I believe that Blair, the Prime Minister who took us into the war, will probably get a great deal out of it. I suspect that he will end up as a well-paid director of at least one big American company when he stops being Prime Minister. As I've already predicted, I wouldn't bet against him ending up on the board of the

Carlyle Group – the infamous enterprise set up with the Bushes and the Osama bin Laden family on board.

12

Securing oil supplies was an important element in many major wars of the twentieth century. It was certainly the major factor in America's recent illegal wars. The war against terrorism was merely a convenient and publicly acceptable excuse for unacceptable behaviour. Peak oil has led directly to our loss of freedom.

13

The prospect of Saudi Arabia running out of oil has hung over us all for several decades – though you won't know this if you have been relying for news upon such British Government mouthpieces as the BBC and the national press.

At a secret 1974 USA Senate hearing investigation, it was reported that back in 1972 the American oil companies in Saudi Arabia had begun to realise that they were taking so much oil out of the Saudi Arabian oil fields that they were damaging the fields.

However, since the American oil companies knew that they were soon going to lose ownership of the oil fields to the Saudi Arabian Government they deliberately decided to 'milk these fields for every saleable drop of oil and put back as little investment as possible'.

This allegation was repeated in 1979 when investigative reporter Seymour Hersh published an article in the *New York Times* questioning the capacity of Saudi Arabia's oil fields. Hersh claimed that the Saudi Arabian oil fields had been systemically over-produced in the early years of the 1970s because representatives of America's major oil companies (which at that time controlled Saudi Arabia's oil fields) suspected that the Saudi Arabian Government was about to nationalise their oil fields. The American oil companies wanted to get oil out of the ground as rapidly as they could – without worrying about the fact that if you take too much oil out of an oil field you risk permanently damaging it.

In 1979 the US Senate Subcommittee on International Economic Policy of the Committee on Foreign Relations took another look at the Saudi Arabian oil fields. The Senate's advisers suggested that the 9.8 million barrel per day production rate was probably as good as it was ever going to get. In other words, even if money were invested in them, the key oil fields in Saudi Arabia would all be in decline before the year 2000. This information was considered too alarming for the public and so the source documents for this conclusion were sealed from the public view for another 50 years – until long after the prediction would have been proved either right or wrong, and probably long after those who were responsible for it had gone on to worry about other things.

Predictions are only predictions, of course. Good guesses. Estimates. But this one seems to have been spot on. By the end of the 1990s almost all OPEC producers were close to their peak production rates. Saudi Arabia had managed to increase its oil production in the 1990s in order to help the world cope with the embargo on Iraq's oil exports. The problem is that by doing this the Saudi Arabians probably damaged the long-term viability of their oil fields.

Here's a piece of irony. The American sanctions, designed to force the Iraqis to let the Americans have access to the Iraqi oil, probably resulted in permanent damage being done to the huge Saudi oil fields.

14

Only a small number of new oil fields of significant size have been discovered in recent decades. By the year 2000 it was clear that the bulk of the world's oil production was coming from a small number of ageing oil fields. The world's oil supply was definitely starting to run out.

As a result of the rise in the oil price, shares in oil exploration companies have reached record highs but the seismic specialists and drilling rigs aren't finding much new oil. Most wells are coming up dry and none are proving to be indicative of big oil fields.

15

There are of course many people who believe, apparently sincerely, that the supply of oil in the ground is unlimited. Back in the 1950s and 1960s there were many people in America who used to believe that about American oil supplies. But American oil supplies reached a peak of 9.5 million barrels of oil a day in 1970 and since then American oil production has been on a downward slide. The entire American oil industry now produces just between 5 and 6 million barrels of oil a day. Since America stopped being a major supplier of oil, Saudi Arabia has been the world's most important source of oil and many commentators have for a long time believed that the Saudi Arabians could increase the supply of oil they produced just as easily as one can open a tap.

They should, perhaps, have read that Senate report about the oil running out.

By the start of the new millennium every key oil producer around the world had started to acknowledge that they were producing more or less at peak sustainable rates. Many of OPEC's key oil fields were in permanent decline and some OPEC countries had stopped exporting oil at all. In 2004, for example, Indonesia became an oil importer for the first time in its history. By the middle of 2004 there were concerns that the Russians were overproducing oil and working their oil fields too hard, in order to maximise their current profits. (Russia has developed close links with India and China. Russia has oil and no money. India and China have bucket loads of money but no oil.)

16

'Oil is too important to be left to the Arabs.'
HENRY KISSINGER

17

Even big oil companies are having to admit that they don't have as much as they said they thought they had. Royal Dutch Shell astonished the oil world by downgrading its proven reserves by over 35% in 2004.

All this put even greater pressure on the Saudi Arabian oil fields. The increasing fall in supply from most countries around the world has coincided with a sustained increase in demand. Saudi Arabia, which long ago gave itself the task of filling in when world oil supplies look insufficient, is now probably causing permanent damage to its oil fields by increasing production in order to keep up with the demand for oil. When the valves are opened too wide (to get out extra oil) the pressure within an oil field falls. When the pressure falls it becomes increasingly difficult to get oil out in the future. More importantly, as the oil is drained out, water tends to pour into the void – further damaging the oil field.

18

For years the world has believed that there is so much oil underneath Saudi Arabia that it can never run out. Sadly, there has never been any reliable evidence to sustain this optimistic view.

Twilight in the Desert is surely one of the most important books to have been published in the last half a century. The author, banker and oil expert Matthew R. Simmons, explains the size of the threat facing the world in precise and unemotional detail. Simmons has examined the fading of Saudi Arabia's oil supply and suggests that it is the coming failure of Saudi Arabian oil supplies which will bring about the peaking of global oil supplies – at the very time that the global demand for oil is rising faster than ever before.

Simmons points out that 90% of all the oil that Saudi Arabia has ever produced has come from just seven giant oil fields which have now all matured and grown old. The three most important oil fields in Saudi Arabia have been producing oil at very high rates for over half a century. Ghawar, the biggest single oil field, the King of oil fields, has been producing oil since 1951 and in that time has produced 55 billion barrels of oil. Throughout the last half of the twentieth century the oil produced from Ghawar, made up between 55% and 65% of Saudi Arabia's total oil production. But now the end is nigh.

'Twilight at Ghawar is fast approaching,' says Simmons. Just how quickly the oil will run out is something no one knows. Once peaking occurs, however, the decline in output tends to fall. It doesn't reach a plateau and just stay there. It is not uncommon for the output from a major oil field to halve in just a few years. Indeed, it is the norm. A survey of major oil fields showed that all of them declined by more than 50% within ten years of peaking. The Brent oil field was producing 450,000 thousand barrels of oil a day in 1985 but, just five years later, in 1990, the production was down to 100,000 thousand barrels of oil a day. Both the Brent oil field and the Forties oil field (the UK's two largest oilfields and the mainstays of the North Sea oil field industry) were largely empty by the year 2000 – around 30 years after their discovery. The Samotlor oilfield was producing nearly 3 million barrels of oil a day in 1986 but by 1994 the oil production was down to below half a million barrels of oil a day.

China's need to import oil stems not only from the fact that the nation's demand is rising rapidly. The huge Chinese Daqing oil field has been producing over one million barrels of oil a day for over 35 years but in early 2004 China's energy planners publicly discussed the likelihood that Daqing's output would be down by 40% by 2006 or 2007.

If Ghawar and other major oil fields fall only as quickly as the world's other oil fields (and, remember, Ghawar and others have been worked very hard for many decades and it is not unreasonable to expect that they could fall even more rapidly) the world oil supply will be devastated within less than a decade. Remember that despite the spending of huge amounts of money on looking for oil there have been no major oil field discoveries for years.

The chances are that it will not be possible to replace dying oil fields with new ones. And so the oil age is coming to an end.

The oil produced in Saudi Arabia is crucial largely because of the quantities involved. For decades the oil produced by the Saudis has made up around half of the oil produced in the whole of the Middle East. Saudi oil reserves make up nearly a quarter of the world's oil reserves. And, over the years, the willingness of the Saudis to increase their production whenever the world is short of oil has helped to even out the global supply. Today, the Saudis are paying the price for all those years of overproduction.

19

'There is no risk that we are running out of oil...'
GEORGE MAGNUS, SENIOR ECONOMIC ADVISER AT THE UBS INVESTMENT BANK IN THE *FINANCIAL TIMES* ON 17TH AUGUST 2005.

20

The Saudi Arabians are not the only ones who are running out of oil. The world's second biggest oil field is the Burgan oil field in Kuwait. For almost sixty years this oil field has been pumping out vast quantities of oil. It accounts for over half of Kuwait's proven oil reserves.

But Kuwait recently revealed that the Burgan oil field is past its peak output. The oil field's planned output will drop from two million barrels a day to around 1.7 million barrels a day. And the fall will continue – probably quite steeply.

More scary evidence that the world's oil supplies are rapidly running out.

You didn't read about this in your daily newspaper did you? Nor, I suspect, did you hear about it on the BBC.

21

We desperately need energy reform; we need a new energy blueprint.

The twilight in the desert, of which Simmons writes, will soon be darkness for us all. We need to find alternatives, real alternatives; energy sources which can provide us with heat and light and which can enable us to move around.

'What can be predicted, with absolute certainty,' says Simmons, 'is that the decline is coming, and our oil-consuming world is grossly unprepared for it. Somebody needs to get busy writing the script for Act II.'

I suspect that everything Simmons predicts is accurate – with one exception. I think someone has already been busy writing the script for Act II.

Simmons' book was published in 2005 but to me it seems that if a Houston based banker could work all this out then some of George W. Bush's oil industry friends had probably worked it out some years earlier – particularly since they had access to a good deal of other information, including the secret Senate hearings from the 1970s.

I suspect that George's pals in the oil industry realised long ago that as the oil started to run out the price would rocket. They desperately wanted to lay their hands on as much oil as they could. George's pals in the arms industry realised that without oil their planes and tanks and ships wouldn't be going anywhere. And if they couldn't go anywhere they wouldn't be able to fire their weapons of mass destruction.

I believe that George W. Bush's backers, the American neo-conservative Zionists, saw what was happening some years ago. They have tried to create a world in which they will control what oil exists, benefit from the shortage of oil and be free to introduce an endless variety of legislation designed to limit our freedom and expand their power. The legislation which has changed the world since 11th September 2001 was clearly brought in to enable a relatively small number of money and power hungry men (and women) to control the world and to control potential rioters.

The oil industry needed an excuse to get hold of what was left of the world's oil (much of it in Iraq and Iran) and the arms industry desperately needed an excuse to persuade the taxpayers that the armed forces should have the oil.

The Zionist neo-conservatives and the racist right-wing American Christian fundamentalists also saw this as an opportunity to start a religious war and crush the world's Muslims.

Bingo.

Now it all falls into place.

Now it all makes sense.

22

Does Blair know the full story? No, I suspect not.

Blair and his Labour Party comrades are too stupid, too vain and too parochial. I think Blair is just one of a number of stooges (though possibly the most important). The bad guys (the neo-conservative Zionists) who control Bush want power and money. Blair and his buddies are just useful – and easily and cheaply bought. Blair, driven by greed and vanity, has tied us to America so that he can pay off his mortgage.

23

The importance of the concept of peak oil as a stimulus to power hungry politicians, money hungry businessmen and empire builders of all kinds is difficult to over estimate.

If we had caring, thoughtful, responsible politicians who cared for our welfare they would now be urgently planning for the different world we will soon inhabit.

We need urgently to assess the viability of other sources of energy. Some, which seemed too dangerous before, will now seem acceptable. We must, for example, start building nuclear power stations (the French, the Chinese and the Americans already have them, and are planning to build many more and the Russians are limiting uranium exports to conserve material for their new nuclear reactors).

Much higher oil prices will make many previously unacceptable forms of energy more competitive and will close our eyes to the problems associated with them.

Windmills, wave farms and solar panels cannot possibly provide us with more than a fraction of the energy we need and anyone who believes they can is clearly either from a different planet or is assuming that everyone around will be prepared to give up luxuries such as lighting, heating, cooking, hot water, television and so on.

It is clear to anyone with a brain (including thinking environmentalists who have studied the evidence) that the only safe, effective way for us to obtain our energy in the future is from nuclear power plants. But this logical approach is avoided, partly because it offends a minority of loud-spoken objectors who still think of Chernobyl, but mainly because it offends those leaders of the oil industry who have their heads stuck as deep in the sand as an oil drill in modern Saudi Arabia. The future is nuclear. There is no other choice. Those who complain that nuclear power isn't safe should know that each year the deaths from coal mining exceed the number of deaths sustained during the entire history of nuclear reactors.

24

We need to examine how we can make the best use of our dwindling supplies of oil. The danger at the moment is that as the amount of oil available starts to fall those who deal in oil will treat their product in much the same sort of way that a slum landlord treats his properties; taking what profits they can and doing as little as is necessary to keep the system working. If oil disappears and companies are subjected to windfall taxes as prices rise (as is happening in Britain) there will be little incentive to reinvest, to spend money on old and inefficient pieces of infrastructure or to spend money on exploration.

We need to find out exactly how much oil is left so that we can make best use of our resources – and so that we do not suddenly find ourselves looking at the last drop and wondering what happened. We need to find out how much it is going to cost to extract the oil that does remain. At what price will it be viable to extract that oil? We need to be prepared for a world in which oil is going to get increasingly expensive. A barrel of oil will never again be sold for a few dollars. Barrels of oil will soon cost $100, $200 or more.

We need to decide on our priorities – which should not automatically include the military. How can we best make use of our diminishing oil supplies? Whose needs are greatest? There will have to be priorities and, to avoid arbitrage, individual countries will need to cooperate. Do the requirements of airlines and racing cars come above or below the needs of hospital generators?

The world economy will never be the same again after peak oil. The world will function. But things will be different.

Most importantly of all, we need to look seriously at ways to conserve energy. Ironically, Governments create more waste than anyone. The biggest waste of oil is through traffic congestion. When thousands and thousands of motorists sit in their cars, inching forwards at a few miles an hour, the amount of oil that is consumed is phenomenal. Much oil is wasted not by drivers going too quickly but by drivers going too slowly.

In China, roads which need repair are worked on at night, under floodlights, to cut down the number of traffic jams. The Chinese Government realises that the cost of paying overtime and setting up lights is far less than the cost to the economy of thousands of motorists sitting in traffic jams burning up petrol. Motorways with lanes closed and no sign of activity have become a common sight in Britain but these unnecessary closures cost millions in terms of fuel wasted and hours lost. Arbitrary speed limits, often introduced on motorways solely as a way for governments and police forces to make money from speed cameras rather than in an attempt to reduce accidents, must be abandoned. It seems to me that most traffic jams in Britain are caused by the police – sometimes deliberately (by trying to make more money by introducing impractical speed limits) but often through sheer incompetence or laziness in failing to remove unnecessary speed restrictions.

More people will have to work at home. The Internet will have to change from being little more than a mail order medium to being a genuine way of working together. Mass transportation systems will have to be cheaper and more efficient.

25

We need thoughtful, creative politicians to ask the right questions and find some good answers.

But we don't have thoughtful, responsible politicians. And our politicians certainly do not care for our welfare. No politicians have publicly acknowledged the problems of peak oil. No politicians have raised the questions that I've listed above (let alone tried to provide any answers).

Why not?

Most politicians don't think further ahead than the next election. This is particularly true of Britain where the so-called democratic system means that 'winner takes all'. The leader of the party which wins the general election gets everything. Everyone else gets nothing.

Chapter Five

How And Why Britain Became A Terrorist Nation – Led By A War Criminal

1

Iraq, with the world's second largest oil reserves (over 10% of the world's oil is in Iraq), was the obvious target for an oil hungry America. It was controlled by a dictator and had a small population. The people were weakened by the Anglo-American sanctions. The armed forces had very few weapons.

But George W. Bush (or, more accurately, his neo-conservative Zionist string-pullers) knew that they had to move fast. France, China and Russia were setting up secret deals to buy Iraq's oil as soon as the sanctions ended. And Bush's pals knew that the price of oil was bound to rise and rise and rise.

The neo-conservatives didn't want to involve the United Nations because that would have involved including France and Russia in sharing the spoils. They wanted Iraq's oil for themselves. All of it. And they wanted the UK to support their invasion, not to share the spoils, but to give the war some international credibility. The Americans got that by buying Blair (the vainest man alive) with welcomes at the White House, public popularity (something he no longer has at home) and the inevitable prospect of directorships and huge fees for lecture tours and books afterwards.

2

There has been a Christian community in Iraq longer than there has been a Christian community in America. There have been Christians in Iraq since the 16th century. Before the Anglo American invasion of 2002 the Christians and the Muslims lived together quite happily. But today the Christians are leaving in droves to avoid being killed by the Muslims.

Before the recent invasion there were over one million Christians in Iraq. Considering the fact that Western (Christian) abuse of Muslims goes back nine centuries to the Crusades this wasn't bad. It was, in fact, a pretty amazing sign of tolerance. The Christians and the Muslims were living fairly comfortably together. A year or so after the Americans invaded there were 850,000 Christians left. Christians were leaving Iraq because the Americans had made the country too dangerous for them.

3

Any doubts about the fact that the invasion of Iraq was at least partly a religious war were removed when George W. Bush announced in October 2005 that his god had told him to invade Iraq and, presumably, to kill 100,000 entirely innocent women and children so that Christian Americans could have the oil. Since Bush is a fervent, not to say fanatical, Christian and there are 70 million Evangelical Christians in the USA (of whom the most prejudiced are a considerable threat to world peace) this statement seemed designed to make it clear that America is fighting a religious war against the Muslims. It is difficult to see how this could do anything other than encourage those extreme Muslims who also regard themselves as fighting a long-term war against the Christians.

4

Blair didn't lead us into war, he lied us into war.

5

Benito Mussolini defined a fascist state as one ruled by big business corporations.

6

When it became clear that Iraq's secret weapons of mass destruction consisted of a pea shooter and a catapult in a kid's school desk Blair's Government claimed that the war against Iraq had been started to uphold the authority of the United Nations.

Big fat lie.

Kofi Annan, the Secretary General of the UN had already condemned the whole operation as an illegal violation of the UN charter, effectively accusing Britain and America of international gangsterism – and war crimes.

Blair and Bush are war criminals and will one day face a war crimes tribunal. Not arguably. Not in my opinion. Officially. And not just once. They are serial war criminals.

How many illegal wars does our Prime Minister have to start before people put down their TV remote control and start to protest?

7

'The first panacea for a mismanaged nation is inflation of the currency; the second is war. Both bring temporary prosperity; both bring a permanent ruin. Both are the refuge of political and economic opportunists.'
ERNEST HEMINGWAY

8

The Anglo American invasion of Iraq was initially justified on the grounds that Iraq had weapons of mass destruction with which it could, within 45 minutes, launch an attack on us. When this was proved to be a lie Bush and Blair claimed that the purpose of the invasion was to get rid of the country's leader. But on the eve of the invasion Bush and Blair announced that they would invade even if Saddam and his family left the country. So that wasn't the reason either and the Americans were reduced to using their old favourite (and slightly surreal argument) that the absence of evidence proving that something was going on proved that something was going on but was being hidden very well. (If you or I came out with anything like this, men in white coats would doubtless drag us away and lock us up.)

9

*'Fifty years ago, when I was a boy, it seemed completely self-evident
that the bad old days were over, that torture and massacre,
slavery and the persecution of heretics, were things of the past.
Among people who wore top hats, travelled in trains and took a
bath every morning such horrors were simply out of the question.'*
ALDOUS HUXLEY (WRITING IN 1959)

10

Four former ministers have joined a parliamentary campaign for
Blair to be impeached both for his handling of the Iraq war and for
deceiving the House of Commons by making assertions about
Saddam Hussein's weapons of mass destruction which were
contradicted by his own intelligence assessments. It has also been
argued that he could be charged with making a private agreement
with Bush to take Britain into an illegal war which the people didn't
want.

11

*'I gave my life for freedom – this I know
For those who bade me fight had told me so.'*
WILLIAM NORMAN EWER 1917

12

Before the 2002 war started, Bush (and presumably Blair) ignored a
warning from a high level American task force and from numerous
intelligence and security agencies which concluded that a war with
Iraq would increase the chances of the USA (and presumably the
UK) being attacked with weapons of mass destruction. Bush and
Blair were also warned that an invasion of Iraq might precipitate a
humanitarian catastrophe.

13

*'It would be easy to say that we owe it all to the Bush family from Texas, but
that would be too simplistic. They are only errand boys for the vengeful,*

bloodthirsty cartel of raving Jesus-freaks and super-rich money mongers who have ruled this country for at least the last 20 years, and arguably for the past 200. They take orders well, and they don't ask too many questions.'
HUNTER S. THOMPSON (*KINGDOM OF FEAR*)

14

The Labour Government has refused to tell the people the legal advice it received about the legality of the invasion of Iraq. We paid for the war and the advice but we don't get to see it. Blair's Government claimed that they couldn't (wouldn't) release this information because of client- lawyer confidentiality.

This is, of course, something now denied to ordinary citizens. As usual, it is one law for them and one law for us.

15

'Individuals have the duty to violate domestic laws to prevent crimes against peace and humanity from occurring.'
NUREMBERG WAR CRIMES TRIBUNAL 1945-6

16

British soldiers who were charged with brutally assaulting Iraqis faced a *maximum* two years in prison.

17

'When bad men combine, the good must associate; else they will fall one by one, an unpitied sacrifice in a contemptible struggle.'
EDMUND BURKE

18

The Americans have consistently provided Israel with increasingly powerful weapons. It is now widely believed that it was Israel's destruction of Iraq's nuclear reactor in 1981 (with American planes) which was the trigger for attempts by Saddam Hussein to initiate a serious nuclear weapons programme. The Americans are constantly supplying the Israelis with ever more powerful weapons and, therefore, destabilising the Middle East. When the leader of Iran made some predictable but fairly hard-line remarks about Israel this was seized upon as an unacceptably racist remark. Blair, ever the American lapdog, responded on cue. He leapt around yapping and snarling and made it pretty clear that when the Americans wanted to invade Iran he would provide British back up. In my book *Rogue Nation* (written before America and Britain invaded Iraq) I predicted that Iran would be next. It has, all along, been clear that the American and British Governments would prepare us for this by demonising Iran. Bush has to start a war against Iran because he needs their oil too.

19

Let's not beat about the bush. Blair and politicians who supported his illegal invasion of Iraq are war criminals. Soldiers who fought in the illegal war in Iraq are war criminals. Every MP who voted for the invasion of Iraq should be arrested and tried as a war criminal. Anyone who voted for Blair in the 2005 general election will, if justice ever prevails, be judged to be a war criminal. Indeed, according to the conclusions of the Nuremberg war crimes tribunal, it seems entirely fair to say that anyone who did not protest against the illegal invasion of Iraq is a war criminal.

20

Bush's growing religious war against the Muslim world has revived and given extra strength to the militants and has done wonders for Al Qaeda recruiting. The number of suicide bombers has risen since the invasion of Iraq and the clear and simple statements from the bombers themselves (recorded on the eve of their suicidal attacks) make it clear that Blair is lying when he claims (either with awesome naivety or a breathless disregard for a globally perceived truth) that the bombing attacks on London had nothing to do with the invasion of Iraq. (As an aside, isn't it curious that we tend to have a high regard for Japanese Kamikaze pilots, who flew their final missions with enough fuel to reach their targets but not enough to fly back, who carried a single bomb on their planes and who crashed their planes directly into their targets, but we are encouraged to feel nothing but contempt for Palestinian suicide bombers who are practising the same technique). The Anglo-American alliance has pushed Arab nationalists and Islamic militants closer together and has alienated secular and moderate Muslim opinion, making it increasingly difficult for Muslims to defend western policies anywhere in the world.

21

'For the word 'terrorist' substitute the word 'government' and everything makes sense.'
GRAFFITI

22

The official pretexts for war collapsed one after the other and eventually Bush simply declared that America (with Britain tagging along behind) had the right to use force even if a country had no weapons of mass destruction and had no programmes to develop them but had the 'intent and ability' to do so. This is so subjective that it simply gives the USA (and Britain) the right to attack any country in the world that it wants to attack. (It has been revealed that the Americans intended to attack Iraq long before 11/9).

Neither Bush nor Blair cared about the fact that they were risking the lives of their own citizens. Power, oil and money were all that mattered.

Anyone who harbours hopes that the Americans might leave Iraq to find its own independence, should be aware that although America says it intends to leave Iraq it is nevertheless planning to build 14 permanent bases there. It will also maintain an embassy the size of Alaska. The new American embassy in Baghdad is one of the biggest in the world, with over 3,000 officials employed to control every aspect of Government in Iraq except garbage collection and hospitals. (Control over those has been handed to the Iraqi Government which was appointed by the Americans and which the Americans, who claim they are in the business of 'nation building', describe as 'the first democracy in the Arab world'.)

Does that sound like anything to you? The Vichy regime in France under Marshal Petain, perhaps?

The Americans don't realise that they are the problem, and cannot possibly ever be the solution.

23

Before the invasion of Iraq began I wrote that it would turn out to be another Vietnam. This forecast was widely dismissed as nonsense.

24

'Terrorism is a war of the powerless. War is the terrorism of the powerful.'
BISHOP SPONG

25

We are in a war without end. But this is not a miscalculation. The American Government always knew that they were going to have to stay in Iraq. Probably for ever. The oil and armaments industries want an endless war. The mistake liberals make is in assuming that all this was a shock to the Bush Government. It wasn't. Permanent war was always the plan.

26

The British and Americans like to keep showing footage of Saddam's statue being toppled (usually managing to keep out of shot the American soldiers who were doing the toppling). But long after the American and British invasion had defeated the Iraqi military Saddam Hussein remained one of the six most popular politicians in Iraq. 'If there were genuinely free elections in Iraq I wouldn't bet against Saddam being elected president,' said one Iraqi while Saddam was on trial.

27

In Afghanistan, books printed by the Mujahedeen Government teach children the alphabet like this:
J is for Jihad, our aim in life
I is for Israel, our enemy
K is for Kalashnikov, we will overcome

M is for Mujahedeen, our heroes

T is for Taliban

And in maths children are taught from books which don't do the usual calculations involving baths and bath taps but which, instead, involve guns and bullets. For example: 'X has a Kalashnikov with six magazines. There are twenty bullets in each magazine. X uses half of the bullets and kills sixty infidels. How many infidels does he kill with each bullet?'

28

Tony Blair's place in history (his third greatest concern, after personal vanity and wealth) is assured. But he will be remembered not as the first Labour PM to win three elections but as the first sitting British PM to be a war criminal. Some legacy. Not many British children have ever been able to say: 'My Dad is a war criminal'. Blair's kids can say that.

29

Has there ever been a more disreputable, more hypocritical, dishonest man in charge of Britain? I can't think of one. Blair has defied and ignored the will of the people time and time again. He has taken us into war after war and has single-handedly, and with no good reason, made Britain one of the three major terrorist targets in the world. (The other two being Israel and America – hardly nations with which we can be proud to be associated.) Bush and Blair are today's Hitler and Mussolini.

Britain is linked inextricably with America – the world's number one terrorist nation – and obediently supports the illegal activities of Israel in order not to upset the Americans. Britain, now fighting a religious war in order to support the aims and ambitions of zealots in the USA and Israel, has become part of the modern axis of evil. We are responsible for what America's soldiers do. If two men rob a bank and one kills a guard the robber who did not pull the trigger is still held responsible. When America uses landmines and cluster bombs (both illegal) Britain is responsible. When American troops torture Iraqi prisoners (which they do) Britain is responsible. When the Americans attack innocent Iraqi civilians with white phosphorus grenades Britain is responsible. White phosphorus grenades are so nasty that at first even the Americans denied using them. But use them they did. White phosphorus sticks to the skin while it burns at an intense heat. Iraqi women and children have been burned to death in this way. This is no better than the indiscriminate use of napalm bombs in Vietnam. The Americans are, it seems, unable to avoid reverting to type. Britain and America are now inextricably linked. Blair and Brown and Blunkett and Straw and the rest of them have turned us into Nazi style monsters. A nation of gangsters, bullies and steel-hearted bastards who will kill brown-skinned children in the name of nothing in particular and not even bother to count the bodies. Thanks to Blair's personal greed and vanity, we have become hired killers. Get out of our way. We're coming through and we've got the weapons of mass destruction. The Americans have declared themselves to be immune to prosecution as war criminals. While they have the biggest bombs they will doubtless remain immune. But that immunity will not last for ever. And I do not doubt that Blair and his gang, who have no immunity, will themselves one day face trial as war criminals. The list of offences with which Blair will be charged will be long. It seems, for example, that he may well have been aware that the Americans were kidnapping and then torturing suspects in a process known as 'extraordinary rendition'. If Blair did know that the Americans were breaking the law in this way (and it seems inconceivable to me that he did not) then that would be another crime to put on a very lengthy charge sheet.

30

'Any action intended to cause death or serious bodily harm to civilians
or non-combatants, when the purpose of such an act,
by its nature or context, is to intimidate a population
or to compel a government or an international organisation
to carry out or to abstain from any act, cannot be justified
on any grounds and constitutes an act of terrorism.'
UNITED NATIONS

31

To be born English or British used to be regarded as an asset in the world. The English might have been feared, but they were also respected. No more. Today, thanks to the Labour Party and the leadership of Tony Blair, to be born British is to be born grossly and permanently disadvantaged; despised and loathed by citizens of the world; regarded as a citizen of a second-rate poodle state. Americans can at least wander the world with some arrogance: they are perceived as rich, aggressive and fearsome; their Government provides its citizens abroad with a considerable amount of protection. No other country can imprison an American without fearsome consequences. The extradition of American citizens is almost unknown. Britons, on the other hand, get no protection from their Government. Britons can be whisked hither and thither without protest. Britons are regarded as the citizens of the gangland leader's right hand thug. We are easy prey. Expendable. Extraditable. Kidnappable. Imprisonable. Africans and Asians who don't dare sneer at Americans will happily sneer at Britons. The Greeks who arrested British plane spotters would never have dared to arrest American plane spotters.

32

When America claims it is invading Iraq to protect the world from chemical weapons and to prevent Iraqis being tortured, the accusation 'hypocrisy' is unavoidable when we discover that the American troops are using chemical weapons to kill Iraqis and then torturing the ones they haven't managed to kill outright.

In these difficult times we all have to think carefully about our responsibilities. Should members of the armed forces agree to fight illegal wars just because the Prime Minister tells them to? According to the principles created at the Nuremberg Trials they should not. Soldiers who fight an illegal war, and who kill innocent citizens at the behest of a war criminal are themselves war criminals too.

Before Britain invaded Iraq two soldiers refused to go. Nothing happened to them. Neither the Government nor the army wanted to risk a trial at which the defence would undoubtedly claim that it would be wrong for soldiers to fight an illegal war. Soldiers in the

British armed forces had a legal and moral responsibility not to fight in Iraq and should have found the courage to stand up against the Prime Minister's lawless determination to abuse his authority and their power. I have sympathy for British troops in Iraq only in the way that I have sympathy for Nazi troops who didn't really believe in Hitler but were too frightened of the consequences to stand up to him.

So don't tell me that the soldiers who went to Iraq were brave. They were just doing their jobs. The ones who were really brave were the ones who refused to go. The rest might as well have just joined Blair and Brown and Blunkett as honorary members of the Klu Klux Klan.

At Nuremberg, after the Second World War, many German soldiers discovered that the excuse 'I was just doing my job' is no excuse when charged with war crimes. Our 'boys and girls' in the desert would do well to remember that.

33

'The war on terror is the first great war of the 21st century.'
GEORGE W. BUSH, PRESIDENT OF THE USA
(OBVIOUSLY EXPECTING MORE WARS)

34

The world hates America. It's not difficult to see why. Now, entirely thanks to Tony Blair's greed and vanity, the world hates us too.

35

'I will accept nothing less than complete victory in the war on terror.'
GEORGE W. BUSH, PRESIDENT OF THE USA AND DOOMED TO
DISAPPOINTMENT

36

One of the arguments for waging war on Afghanistan and Iraq has been that the men in these countries do not treat women with proper Western-style respect.

In autumn 2001, after I had written an article expressing concern that America might take advantage of the events of 11th September to justify starting wars against Muslim countries, I received a stern letter of complaint from a reader who accused me of supporting Osama bin Laden, the Taliban and terrorism in general.

My reader argued that the Americans were entitled to invade Afghanistan if for no reason than in order to free the women of that country who, he argued, were entitled to be treated with more respect.

I wrote back to him agreeing with his point that women should be treated with respect (I added that children, animals, the elderly, the mentally ill etc. should also be treated with more respect than they are in modern Western societies).

But, I asked him, if he was seriously suggesting that we should now bomb all countries which do not treat women with respect? Carpet bombing a country which needs rebuilding and where the women are treated badly doesn't seem like much of a solution.

I pointed out that if we are going to declare war on countries which support terrorism then we should declare war on America – which has funded the IRA for years.

And I finished: 'And if we are going to declare war on countries which have policies which we find repugnant...well...who, pray, is going to pay for all the bombs we will need?'

37

A few months after the invasion of Iraq, while Bush was standing on an aircraft carrier dressed up like an extra from a second rate war movie, Blair celebrated what he called the official end of the war on Iraq (and what a remarkable piece of wishful thinking that was) by using taxpayers' money to send British feminists to Iraq to teach Iraqis about women's rights. Along with designer frocks obtained at a discount this was, according to at least one newspaper story, something that Cherie Blair felt quite strongly about.

38

Not many months later a British Muslim schoolgirl won the right to wear to her British school the sort of clothes the Blairs had said we had invaded Afghanistan and Iraq to stop women having to wear.

And many English women who marry Muslim men happily submit to their way of life.

Very much in touch with the hopes, aspirations and preferences of the ordinary people they kill are our leaders the Blairs.

Actually, it does seem to me that when you fight a war to force people to submit to your own religious and cultural mores you are fighting a crusade; a religious war. And that is just a tiny bit arrogant, patronising and imperialistic.

Blair (and presumably Bush) is fighting a racist war as well as a war for money and oil.

39

After the Second World War Albert Speer, third ranking member of the Nazi hierarchy during the Second World War, pleaded guilty at Nuremberg and was sentenced to life imprisonment. He said that he, like others, was often asked: 'Didn't you know what was going on?' and he always replied: 'We wanted not to know.'

That it seems, rather sadly, is the response of many Britons today.

40

It used to be that Britain didn't start wars. We fought them (often to protect the weak) but we didn't start them. We were the white-hatted cowboys who never drew first. Blair changed that. We're now the bad guys. The guys in black hats who shoot first and swagger off with the loot.

41

Iran will be next.

As I forecast in my book *Rogue Nation*, the Americans claim that they want to bomb the sand out of Iran because the Iranians are daring to build their own nuclear deterrent. If the Iranians are building nuclear warheads they are doubtless conscious of the fact that *really* having weapons of mass destruction acts as a great deterrent since, in the true tradition of all bullies, the Americans are less likely to attack countries which can defend themselves. (That's why they haven't yet attacked North Korea.) The Iranians doubtless also know that having nuclear warheads would put them in a strong negotiating position. They are doubtless also aware that the USA and the UK have, counting the two wars against Iraq and the sanctions in between, been responsible for the deaths of far more innocent people in Iraq than Saddam Hussein. (The success of the well-armed IRA in negotiating with Blair's feeble Government cannot have escaped notice around the world. The IRA got a lot of political mileage out of giving up weapons. Indeed, the unfired weapons doubtless proved far more effective than the ones that had been fired.)

The Americans don't mind Pakistan having nuclear capability because Pakistan's leadership has rolled over and allowed the Americans to do with them what they will. And they don't mind Israel (the constant cause of unrest in the Middle East) having nuclear weapons because American Jews vote noisily and contribute generously to the right political campaigns.

The Americans say they want to bomb Iran to stop the Iranians being able to defend themselves against being bombed.

But that's not really true. At least, it's not the whole truth.

The main reason why America wants to start a war with Iran can be summed up in one word: money.

The Americans want to drop bombs. Lots of bombs. When the American Government drops bombs the American bomb making industry sells more bombs and makes more money. If the Government just stockpiles the damned things the orders stop flowing. The neo-conservative religious maniacs who run America want an everlasting religious war with the whole Muslim world. They want all those damned heathen foreigners bombed to smithereens.

Iran is a powerful, independent country which has a lot of oil. It is making its own security and oil deals with China, Russia and Venezuela. It sits in a strategically crucial position between the Middle East and Central Asia.

All that is reason enough for the Americans to want to invade Iran.

But there is more.

The Iranians plan to establish their own oil exchange at which petrochemicals, crude oil and oil and gas products can be traded. The aim is to make Iran the main centre for oil deals in the Middle East.

And, as I have pointed out in previous books, they're going to trade oil in euros, not American dollars.

The American dollar has been kept artificially strong for thirty years. Having a strong dollar – the only currency in which oil is traded – has enabled the Americans to run up a huge Government deficit and gargantuan trade deficits. Other countries have been paying for the American miracle. All those fat American tourists, waddling around the world with fistfuls of dollars, are wealthy beyond their own dreams because their nation has conned and stolen money from just about every other country on the planet. Millions have died of starvation to pay for the American economic 'miracle'. The American dream has been everyone else's nightmare.

Iraq was the first country to announce its intention of selling oil in euros instead of dollars. Although there were undoubtedly political reasons for this decision (it is fair to assume that Saddam Hussein wasn't a fan of America) the economic logic behind the intention was sound. The European Union imports more oil from OPEC producers than the USA and 45% of the imports into the Middle East come from the EU.

Iraq's decision was announced back in November 2000 and it was one of the additional triggers for the American invasion. Once the Iraqis had decided to threaten the American currency monopoly on oil sales the neo-conservatives had an easy task in 'selling' the idea of an invasion to the rest of the American hierarchy.

One of the first things the American invaders did when they got into Iraq was to return oil sales to dollars instead of euros. The invasion was designed to instal a pro-American puppet Government in Iraq, to establish plenty of American military bases there, to secure the Iraqi oil for American motorists and the American military and to ensure that Iraq sold oil in dollars not euros.

42

As soon as they understood the significance of 'peak oil' the Americans realised that we had entered the endgame of the oil era. If America doesn't control the world's oil then China will do so. China's thirst for oil is growing at an astonishing rate. And China, remember, has already done oil deals with Venezuela, Saudi Arabia, Nigeria – and Iran. The Chinese even alarmed the Americans by trying to buy an American oil company.

The Americans and the Chinese may, on the surface, appear to be friends. But beneath the surface both countries know that what happens in the next few years will decide which country rules the world for the next century or two.

At the moment both countries need one another.

America needs China for its cheap television sets and other consumer products. Without China's help the cost of living in America would soar. And America would be in an even worse economic mess than it is at the moment.

China helps sustain America by investing their dollar earnings back into American Treasury Bills. If the Chinese didn't invest their money in dollars the Americans wouldn't be able to afford to buy any more Chinese goods (however cheap they might be).

So, at the moment it suits the Chinese to support America.

But, as the dollar continues to decline (as it inevitably will) so the Chinese will gradually sell their dollar investments and put their savings into something else (probably euros.)

When the Chinese do this, the American dollar will collapse and so will America.

The world's most arrogant nation will be just another failed empire.

The Americans have to invade Iran. As they see things, they really don't have any choice. They can't afford the money to invade Iran. They don't have the men to invade Iran. They can't really risk upsetting Iran's allies (such as China). They know that Iran won't roll over as easily as Iraq did. They know that the rest of the world will disapprove. But they'll do it.

In his State of the Union address on February 2nd 2005, Bush said: 'Today, Iran remains the world's primary state sponsor of terror, pursuing nuclear weapons while depriving its people of the freedom they seek and deserve.' Much the same was said to excuse the invasions of Afghanistan and Iraq. A couple of weeks later Bush pledged to support Israel if it bombed Iran in an effort to destroy Iran's ability to make a nuclear bomb.

So when Bush and Blair criticise Iran and complain that the Iranians are killing American and British soldiers in Iraq we know that their complaints have a strong political motive. Bush and Blair are preparing us for a war against Iran. The Americans cannot invade

Iran without an excuse. They have made such a mess of the invasion of Iraq that not even the American people would accept another war without some justification.

(As an aside, I think it is possible that Blair's constantly postponed retirement is a result of American intervention. The Americans know that Blair will do whatever they want him to do. They may not be so sure of Gordon Brown's compliance. Blair cannot retire until the Americans tell him that he can because he desperately needs the jobs which I believe they have promised him. If America invades Iran, Blair will have to try and take us into that war too. Are there any politicians in Britain strong enough to stop him? Wasn't it convenient that Robin Cook died so mysteriously?)

At some time in the near future we will, I suspect, hear that the Iranians have attacked either Israel or an American warship. The attack won't be genuine, of course. It will have been arranged by the Americans themselves, or by the Israelis. The American leadership will happily sacrifice a few thousand of its own citizens in order to justify another invasion. And then there will, again, be war.

43

'There is no justification for Iran or any other country interfering in Iraq.'
TONY BLAIR

44

In autumn 2005, in what was clearly an attempt to prepare the way for a war on Iran, Britain's Labour Government blamed Iran for the deaths of some British soldiers in Iraq. The British Government accused Iran of being dishonest and harbouring hostile intent. Blair has obviously never heard the words 'pot', 'black' and 'kettle' used in the same sentence.

45

When the Americans invade Iran they will be making an even bigger strategic mistake than they made when they invaded Iraq.

It seems inconceivable that America's leaders could make such a stupid mistake.

But they probably will.

George W. Bush and his leaders think they are bright.

But they really are as stupid as the rest of us suspect they are. George W. Bush is said to have told his advisers that he only wants to hear good news. Experts whose advice doesn't fit in with the neo-conservative plan for dealing with the peak oil problem are dismissed or ignored.

The Iranians have better weapons than Iraq had before the invasion. And having seen what has happened in Iraq they will have doubtless done as much as they can to improve their capability and preparedness.

But the Iranians know that their best chance is to fight a guerrilla war, rather than to meet the Americans in a pitched battle.

And, unlike Iraq, Iran has good relationships, and strong economic and military ties, with a number of other countries. It has good relationships with China, Russia, Japan and the EU. An American invasion of Iran could well lead to a confrontation with the first two of those. Putin's Russia has been quietly selling its advanced missile systems to Syria, Venezuela and Iran. China is a sleeping giant with huge military capabilities. Even Japan should be taken seriously by the American planners. Japan obtains about 15% of its oil from Iran.

The Americans see themselves as invincible. They aren't. Around the world America is increasingly regarded as a liability. Its huge debts are being sustained by other, poorer countries where resentment is building. It uses up natural resources with great greed – leaving insufficient for other countries. It has refused to sign the Kyoto accord and is, therefore, constantly being blamed for the consequential environmental problems caused by global warming. To most of the rest of the world America is the planet's most dangerous and most feared terrorist nation. As accomplices to America we too are now the terrorists.

The American invasion of Iran will further divide the world into two camps: America and its allies, and the rest. If the Labour Party keeps Britain alongside America (which I suspect it will) then Britain will be destroyed along with America.

The inevitable new war on Iran will serve two purposes: it will enable the Americans to gain direct access to yet more of the world's diminishing supply of oil and it will be an excuse to introduce ever stricter rules and regulations limiting our freedom and our rights.

46

'My opposition to war is not based upon pacifist or non-resistant principles. It may be that the present state of civilisation is such that certain international questions cannot be discussed; it may be that they have to be fought out. We ought not to forget that wars are a purely manufactured evil and are made according to a definite technique. A campaign for war is made upon as definite lines as a campaign for any other purpose. First, the people are worked upon. By clever tales the people's suspicions are aroused toward the nation against whom war is desired. Make the nation suspicion; make the other nation suspicious. All you need for this are a few agents with some cleverness and no conscience and a press whose interest is locked up with the interests that will be benefited by war. Then the 'overt act' will soon appear. It is no trick at all to get an 'overt act' once you work the hatred of two nations up to the proper pitch.'

HENRY FORD

47

Where will the USA (and UK) find the soldiers for a war on Iran? A draft will have to be introduced.

The American Pentagon is already building a database of high school and college students. They're collecting names from websites and commercial data brokers.

Even if they aren't in the armed forces your children and grandchildren could die in Iran.

48

Terrorists are defined as those who favour or use terror-inspiring methods of governing or of coercing a government or community. This means that the Israelis are terrorists just as much as the Palestinians. And it means that Blair and Bush and their supporters are terrorists too.

Bush's infamous claim 'you are either with us or you are with the terrorists' becomes confusing when you realise that Bush is himself the world's most notorious and evil terrorist.

49

A growing number of Americans now also want to invade Venezuela. Although the Middle East is traditionally regarded as the source of all oil, Venezuela has, in recent years, become one of the world's biggest oil suppliers. Tough-talking Americans want their Government to invade Venezuela, and replace the present Venezuelan Government with puppets.

There are, although it seems difficult to believe that even Americans can be this stupid, some Americans who want to start some sort of war with China. Oh boy. For those who believe America is all powerful and can defeat any country (including China) I would point out that one in every six people on the planet is Chinese. The Americans have about as much chance of defeating China in a war as I have of becoming Chairman and Chief Executive of Haliburton.

Chapter Six

Our Special Friends And Closest Allies: What Sort Of People Are These Fat And Greedy Bastards And What Do They Believe In?

1

People who lived in Australia, India, Canada, New Zealand, South Africa and the American colonies during the great days of the British Empire were greatly affected by what was happening in England. When new laws were passed in England they affected the citizens of dozens of other countries, thousands of miles away. The men who ruled England were, effectively, also ruling a good deal of the rest of the world.

Today, it is America which rules the world. (Though it is amusing to remember that the American Revolution against English rule was triggered when George III raised the tax on tea. If George III hadn't been so greedy, America would probably still be a part of the Commonwealth.)

2

As the world's richest nation (albeit one which has gained its wealth through deceit, dishonesty and violence) the USA might reasonably

174

be expected to offer moral leadership, abide by international law, be generous to neighbours, show respect for the planet, treat people humanely (its own and others) and share its knowledge with less fortunate nations.

No chance.

The Americans, a bunch of unreconstructed crypto-fascist reactionary imperialists, have no sense of style or taste (look at the clothes they wear) and not much of a sense of humour. Nor do they have much in the way of brains (whenever there is a well publicised violent death in Europe, Americans cancel their air tickets and choose to remain in a country where the daily death rate is comparable to the annual rate in Britain). The Americans have the biggest, worst prisons in the world and they practise and approve of torture.

Ever since the first American settlers paid the Menhaden Native Americans $24 in beads for what became Manhattan, the Americans have created their wealth out of exploitation. Largely through greed, theft and thuggery a small number of them have accumulated a fair amount of wealth. This fortunate few flaunt their ill-gotten gains with all the sensitivity illustrated by combatants on the Jerry Springer Show. Early on in its history the American Government encouraged early white hunters to kill whole herds of buffalo because they believed that if the native American Indians had no buffalo (animals which they used both for food and clothes) they would give up their lands and go away. The American Government didn't care where they went as long as they got out of the way. Things have gone downhill ever since.

3

When England conquered the world we gave our victims cricket, pageantry, our heritage and a sense of style. The Americans have given the world cancer-inducing hamburgers and, not having any of their own, they have stolen everyone else's heritage.

4

In terms of foreign aid provided to struggling countries, America is the meanest nation in the world. It never seems to occur to Americans that if they used their money to help the sick and the poor of the world (instead of bombing them) they would appease their enemies and make many friends. And in the end, by creating more customers for their goods and services, they would, of course, actually make more of the thing they love most – money. Muslim Extremists have realised that they can earn respect and win hearts and minds by providing aid to people whose very survival is threatened. Actually, even Columbian drug lord Pablo Escobar realised this. But not the Americans.

The single word that best sums up the Americans is 'ruthless'. The American way is to bomb countries and steal things, rather than to give troubled nations and starving populations a helping hand. Their idea of generosity is to sell African countries cheap laptops so that every child can shop at American websites. (They either don't know or don't care that the African children would much rather have food and water. To starving children to whom electricity would be a luxury, a laptop at any price is simply too expensive.)

5

When England ruled the world style was merely the way in which the substance was presented. These days, led by the Americans, life is all style and very little substance.

6

The actions of the United States of America have had an overwhelming effect on the stability of the world in recent years. Since 2002 most nations in the world have regarded America as a far greater threat to world peace than Saddam Hussein (or, indeed, any other tyrant). America is the true terrorist nation; wherever it goes it takes violence and destroys hope. The Americans have acquired a well-deserved reputation for getting their way by supporting coups, financing destabilising movements and causing economic sabotage. Although often claiming (with rare quantities of hypocrisy) to sell morality and democracy to the world America is, in truth, the world's most immoral and undemocratic nation. Indeed, it is possible to argue that it is the most immoral and undemocratic nation that has ever existed.

7

When she was reminded that 500,000 Iraqi children had died in the 1990s as a direct result of American and British sanctions preventing the Iraqi people from having access to clean drinking water or medicines, a slug called Madeleine Albright, representing the American Government, said she thought it was a price worth paying. Well, they weren't Americans were they?

8

Using nothing more subtle than brute force and ignorance the arrogant Americans are now imposing their rules on citizens virtually everywhere. Even if you don't plan to visit America your life will be controlled by America in many significant ways.

9

Hollywood makes endless movies in which the USA is threatened by Muslim terrorists. The American movie makers assume that these films will ensure that everyone sees the Arabs as the 'bad guys'. What they don't realise is that two thirds of the world's population is rooting not for the toothy, tanned Hollywood star but for the terrorists.

10

The IMF and the World Bank were founded after the Second World War and are now probably the world's largest, richest and most malignant bureaucracies. They are controlled by, and work for, America. Their analyses are laughable (though pompous) and their recommendations and prescriptions range from irrelevant to useless. The only people who benefit from the existence of these organisations are the twelve thousand highly paid bureaucrats who work for them (and who, it need hardly be said, enjoy wonderful salaries and pension programmes) and the thousands of bureaucrats who are employed by national governments to deal with them.

11

Airlines everywhere (whether flying to the USA or not) must follow security measures imposed by the USA. If you want to fly in an aeroplane anywhere you must adhere to American rules. If you want to fly to America, through America or over America your name must be given in advance to the American authorities for approval. (I find it difficult to understand why anyone would want to fly to America. Anyone who applies to visit the USA should surely – by Catch 22 – be denied approval on the grounds that they must be mentally unstable.)

12

If you want to open a bank account anywhere in the world, or deal in shares, you must sign papers which satisfy American rules and you must clarify your personal relationship to the USA.

13

The American navy now has the right to board any ship anywhere in the world. The Americans have arbitrarily taken away the freedom of the seas.

14

'Even in countries with no roads to speak of,
Mercedes service is available – often to the exclusion
of things like food – thanks to all the US foreign aid,
the International Monetary Fund, and World Bank money being
shipped in. It is no secret that this money is aimed at nourishing only
those corrupt enough to get their hands on it, while at the same time
fattening the bureaucrats on both sides of the transaction who
diligently work the trough. And none of them is driving a Chevy.'
JIM ROGERS, ADVENTURE CAPITALIST

15

The Americans impose such absurd rules on foreign companies listed on the American stock market that huge numbers of companies are now de-listing. Most German companies want to abandon their American listing. French and British companies are following suit. Many investors will no longer buy American stocks, many travellers avoid the USA and some banks outside America now refuse to take American clients. Here, for example, is a quote from a letter recently sent to American customers by a manager representing a European bank:

'I regret we can no longer offer you banking services. Recent changes in our procedures, mainly as a result of the US Patriot Act, preclude us from maintaining accounts for American nationals. I am not able to recommend another bank for you. I suspect that most are in a similar position as ourselves.'

16

The Americans control the world's Web address system and control the distribution of domain names. Although virtually every other country in the world has demanded that the Americans relinquish this control, the Americans simply refuse to abandon their exclusive control of the system (invented let us remember by an Englishman) which enables the world's computers to communicate with one another. (In the long run, if the USA insists on retaining control of the present system, then rival networks will undoubtedly be created.)

17

'For the past 26 years, we never put pressure or problems on to the world. The USA has the reverse attitude, whenever they have a problem they blame others. The appreciation of the renminbi will not solve the problems of unemployment in the USA because the cost of labour in China is only 3% that of USA labour – they should give up textiles, shoe making and even agriculture.'
LI RUOGU, THE DEPUTY GOVERNOR OF THE
PEOPLE'S BANK OF CHINA

18

Food which has been prepared with genetically engineered crops is now compulsory everywhere. The Americans have insisted that it be so. Protests from European citizens have been ignored.

19

'The prevailing quality of life in America – by any accepted methods of measuring – was unarguably freer and more politically open under Nixon than it is today in this evil year of Our Lord 2002.'
HUNTER S. THOMPSON

20

Like the police in other EU countries, the American police can now extradite British citizens without any evidence proving that they are guilty of anything. The Americans have demanded, and been given by the British Government in general and Blunkett in particular, the right to extradite Britons. They don't have to prove that you've done anything wrong. If the Americans want you they can take you. You have no choice but to go. Thanks to Blair, Blunkett et al the British Government will do nothing whatsoever to protect you. Shamefully, although the Labour Government was quick to ratify this deal with the USA (betraying the interests of its own citizens in the process) the Americans have failed to ratify their end of the deal. So although Britons can be automatically extradited to the USA on the whim of an American prosecutor (there is no need for the Americans to produce evidence that there is a prima facie case to answer), Americans are still protected from being extradited to the UK. That half of the deal never went through. So, the American Government can help itself to whichever British citizens it wants. Without providing any evidence that they have done anything wrong. But the British Government cannot help itself to American citizens.

Is there no end to the extent to which the Labour Government will go to ingratiate itself with the Americans?

21

'The mass of men lead lives of quiet desperation.'
HENRY DAVID THOREAU

22

Passports issued by all countries must now satisfy American requirements. Whether or not you want to visit America your passport must satisfy American demands. The European Union is toeing the line and biometric passports will in future be compulsory. Passports must include iris prints, face prints and/or finger prints. (Only American citizens are exempt from these demands). The Americans already take photographs and fingerprints of people stupid enough to visit their country. Inevitably, all these new regulations, demanded by the Americans, mean that passports will become more expensive.

23

'The Brits – regardless of any special relationship – are seen as foreigners. We tend to keep the Union Jack well hidden.'
THE CHIEF EXECUTIVE OF UK DEFENCE GROUP CHEMRING DISCUSSING THE PROBLEMS OF DOING BUSINESS WITH OUR ALLIES IN THE AMERICAN GOVERNMENT.

24

'The Patriot Act is the worst thing to happen to the US since Pearl Harbour.'
HARRY D SCHULTZ (WRITING IN THE *HSL LIFE STRATEGIES* NEWSLETTER, OCTOBER 2004)

25

Inside America the Patriot Act has given not-terribly-bright people in official uniforms vast powers over ordinary citizens and visitors – wherever they are from. For example, you can now be arrested in America for carrying a pen. Pens and pencils are items which can be used in forgery and are, therefore, useful to terrorists. You think I'm joking don't you? I wish I was and I sincerely hope that you never find out that I'm not. The possession of forgery devices is now a felony in the USA.

Thanks to the Patriot Act, America's Homeland Security has extraordinary powers and access to a wide range of other

Government information. For example, by using data from the USA Census Bureau, Homeland Security was able to identify Arab-Americans so that they could be rounded up and deported. Still, I suppose that's better than gas chambers.

26

'One single book can significantly change the reader's attitude and action to an extent unmatched by the effect of any other single medium.'
CENTRAL INTELLIGENCE AGENCY

27

If you are British and want to buy shares in an American company you must fill in a very scary American tax form – complete with some very nasty warnings but no instructions. Simply being able to prove that you are a British citizen and taxpayer cuts no ice. Those brave enough to fill in the form should remember that Britons can now be extradited to the USA merely on a whim. Americans, of course, can buy shares in British companies without any bother.

28

America is now as bad as China in obstructing the press. While I was writing this book I discovered that three different federal judges had found a total of eight American journalists to be in contempt of court for refusing to reveal their sources. All faced jail. Governments everywhere are increasingly secretive and increasingly opposed to press freedom. America is leading the way.

29

'The Americans will always do the right thing, after they've exhausted all the alternatives.'
WINSTON S CHURCHILL

30

The Americans do not acknowledge the Geneva Convention for the treatment of prisoners. Indeed, an Attorney General of the USA has described the Geneva Convention as 'quaint'. Nevertheless, the Americans are quick to demand that the Geneva Convention be observed when Americans have been captured. If American soldiers who are taken prisoner aren't given air-conditioned rooms with satellite television and room service the Americans become hysterical. There is nothing more typical of American hypocrisy than the sight of American politicians protesting that Iraqis, who are defending their country against an illegal and immoral invasion conducted by forces led by incompetent thugs, aren't obeying the 'rules of war'. In January 2002 the Americans opened a concentration camp at Guantanamo Bay where they held and tortured hundreds of innocent captives. In September 2005, there were still 500 prisoners in the Guantanamo Bay camp. More than 100 of these were on hunger strike against their indefinite detection without charge. Many had been held for nearly four years. The Americans were force-feeding the prisoners to avoid the embarrassment of having them die in the camp. Force-feeding of prisoners is prohibited under the World Medical Association's 1975 Declaration of Tokyo, which has been endorsed by the American Medical Association. George W. Bush vetoed an amendment passed by Congress which was intended to ban American soldiers and spies from torturing prisoners. The amendment passed by the American Congress and vetoed by Bush stated that: 'no individual in the custody or under the physical control of the United States Government, regardless of nationality or physical location, shall be subject to cruel, inhuman or degrading treatment or punishment.' Bush's defence secretary has publicly declared that America doesn't take notice of the Geneva Conventions and his Justice Department has produced a memorandum explaining how torture is part of the President's war powers. Moreover, the Washington Post (an American newspaper) has revealed that the CIA maintains a string of jails where it can keep people indefinitely and in secret.

31

The Americans put tariffs on everything that Americans can't make or grow as cheaply as other people can. And the list of producers and farmers the American Government needs to protect is embarrassingly long (including everything from steel to rice) and contains some surprising examples. For example, the American Government has put a tariff on tomatoes grown in Canada because growers there (in a country probably better known for its snow and ice than anything else) can produce tomatoes cheaper than can growers in Florida (well known for its almost constant sunshine). The heavily subsidised American farmers are earning so much that they are constantly expanding – buying more land in order to make greater profits. Naturally, as they expand, the price of the land goes up and so the farmers have an everlasting excuse for demanding bigger and bigger subsidies.

32

Many American Jews are opposed to Israel's policies. In February 2002, over 20,000 orthodox Jews demonstrated outside the Israeli consulate in New York in opposition to the State of Israel. 'Israel does not represent World Jewry' said one placard. 'We are against Israel because we are Jews,' said another. Jews, as well as Muslims and Christians, object to Zionist policies.

33

'The Americans don't really care if they lose dispute settlement cases. If we don't want to be treated as a US colony, then we have to assert our rights...The American mood these days is one of belligerence and a misguided belief that it can set its own rules and essentially do what it wants.'
TORONTO STAR, 29.7.05

34

The Americans have decided that they own the Moon and Mars and are selling bits of it to one another at £20 an acre.

35

When USA President Bill Clinton decided to drop in to the signing of a treaty in Arusha that was supposed to end civil war in Burundi his main aim in going there was to stage a photo opportunity with

Nelson Mandela and get a few more American votes. Clinton's entourage arrived in Arusha a week before the signing (even though the President wasn't due to spend a single night there). The American secret service cut off all the phones in the city except its own and then broke new grounds in arrogance by hauling the Tanzanian President from his limousine and searching him before allowing him to enter the building where the signing was taking place. His bodyguards were confiscated and he was made to enter the building alone. To put this into perspective you have to imagine yourself in America. The French President is visiting Washington. When the American President arrives at the venue, French secret service agents force him to get out of his limousine and walk into the building. But first they search him and his car. Do you think the Americans might be just the teeniest weeniest bit offended?

36

When the American President visited India for five days the people and equipment accompanying him were flown into India in 36 cargo planes, seven tanker planes and 39 other planes. The President was accompanied by the USA Air Force which flew 1,150 sorties. Not even the Rolling Stones take that many people or that much equipment when they are on tour. Such visits have a negative effect on local communities. No American Presidential visit creates goodwill for America any more. (I wrote about George W. Bush's outrageous visit to London in *Confronting the Global Bully*).

37

Americans think they are disliked because they are 'rich and free'. That's self-deluding nonsense. Americans aren't rich (most of them live in poverty – as was demonstrated only too well in the aftermath of Hurricane Katrina) and America as a nation is poor compared to Switzerland.

38

'Facts do not cease to exist because they are ignored.'
Aldous Huxley

39

The Americans boast that they are military superpower. But that is something of an exaggeration. Their navy has 12 aircraft carriers today. At the end of the Second World War (having made vast amounts of money out of selling unwanted and clapped out hardware to Britain) they had more than one hundred large carriers. The average American air force plane is 20 years old. The Americans used up nearly all their cruise missiles in Afghanistan (firing them at wedding parties and harmless hamlets).

40

American companies complain bitterly that their products and patents are copied by Chinese companies. But throughout history no one has stolen more than the Americans have. Americans are natural thieves and they have been stealing from the rest of the world for as long as they have been there. In the 19th century intellectual piracy was commonplace and authors such as Dickens were infuriated by the fact that American publishers simply stole their work. More recently, as I have explained in earlier books, Americans have stolen the copyright on seeds and taken out patents on parts of the human body. Google, an American Internet company has made it its mission to make all the world's information available online (as long as it is online on its own website of course). Google decided to scan in millions of books from leading libraries in the USA and the UK, ignoring the fact that many of the books were still under copyright. Google, with the arrogance of Americans, decided they had the right to copy without permission and that they would make books available online – without paying for this or even obtaining permission. When publishers protested, Google, the latest in a long line of corporate thieves, said that copyright holders could tell Google which books they preferred not be scanned – but the default authority which they had given themselves would give Google permission to 'steal' copyright. 'Don't be evil,' say the co-founders of Google, with that brand of unthinking hypocrisy so popular in the USA. 'We believe strongly that in the long-term, we will be better served – as shareholders and in all other ways – by a company that does good things for the world...'

Jim Gerber, Google's 'director of content partnerships' (it seems to me that Mr Gerber's job may be about content but it isn't much to do with partnerships) was quoted as saying: 'In the future, the only thing that will get read is something that will be online. If it isn't online, it doesn't exist.'

Now Mr Gerber may believe this, in the same way that the idiot who talked so confidently about computers bringing in the paperless office probably believed that, but the fact is that neither the computer nor the Internet will destroy books. And if Mr Gerber seriously believes that offering your work free to the world is the only way to be read he is forecasting the end of the professional author and a whole host of other things too.

From where I sit Google is evil. Maybe not evil in the George Bush and Tony Blair way, but evil nevertheless. Google claimed to be acting in the public interest but they were still planning to sell advertisements alongside the stolen material. They made no mention of donating all the profits to good causes (destitute authors for example).

In the traditional American way of looking at things, stealing other people's property is a 'good thing'. Even the *Financial Times* was critical: `...Google's approach smacks of the high-handed attitude often taken by technology companies towards copyright owners.'

'No matter what benefits this scheme could bring,' went on the *Financial Times*, 'authors must be asked before their work is reproduced. Google ought not to use the slippery device of assumed permission to harvest intellectual property for its own purposes.'

But no one in the publishing industry seemed to have the balls to take on Google. They were, perhaps, afraid that if they did so they, and their book titles, would disappear from the Google search engine completely.

I've had what is called a 'presence' on the Web for well over a decade (since the very first clumsy days of the Internet's existence) and the biggest problem the Web has created for itself is that users expect to get everything free. It seems that millions would prefer to have access to free false information (paid for by some company with a vested interest in promoting a particular product) than truly independent information and advice for which a fee has to be paid.

Now, thanks to Google, book readers will be able to get hold of whole books entirely free of charge. It doesn't seem to have occurred to anyone at Google that their initiative could spell the end for professional authors. How, pray, are authors and publishers supposed to survive if they can no longer sell their books? Google is creating a future in which the only new material will be press releases.

Only an American company soaked to the fundamentals in hubris would have the arrogance to say: 'We are going to steal your stuff. It is not enough for you to tell us that we cannot do this. If you don't want us to steal your property you must identify each item you don't want us to steal. And every time you buy something new you must contact us and tell us that we can't steal that either. If we don't hear from you we will assume that you have given us the right to steal your property.'

Even some parts of the American media have raised eyebrows at Google's plans.

'An opt in scheme would be so much more polite than asking copyright holders to opt out,' wrote *Fortune Magazine*.

41

Americans seem bizarrely unaware of the way their country is perceived, or indeed, of the reality of the world they seem determined to conquer. Many genuinely seem to believe that the world owes America respect and thanks. In a dour rather self-serving book called *Paris to the Moon* a New Yorker writer called Adam Gopnik wrote that in the late 20th and early 21st century 'there was as much peace and prosperity in the world as there has ever been and at the same time a lot of resentment directed at the United States, the country where the peace and prosperity came from.' Huh?

42

Since the future of the world is now being decided by oil, and since our future depends on the relationship between the Americans and the Arabs, a short look at the history of this relationship is worthwhile.

The most important relationship of all is the unusual one between Saudi Arabia and the United States of America.

Like most Middle Eastern countries, Saudi Arabia is, as a nation, a fairly modern creation. In 1902 Abdul Aziz, later to be known as King Ibn Saud, captured Riyadh, expelled the Rashid dynasty and broke off the long established links with the waning Ottoman Empire which had for many years had great influence over that part of the Middle East. After two decades of war Abdul Aziz established his control over what we now know as Saudi Arabia.

Abdul Aziz was one of the first people in the world to realise just how dangerous it would be if Zionist attempts to create a Jewish homeland in Palestine were successful. He warned that a Jewish nation in the middle of a Muslim dominated region would create a powder keg. In 1937, Abdul Aziz urged the British Government (which then had far more of an influence over the Middle East than the American Government) to keep Palestine under British sovereignty and not to break a bit off to create a Jewish state.

After the Second World War, Abdul Aziz, by then known as King Ibn Saud, met American President Franklin D. Roosevelt. Though both men were old and frail it was a crucial meeting and both men were quickly made aware of the cultural differences between them. For example, when Roosevelt commented on how wonderful it would be if the deserts of Saudi Arabia could be made to flourish, King Ibn Saud replied by explaining that he liked deserts and that they were good, not bad.

The most important part of their discussion referred to the Jews. The King made it clear to Roosevelt that he was alarmed by the speed at which Jews were buying arms with which to fight the Palestinian Arabs and the rate at which they were buying up Palestinian land. King Ibn Saud warned that if the Jews were allowed to come to Palestine they would establish a different culture which would lead to war between the Muslims and the Jews. King Ibn Saud urged that if the Jews were to have their own country it should be in Europe, not the Middle East.

When Roosevelt returned home he sent a handwritten note to King Ibn Saud pledging that there would be no decision about Palestine without consulting both the Arabs and the Jews. 'I will take no action in my capacity of Chief of the Executive Branch of this Government, which might prove hostile to the Arab people.' To the Arabs this was a crucial promise and the fact that Roosevelt died eight days after he had written the note didn't alter its importance. The Arabs were dismayed when the Americans cold bloodedly reneged on their former President's promise. They should not, perhaps, have been quite so shocked. The whole modern history of the Middle East is littered with British and American promises which have been made, accepted and then ruthlessly broken.

Roosevelt's broken promise, and the formation of the Jewish state of Israel within the borders of Palestine and in the middle of Muslim lands, has affected the relationship between the Arab world and America in particular and the West in general. A quarter of a century after that meeting King Faisal still remembered the pledge Roosevelt had made to his father. When President Truman announced that he would support the United Nations resolution creating the State of Israel he was warned by George Marshall, his Secretary of State: 'Mr President, you can't do this. The Arabs will never forgive us.' It is reported that Truman, with all the parochialism of a professional politician, responded that Arabs didn't vote in American elections but that Jews did. (Ever since then American Middle East policy has been based on the same belief and American politicians have constantly forgiven all Israeli sins.)

The leaders of Saudi Arabia may have forgiven and forgotten the betrayal (partly, in return for military support from the Americans and partly because the Americans have provided the biggest market for their oil) but many Arabs have not forgotten the way the Americans have consistently taken the side of the Israelis. Zionist Jewish Americans have a great deal of money and a good deal of power and they are not shy about using both in support of Israel.

America has given vast amounts of arms and money to Israel and has always bent over backwards to support Israel in Middle Eastern disputes. Suggestions that there might, just might, be a link between American support of Israel and anti-American feeling among Arabs is, bizarrely and inaccurately, usually a signal for accusations of anti-semitism.

(To describe criticism of Israel as anti-semitic is absurdly dangerous, overtly manipulative and a deliberate misunderstanding both of the intentions of the critic and the meaning of the words 'semitic' and 'anti-semitic'. Around 100 million Arabs are semites. The Americans misuse the term to suggest opposition to Israel, dismissing Arabic semites as inconsequential and irrelevant. America is, in truth, the most anti-semitic nation on earth.)

43

The Labour Government makes a great deal of its so-called 'special relationship' with the USA in general and with the George W. Bush administration in particular, so it is important for us to understand the nation and the politicians with which we are now almost inextricably linked.

In practice, the special relationship is very much a one-sided business. The Americans knew well that IRA terror campaigns (including the one which nearly killed Margaret Thatcher) were financed by collections made quite publicly in America. They didn't worry about it. Nor did it worry America when Iceland unilaterally extended its fishing water limits from 12 to 50 miles in 1972. The UK objected strongly but the USA supported Iceland and helped them do a vast amount of damage to the British fishing fleet by cutting our nets.

The Americans have never regarded the British as important allies. Officially, the Americans regard Japan and Israel as their primary allies. To America, Britain is just a slave nation.

44

America has long been a nation of aggression, violence and dishonesty. The Americans shamelessly lied, tricked and cheated the North American Indians, the original residents of the country, out of their land. As Harry D Schultz, veteran American newsletter publisher wrote: 'enslaving the blacks and stealing the Indians' lands and killing five million of them...made a shaky foundation for nation building.'

American imperialism is nothing new. Back in the very early days of America, in the late 18th century, William Cobbett described the American Government as: 'the most profligately dishonest that I have ever seen or heard described...the most corrupt and tyrannical that the world ever knew.'

And in the 1960s Che Guevera described America as the biggest problem facing the world; claiming that England had never been as imperialist as America had become.

Since then it's pretty much been all downhill for America.

It is difficult to believe, but the credibility of American presidents has deteriorated steadily since Nixon; a man who now stands out in modern American history as a beacon of probity.

45

It is often said, by apologists for America, that it is only Bush and a few of his cronies who are responsible for all America's terrible deeds. It is claimed that Bush and his supporters are too stupid to understand the harm they are doing and too immoral to care even if they understood. Other Americans, we are assured, are nice people.

I'm not at all sure that this is true.

Millions and millions of Americans are crude, belligerent and greedy. You don't have to travel much or far to discover that Americans are the most disliked race on the planet and that this dislike is not entirely a result of their Government's aggressive and imperialist policies. A few Americans are cultured, sensitive and just, and are embarrassed by their Government and their nation's lack of culture and lack of style. But most of the Americans who can afford to travel are simply not very nice people. They treat everyone else as inferior and stomp around the world like conquering heroes.

46

After the Tsunami hit Asia many local people believed that America had deliberately caused the great tidal wave that killed so many and caused such widespread devastation. I was sent copies of Asian newspapers which carried long articles explaining why the Americans were responsible. None of this was reported in British or American newspapers.

I doesn't matter if this belief was true or not. The theories may have been born of paranoia. They may have been factually based. What does matter – very much – is that perception is more important than reality and many people believed that America was responsible for the Tsunami.

If the Americans were wise they too would realise that it matters.

47

Former New York mayor Rudi Giuliani called President George W. Bush 'Churchillian'. This can only be described as a terminological inexactitude. Unless Bush is a keen bricklayer.

48

There are plans in the USA to define 'political paranoia' as a mental disorder. Henceforth, individuals who have 'paranoid' delusions about voter fraud, political persecution and FBI surveillance will be classified as suffering from a psychiatric illness. People who believe that the American Government had something to do with the attack on the twin towers in September 2001, or who suspect that the invasion of Iraq was planned to get the oil or who – well, whatever – will be 'offered' treatment with medication for their paranoia.

49

On December 13th 2003, while most of America was busy toasting the victory of American forces in Iraq, President Bush signed the Intelligence Authorisation Act. The Act increased funding for intelligence agencies in America, dramatically expanded the definition of institutions which can be surveyed, and authorised the FBI to obtain private records of any individuals suspected of 'criminal' activity. The Act was not reported in America's corporate owned mass media.

An explosion in the availability of surveillance-enabling technologies has led to an explosion in the number of American organisations designed to use them. Bush has, for example, also given Americans the Information Awareness Office and the Total Information Office (later renamed Terrorist Information Awareness) which is itself a branch of the USA Department of Defence's Defence Advanced Research Projects Agency, and the Multistate Anti-Terrorism Information Exchange (known, believe it or not, as MATRIX).

50

Just before Christmas 2005, European politicians had the audacity to criticise America's habit of illegally arresting and kidnapping innocent citizens and then transporting them around the world to secret locations where they could be tortured and interrogated. This is what the Americans call 'extraordinary rendition' of suspects, though one assumes that if other people did it to Americans it would be called illegal kidnapping and condemned rather roundly with large amounts of bombs being dropped on those living in countries neighbouring the places where the torturing was going on. (Suspects, incidentally, may turn out merely to have names which are rather similar to the names of people the Americans think they want to question).

When suspects are subjected to 'extraordinary rendition' they are effectively kidnapped and taken away to countries which are said to include Afghanistan, Poland and Romania. In these countries perfectly innocent suspects are taken either to secret CIA concentration camps, where they are beaten-up in an attempt to force them to confess, or handed over to groups of home-grown interrogators who do the beating-up on contract for the Americans. I suppose the Americans use this facility when they run out of steel-toed boots and the special little gadgets torturers need in order to fix electrodes onto testicles.

When all this was questioned, a thoroughly nasty little American woman called Condoleezza Rice said that beating up innocent people 'saved innocent lives' and prevented terrorism attacks in Europe. She did not explain how this worked but she did say that she expected people to cooperate and keep quiet about sensitive anti-terror operations. The unspoken threat seemed to me to be that if people didn't keep quiet about American operations they would be kidnapped, carried off to foreign places and beaten up or killed.

When pressed further by European politicians and journalists Ms Rice back-pedalled and said that the Americans would not do more torturing. But she wouldn't promise that the Americans wouldn't hand suspects over so that others could do the torturing.

51

Although the Americans kidnap citizens of other nations they get terribly upset if American citizens are kidnapped. The Americans insist that hostages should be allowed to die rather than be the objects of any form of trading. However, if American citizens are kidnapped then negotiating and trading is allowed. Of course, the citizens who are kidnapped have to be of some importance for this policy to be adopted.

52

A German citizen who had been held secretly by the CIA for five months started a lawsuit against the American administration. The German, a father of five and of Lebanese origin, was detained in Macedonia on New Year's Eve 2003 because someone thought his name sounded like that of an Al Qaeda suspect. He was held for 23 days in a windowless room before the local CIA persuaded the Macedonians to hand him over into American custody. The local CIA chief is said to have had a hunch that the poor chap might be someone the Americans would like to interrogate. The unfortunate German was handcuffed, blindfolded, drugged and stuffed into one of those horrible jumpsuits Americans make their prisoners wear. He was taken to Afghanistan and put in a cold, dirty cellar with no light where he was beaten, kicked and threatened. By March the CIA had, by pooling their brainpower and technological skills, managed to work out that the man's passport was genuine and that he wasn't the man they had thought he was. So, half-full of remorse, the Americans waited another two months and then flew him to Albania and dumped him in a wood. The man is now justifiably suing the American Government and I hope he wins every penny in the whole damned country. The CIA woman who had the hunch will probably argue that it was the sort of mistake anyone could make. I hope a court condemns her to be stripped naked and dumped in a pit of vipers. But I doubt it will happen.

53

Opinions, views, passions and beliefs can, if they are considered to be the wrong ones – prove fatal. That is the democracy of George

W. Bush. If you have the wrong religion and the wrong skin colour and you believe in a style of democracy which differs to theirs (for example, you believe in one which depends upon the idea of citizens having a say in the way their country is run and the policies its government pursues) then you are likely to find yourself locked up; a prime candidate for torture and death.

54

The Americans seem to think of Muslims as, at best, heathens who need to be converted to Christianity and, at worst, as savages and cannibals who need to be conquered and to have the rudiments of civilisation (at least, what Americans think of civilisation) forced upon them. Americans, whose self-assurance is built on the shifting sands of their wealth, feel aggrieved and slightly offended that the Arabs are, by a stroke of good fortune, endowed with vast quantities of oil – something which the Americans need desperately but which the Arabs, not being civilised (in the American way) have comparatively little need for. It is the oil, more than anything, which explains why genuine anti-semitism is the common denominating factor holding together the American, British and Israeli Governments.

55

I have heard Americans claim that by taking the oil away from the Arabs they are liberating them from a huge economic burden for which they are ill-prepared; relieving them of a wealth which will only lead to anxiety and unhappiness. It is the sort of argument a cut-throat might use when relieving a passing pedestrian of her pearls and her handbag.

56

In the Anglo-American struggle for peace not a single stone will be left standing.

57

The Americans start wars for all the wrong reasons. They start wars to cover up political and personal embarrassments, to win elections and to make money. But what can you expect from a country where politicians arrange executions to help them win elections?

58

The Americans become very upset when innocent American citizens are killed by military or terrorist action. And yet it was the Americans who invented the phrase 'collateral damage' to describe the deaths of civilians. Along with the phrase, the Americans invented the immoral and elitist philosophy that it doesn't matter a damn if civilians die as long as they aren't American. When citizens of other nationalities are killed it is called 'collateral damage'. When American citizens die it is called 'terrorism'.

59

It was, also, the Americans who invented the phrase 'friendly fire' to sanitise the deaths of servicemen in other armies. Whenever the British have fought alongside the Americans, the Americans have killed more of our soldiers than the enemy.

60

The Americans collected innocent people who had foreign sounding names, or who seemed foreign, and they put them all into a large concentration camp. Some of the innocent people they kidnapped and imprisoned and tortured were children. They ignored the bits of the Geneva convention that were intended to defend non-combatants and prisoners, and made it clear that if they felt like it they would kill their prisoners without bothering to try them or give them any chance to defend themselves in court.

Subsequently, Islamic militants started capturing American and British personnel in Iraq and doing the same to them. Dressing them in orange jump suits and shackling them. Naturally, the Americans were incensed by this and said that it showed just how barbaric their enemies are.

61

*'The real power in America is held by a fast-emerging
new Oligarchy of pimps and preachers who see no need for Democracy
or fairness or even trees, except maybe the ones in their own yards,
and they don't mind admitting it. They worship money and power, and death.
Their ideal solution to all the nation's problems
would be another 100 Years War.'*
HUNTER S. THOMPSON (*KINGDOM OF FEAR*)

62

The whole question of what is and is not racism has been confused almost beyond redemption. Allegations of anti-semitism are often exaggerated. For example, one well-reported incident of an arson attack on a Jewish community centre in Paris appeared subsequently to have been staged by a Jew. Naturally the accused man was described as 'disturbed'. I suspect that if a non-Jew had been found responsible he would have merely been described as a 'Nazi' and his mental state would have been ignored.

The level of oversensitivity to alleged anti-semitism is now so absurd that it is sometimes difficult to avoid the feeling that the outrage is manufactured to attract sympathy for the Zionist cause and that history is used as an ever-lasting excuse. When I criticised the barbaric way Jews slaughter animals in a short newspaper column I added not one but two firm caveats to the piece, making it clear that my criticism was fired only by an affection for animals and was not in any way a criticism of the Jewish faith or the Jewish people as a whole. Nevertheless, the piece attracted an immediate protest from prominent Jews who complained that I was being anti-semitic and that I and the paper should apologise. Similarly, when I criticised the way the Maltese treat animals this too was criticised for being critical of Jews. I had made no mention of Jews in the article but this was clearly no impediment to my critics.

63

After a Radio 4 journalist cried as the dying Palestinian leader Yassir Arafat was airlifted from the West Bank she was judged to have breached BBC impartiality. The BBC Governors upheld a complaint from a member of the public who accused the journalist of bias for crying.

64

The American attitude towards Jews is nowhere better exemplified than in their absurd persecution of Bobby Fischer. Unorthodox and controversial (to say the least), Fischer is nevertheless one of the greatest 20th century Americans: a brilliant chess player.

Fischer's mistake has been to dare to criticise Jews and to defy the American Government and to criticise American foreign policy. In response the American Government has (rather meanly) spent half a lifetime persecuting Fischer around the world.

65

Suggestions that the Israelis have behaved like Nazis in the way they have treated the Palestinians are met, not with comprehension or understanding, but with outrage.

66

Jews might perhaps understand the world a little better if they were to ask themselves how they would feel if major political strategy in the USA was planned by a cabal of militant Muslims.

67

Arabs are not impressed by the American habit of ignoring deaths when the people dying are foreigners. The Americans don't know how many Iraqis have died in the Blair and Bush illegal invasion of Iraq because no one has kept count (though a generally accepted figure is that it is well in excess of 100,000). No one knows how many innocent Iraqis died in the invasion authorised by George W. Bush's father and during the years of 'sanctions' supported by Clinton (though it is undoubtedly well into seven figures). And no one knows how many millions of Vietnamese citizens died during America's wars in Indochina. No one ever bothers to count the foreigners, though the Americans have, of course, kept careful count of the number of Americans who have died.

68

It's a reasonable guess that the Americans have killed more Iraqis than Saddam Hussein and, most importantly, more indiscriminately. Under Saddam, people knew who was likely to be targeted and could take precautions accordingly. Under American occupation everyone – men, women, children, hospital patients, the blind, the disabled – is a potential target.

69

Whenever America interests have been threatened, America has responded with violence. When American authority and influence in Central America was threatened, avuncular and charming but brain-dead President Ronald Reagan led an administration which responded by declaring a 'war on terror'. (This was in 1981). America quickly started a terrorist war which was almost instantly infamous for barbarity, torture and slaughter.

When Sandinista rebels overthrew the American backed Somoza dictatorship in Nicaragua, local relief and delight was short lived as America moved in.

Very few Americans know the truth about what their country did in Central American countries such as Guatemala and El Salvador, though the horrors were well-documented by independent observers.

It is, perhaps, enough to point out that while the Americans were busy subduing Central American nations (and making money) a dinner party consisting of Reagan's favourite fellow world leaders would have included Iraq's Saddam Hussein, Suharto of Indonesia, Ceausescu of Romania and Zia al-Hug, the Pakistan dictator who was allowed to develop nuclear weapons because his brand of ruthless, brutal fascism fitted in nicely with the American dream.

70

George W. Bush talks often of justice, democracy and freedom as if he knows what these words mean. But the only talent he and his colleagues seem to have mastered is that of hypocrisy.

71

The new Patriot Act in the USA makes news gathering and reporting a crime if the results are 'unfriendly' to the Government's plans. The American Government can now declare an article evidence and lock up the writer. No one can report that the writer has been locked up. If they do then they too will be locked up. And so it goes on.

72

Not all Americans are happy about what is happening in their country. 'America has survived mightier enemies than this in her 200+ year history, without giving up the liberties and constitutional safeguards that make us what we are,' stormed the *Las Vegas Review-Journal*.

In October 2004, in a thundering defence of the Bill of Rights, a federal judge threw out the provisions of the American Patriot Act which the FBI had used to force airlines and hotels to turn over the names, addresses and personal identification information of 350,000 passengers and guests and to order those airlines and hotels to keep quiet about what had happened.

The American civil liberties union challenged the law in federal court and the judge concluded that the ban on companies talking about what had happened was unconstitutional (despite the Patriot Act) because it was a restraint of free speech.

73

The Americans genuinely seem to believe that terrorists always travel under their proper names and give their occupation as 'terrorist'. The reason they haven't been able to catch Osama bin Laden is probably because they have been searching airline passenger lists looking for 'Osama bin Laden' with an address something like 'Cave no 4, The Hills, Afghanistan'.

Mind you, we shouldn't laugh.

If a British bank saw that name and address on an account application form they would doubtless accept it as long as Mr Laden could provide two utility bills showing that he had an account with authorised suppliers.

74

Here is the most hypocritical statement ever made by any politician anywhere in the world. It was made by the USA Deputy Secretary of State Richard Armitage, speaking about Chechen warlord Shamil Basaev (who was fighting for his country's freedom from Russia).

Armitage: 'He has proved beyond the shadow of a doubt that he is inhuman. Anyone who would use (the killing of) innocents for political aims is not worthy of existence in the type of society that we endorse.'

I wonder if Armitage realises that he has condemned Bush, Blair and all their acolytes.

75

Bush calls himself the war president and he has never mentioned the word 'peace' in a speech. Nor, to the best of my knowledge, has Blair.

76

George W. Bush managed the apparently impossible and succeeded in turning a sympathetic wave of post 11th September international support for his country into a veritable tsunami of hatred and contempt.

77

Under the leadership of the George W. Bush administration:

1. America has unilaterally blocked the United Nations' efforts to ban the militarization of space.

2. America has terminated international negotiations to prevent biological warfare.

3. America has announced that anyone who harbours terrorists is as guilty as the terrorists and must be destroyed. (This was the logic behind the invasion of Afghanistan. The Americans wanted the Afghans to hand over Osama bin Laden. But in the absence of any evidence that he had done anything wrong the Afghans, quite properly, refused.) Bush has unilaterally revoked the

sovereignty of nations which harbour terrorists. But America has harboured terrorists for years (specifically those supporting the IRA). Indeed, Bush and his neo-conservative colleagues are all terrorists. If America, controlled by moronic idiots who have been circumcised from the ankles up, wasn't so riddled with hypocrisy it would have to declare war on itself.

4. America has given itself the right to use force to eliminate any perceived challenge to US global hegemony now or at any time in the future. Ever.

5. America has deliberately blocked efforts by the World Trade Organisation to provide inexpensive drugs to people dying from treatable diseases. This was done to please the American pharmaceutical companies (which are heavily subsidised by the American taxpayer). Bush made it clear that he puts drug company profits way before the tens of millions of lives which he could have saved. Nice one, George. Tony and Cherie Blair are doubtless proud to have you as a friend and ally.

6. America has systematically undermined international efforts to reduce threats to the environment, going so far as to deny truths which have been established and accepted by the vast majority of the world's leading experts. Bush and his associates have made no effort to hide the fact that they feel their responsibility is to the profitability of corporate America, rather than the future of the world. George W. Bush doesn't believe that global warming exists. Or, rather, he has been told that he doesn't believe that global warming exists. The oil and arms companies which control him and his presidency find the whole idea of global warming unacceptably uneconomic. Bush has made brazen statements making it clear that profitability comes first, second and third and that everything else comes nowhere. The Bush Administration has failed to introduce any recommendations for limiting emissions, but has restricted itself to suggesting voluntary targets which allow American emission rates to grow for as long as it is necessary to keep profits rising. The Bush administration has shown clear contempt for the concerns both of scientists and of the international community. Bush and his Co.-conspirators regard profit to be far more important than the sort of chaos and destruction which followed in the wake of

Hurricane Katrina. In one of his many unguarded moments Bush admitted that it was not in America's financial interests to ratify the Kyoto Protocol. Actually he was, as usual, a little confused. What he meant to say was that it wasn't in the interest of his chums to ratify the Kyoto Protocol. (It *would* have been in the interests of the American people living in New Orleans to ratify it.) The truth, of course, is that global warming is more of a threat to our future, our lives and our homes than terrorism but it is America which is largely responsible for global warming. Thanks to global warming our ice caps are melting. Our hot weather is going to get hotter, creating droughts and unbearable heat waves, and our storms are going to get stormier with the result that hurricanes will arrive with greater frequency and greater ferocity. The warming up of the oceans is causing more hurricanes – and bigger and more destructive ones. Storms are becoming hurricanes and hot summers are becoming heatwaves. Radical changes in weather patterns are ahead. Droughts and famines are coming. Many diseases (such as malaria) which were common only in underdeveloped countries will spread to the industrialised parts of Europe and America as the earth's temperatures change. Meanwhile, the American coal industry pays huge sums of money to scientists who deride global warming, the oil companies pay so-called experts to claim that global warming doesn't exist and the rancid George W. Bush gratefully grasps at their putrid reassurances. The British Government, totally craven, stands by. Blair seems to like starting wars. If he had the balls he'd start a war against America. But Blair refuses to confront Bush. Could this be because to do so might affect his chances of getting a directorship of the Carlyle Group when he retires? Meanwhile, everyone whose home is flooded should send a 'thank you' note to George W. Bush..

7. America has taken greater control of space. The American Air Force Space Command has changed its targets from 'control' of space to 'ownership' of space, giving itself the sole right to use sophisticated global surveillance and offensive weapons from space. At the United Nations a resolution to prevent the militarization of space was passed by 174 votes to 0 but there were also 4 abstentions – including the USA, Israel, Micronesia and the Marshall Islands. An abstention from the USA means

that the resolution is blocked and disappears from the UN's history.

8. America has voted alone against a new Comprehensive Test Ban Treaty (at the United Nations General Assembly in 2003) and against the total elimination of nuclear weapons (it was supported in this one only by India). The USA voted alone against 'observance of environmental norms in the drafting and implementation of disarmament and arms control agreements' and, together with its old time buddies Israel and Micronesia, voted against steps to prevent nuclear proliferation in the Middle East.

78

Why did Bush fail to help the Americans suffering in the wake of Hurricane Katrina?

We know that Bush is a war criminal who should, if justice were not in such short supply in the world today, be tried for his crimes. But his callous disregard for those Americans suffering in the wake of Hurricane Katrina opens up a new aspect of his appalling character.

Why did Bush take five days before doing anything?

The first, and most obvious answer, is that any normal President would have sent in the troops straight away. No other group of men and women are better able to distribute supplies, build bridges, treat and evacuate the wounded and keep order. But Bush's troops are distributed around the globe, busy killing innocent women and children and British troops. So: no troops.

Second, the vast majority of people suffering in the wake of Katrina were poor (and black). There were 135,956 white people living in the Gulf of New Orleans. They had an average per capita income of $31,971. There were 325,947 black people living in the same area. They had an average per capita income of $11,332. Around a third of the black people in the Gulf of New Orleans were officially living in poverty. These are not the sort of people for whom George W. Bush is going to stay up late at night. He has, after all, spent much of the last four years sending troops to kill vast quantities of poor people. A few thousand more won't make much difference to his karma. If the hurricane had hit Washington or

New York do you honestly think that Bush would have waited five days before doing something – and flying in for a photo opportunity? If the patients who were left to drown in their nursing home and hospital had been rich and white is it not possible that there would have been a national outcry?

Third, the damage done to the rigs off the coast meant that the price of oil would rise. Now, what business is most closely allied to the Bush family? Well done if you said 'oil'. What happens when there is a temporary shortage caused by oil rigs blowing over? The price of oil goes up. Who benefits when the price of oil goes up? People in the oil business. (Remember: the damage done in and around New Orleans did not destroy the oil. It merely interfered with production – and pushed up the price of the oil remaining in the ground.)

79

So unenthusiastic was Bush's Government about spending money helping poor, homeless American black people that they actually begged for help from other countries, apparently without any sense of embarrassment. Afghanistan, Cuba and Iran were among the countries which responded to America's plea for help.

The sight of aggressive, imperialistic, oil grabbing America begging for help from countries around the world (including ones it was still bombing) was one of the most nauseating and hypocritical sights of modern times.

The Americans, let us not forget, constantly boast that they are the richest and most powerful nation on earth. Their appeal for help was driven, it seems, by the fact that thousands of drivers of huge four wheel drive utility vehicles had discovered that because of the hurricane the price of their petrol had gone up. Horror of horrors. White middle class Americans were having to pay a little more for their petrol. (A wise world would have cheered, pointed out that with less cheap fuel to waste Americans might learn a few truths about the energy crisis, peak oil and global warming.)

But after (the entirely predictable) Hurricane Katrina the Americans were reduced to pleading for the rest of the world to help them deal with the consequences. (A hurricane which possibly wouldn't have happened if it hadn't been for America's selfish refusal to ratify the Kyoto Treaty.)

Could this have been because the American Government doesn't have the money or the equipment? Hardly. Or could it be because Bush and his nasty cronies don't want to use their money or equipment to help save poor Americans?

In response to the Americans' plea for help the EU sent millions of gallons of petrol to the USA to enable the Americans to keep their petrol prices low. Did it not occur to anyone in the USA or the EU that it was partly because of cheap petrol prices that Katrina occurred?

80

Here's a small list of the countries which helped the poor American blacks who were abandoned by their own Government:

1. Cuba
Long considered by America to be an enemy, Cuba offered to fly 1,100 doctors and 26 tonnes of medical supplies to help victims in the USA.

2. Iran
It is well known that Iran is next on Bush's bombing list. But the Iranians offered to send help to the American people.

3. China
The Americans are conducting a vicious trade war with China. But the Chinese offered £3 million, doctors and rescue workers.

4. France
The Americans still sneer at the French for refusing to take part in the illegal invasion of Iraq. But the French offered help and said they would send rescue teams.

5. Afghanistan
The people of Afghanistan sent £70,000 to America – to help it clean up its mess. This was the same Afghanistan which America was still bombing.

6. Britain
British taxpayers sent 500,000 emergency rations to help feed the Americans.

7. *Venezuela*

To say that America doesn't get on with Venezuela is an understatement. But the Venezuelan President showed George W. Bush the meaning of dignity and compassion by offering to send cheap fuel, aid and relief workers to the USA.

8. *Sri Lanka*

Still recovering from the Tsunami, the people of Sri Lanka sent money to help America.

9. *Russia*

The Russians offered to send transport planes, helicopters and generators to help out America (which has most of its planes, helicopters and generators involved in various wars).

10. *Mexico*

One of the world's poorest nations sent water, food and medical supplies. The Mexican navy offered two ships, two helicopters and 15 amphibious vehicles. (I can't help thinking that that probably was the Mexican navy.)

Numerous other countries around the world responded to the Americans' plea for help.

Japan offered £300,000 and emergency supplies. Qatar pledged an astonishing £55 million. Singapore sent helicopters.

Oh, and Israel offered to send along some bureaucrats to help coordinate things.

81

The feeling that America is a fundamentally racist country was not helped when Barbara Bush, wife of a former president and mother of the current incumbent, announced, when talking about the unfortunate thousands who had been displaced by Hurricane Katrina and who were packed, in what looked to some observers like slave ship conditions, into a sports arena: 'They all want to stay in Texas...and so many of the people in the arena here, you know, were underprivileged anyway so this is working very well for them.'

82

When I heard that George W. Bush had announced an inquiry into his own incompetent handling of the hurricane Katrina disaster and had appointed himself the head of the inquiry I started to look around for a large rabbit looking at its watch.

This may be life. But not as we know it.

83

Would Britain's very own liar and war criminal Blair have done any better than Bush?

No, I don't think so.

Blair is driven by a desire for money, fame and power. If a hurricane had hit Hampstead or Islington he would have done something. He would have rushed in to be photographed handing designer food to photogenic babies hired from a smart London agency and he would have then rushed home, excusing himself from any confrontation with real people on the grounds of 'personal security'. But if a hurricane had hit Liverpool or Newcastle he would have probably been too busy basking on the beach in Italy or the Caribbean to do anything to help.

If Blunkett had been in charge he would have responded by sending tanks to Heathrow.

84

If what happened in New Orleans had happened in any other country in the world the Americans would have sent in the troops to liberate the people and their oil from a racist and uncaring President.

But who will rescue the people of America from their President?

No one, I fear.

The American Government took advantage of the Katrina disaster to extend still further its control over the population. Once again a crisis was used as an excuse for eradicating freedoms. The alleged absence of law and order and the spreading chaos meant that local citizens welcomed the eventual entry of the military to take control.

'America is drifting inexorably towards military control,' wrote a correspondent in the USA. 'The people are so confused and bewildered by what is happening, and by their fear, that they actually welcome the military taking control. What happened on 11th

September 2001 has begun so many apparently irreversible changes. Liberty and freedom are disappearing fast. The people's fear has enabled Bush to invade Iraq to steal the oil and to protect Israel and is being used to cover the threatening of Iran, Syria and North Korea.'

Survivors of the Katrina disaster reported that they were treated like prisoners rather than refugees and that they were herded into compounds and camps dotted around America. Repeatedly, survivors complained that they were treated in a callous and hostile manner.

'This is exactly what the Pentagon wanted,' wrote another American correspondent. 'The plan was to desensitise the American people to the presence of the military in their midst. The Government wants people to obey the State unquestioningly. They take every possible opportunity to make people afraid because they know that people who are afraid are easy to manage.'

85

On August 8th 2005, the *Washington Post* revealed that the Pentagon had developed plans for using terrorist attacks as a justification for imposing martial law on all or part of America.

We should take note of this for what Bush does today Britain has doubtless already done – but secretly.

My correspondents in the USA make two points about this extraordinary revelation. First, it seems that the shambles which followed when Hurricane Katrina hit New Orleans might well have been a deliberate ploy to ensure that the public greeted this news with relief rather than horror. Second, the leaking of the news about the plan to allow the military to take control of cities, states or even the whole of America seems to have been done deliberately in order to desensitise the American public and to prepare them for the idea of military rule.

Legally, the Pentagon is not allowed to engage in law enforcement but this small impediment seems unlikely to get in the way of the Government's plans which are to allow the military to take charge in a wide range of scenarios including 'crowd control'.

It seems likely that the military and their controllers are taking this stance not because of any terrorist threat to the USA (the only attack on American soil took place on 11th September 2001 and is now widely believed to have been organised by the American Government rather than by terrorists from outside the country) but because the American Government is concerned about the rise in political dissent within the country.

The powerful elite in America (the people who put Bush into the White House and who now tell him which wars to wage) is concerned about the failing political stability in a country which is increasingly polarised. At the top of the heap there is a small group of extremely wealthy people who are constantly getting ever wealthier. Meanwhile, while the rich get richer, other Americans face an increasingly difficult time. Inflation (far higher than' the Government admits) and other problems are creating a constantly increasing underclass of genuinely poor people who live in real poverty and are denied even basic medical care.

Bush and his controllers are terrified of a revolution, rising from beneath and fired by indignation, frustration and anger against an increasingly totalitarian system.

By claiming that the military need to take over to protect the country against terrorism, the American Government expects to be able to able to manipulate ordinary people and trick them into accepting even greater losses of their traditional, democratic rights.

A military dictatorship seems a certainty for America within the next decade or so.

86

Governments used to back their currencies with gold. But these days they don't. New money is just produced as quickly as the printing presses can run. Governments no longer try to back what they print with stores of gold bullion. (One of the first things the Labour Government did in Britain when they took power in 1997 was sell off much of the nation's gold.)

When currencies become weak people tend to buy gold, in preference to holding paper money. When this happens Governments tend to get twitchy. Back in 1934 the American Government confiscated gold from all Americans to stop them dumping their currency and buying gold coins.

The American Government seems to be getting ready to do this again and is re-classifying the sort of gold coins which its citizens can hold without danger of them being confiscated.

Currently many Americans buy gold coins as a hedge against something terrible happening to the world, their country or the dollar. Most know that this can be risky because their Government has a history of confiscating gold bullion when it wants to.

Up until recently, Americans buying gold knew that there was a loophole: holding bullion might be risky but they could safely collect gold coins which had only a slightly higher value than the gold they contained. For example, some British gold sovereigns sell for only about 7% more than the value of the gold they contain and South African Krugerrands often sell for only marginally more than their gold value.

Americans buying these coins thought that they were safe from confiscation.

Bush's Government has changed this.

Now, if they are to be classified as 'collectible', gold coins must be much more valuable than the gold they contain. Moreover, the American Government has given itself the authority to seize all gold and silver bars, all gold and silver coins and all shares in gold and silver mines. To do this they are using a mixture of old laws (including the Trading with the Enemy Act of 1917 and the Emergency Economic Foreign Powers Act of 1977) together with some new ones. They can, they say, seize gold, except rare coins, in *any* emergency.

What sort of emergency?

Well, an epidemic of bird flu will probably do.

The American Government now also has the power to freeze any stock which has foreign ownership, and to help itself to any cash.

People investing in America are clearly at risk. And any compensation paid may be minimal. For example, if the American Government does pay compensation when it confiscates the gold it will do so at the legal value of £42.22 an ounce – a tiny fraction of the price at which gold has been trading for some time.

Finally, informed sources tell me that the American Government plans to use the Patriot Act to prevent Americans sending their own money out of the USA. The Government plans to argue that money sent abroad 'might fund terrorism'.

Why are they doing this? What is the American Government getting ready for?

What do they know that the rest of us don't know?

87

'You have to choose (as a voter) between trusting the natural stability of gold and the honesty and intelligence of members of government. And with due respect to those gentlemen, I advise you, as long as the capitalist system lasts, to vote for gold.'
GEORGE BERNARD SHAW

88

Those who have total faith in their paper currency might like to know that the German mark moved from four per dollar to four trillion per dollar in a few years after the First World War.

Of course, nothing like that could possibly ever happen again. Could it?

89

When the Shah of Iran, was put back in power by the CIA in the 1950s (because the Americans wanted the Iranian oil) he approved a law which meant that American soldiers could not be arrested or prosecuted for anything. Anything. It was this law which started the rise of the Ayatollah Khomeini who said, not unreasonably, that the Shah had reduced the Iranian people to a level lower than an American dog (on the grounds that if an American soldier ran over a dog in the USA he would be committing a crime, but if he ran over an Iranian in Iran he would go free.) The Americans have now extended this law worldwide.

90

The Americans treat their allies and neighbours without respect. I have shown in other books *(Rogue Nation* and *Confronting the Global Bully)* just how poor an ally America has proved itself to be. But it isn't just Britain which has been cheated and short-changed by America.

Look at the way America bullied other countries in which the majority of the population opposed the invasion of Iraq.

In Turkey, for example, 95% of the population disapproved of the invasion of Iraq and the Government eventually decided that it could not support America. The Turkish Government was then warned by America that it would be severely punished. Paul Wolfowitz is reported to have berated the Turkish military for not compelling the Government to do their duty and serve Washington. The Americans demanded that the Turkish Government apologise for its bad behaviour.

91

'How far can you go without destroying from within what you are trying to defend from without?'
DWIGHT D. EISENHOWER

92

The *Toronto Star* in Canada recently reported that North Dakota plans to divert polluted waters from Devil's Lake into Canada's Lake Winnipeg, the 10th largest freshwater lake in the world. This is in clear defiance of the Boundary Waters Treaty of 1909 which states that 'boundary waters and waters flowing across the boundary shall not be polluted on either side to the injury of health or property of the other.' Complaints and representations from Canada have been dismissed or ignored.

From this failure to respond, the Canadians have concluded that the USA only respects the application of treaties when they serve an American interest. Sadly, the Canadians are not the first to notice this.

The Canadians now plan to retaliate. Not, you will be pleased to hear, by polluting American waters but by telling the USA that their desire to transport natural gas from Alaska to the USA via pipeline laid through Canada will be delayed for some years.

Chapter Seven

What Really Happened On September 11th 2001: Who Did It, And Why

1

I have for years fought against believing conspiracy theories. I've read extensively about the Bilderbergers, the Trilaterals and other alleged conspiracy groups, of course. But I have steadfastly refused to believe that the terrible things that have been happening have been the result of some plot by people who regard themselves as our betters.

I am now convinced that I was wrong to be so sceptical.

2

As our freedoms disappear like snow in springtime it gets easier and easier to see why so many millions of people around the world now believe that the attacks which shocked America on 11th September 2001 were organised by the American Government. And why millions more believe that even if the American Government didn't arrange the attacks they knew about them in advance but let them go ahead anyway.

Why on earth would the American Government do such terrible things?

Easy.

What happened on 11th September 2001 gave the American Government (and other Governments around the world) an excuse and opportunity to introduce oppressive new freedom-crushing legislation which had already been prepared and was sitting waiting to be introduced.

And that's a killer fact, isn't it?

The American Patriot Act, and the mass of similar British legislation, had been drafted long before the planes hit the twin towers of the World Trade Centre in New York.

Without that attack neither the American Government nor the British Government would have dared introduced the oppressive legislation which takes away our liberty and gives them untold power.

It makes it easy to be a conspiracy theorist, doesn't it?

3

The Patriot Act. Now there's a fine piece of legislation. This complex piece of pre-prepared legislation (one the American bad guys had prepared much earlier) whizzed through the American Senate on a vote of 99 to 1. Just one American senator voted against it. That was a Mr Finegold from Wisconsin who said that he didn't really know whether or not he was opposed to the bill but he would like to have had a chance to read it before voting for it. Please. The other 99 voted for it anyway. There were just two copies of the 346-page Patriot Act in existence when it became American law. The American Senate members were standing on the lawn outside at the time; thrown out of the building by a convenient anthrax scare. Just time to vote. No time to debate.

4

'The greatest obstacle to discovery is not ignorance –
it is the illusion of knowledge.'
DANIEL BOORSTIN

5

The Patriot Act gave the American Government the right to lock people up without filing any charges. It gave the neo-conservative

Zionist lunatics who run the American Government the right to do pretty much whatever they liked without having to get authority from anyone who might ask questions. All done secretly. Ssshhh. All done secretly because of the threat from the terrorists.

6

I have studied many hours of video tape and DVD footage of what happened in America on 11th September 2001 and the logical, sensible, scientific, intelligent assessment is that the events of 11.9.01 were arranged or orchestrated by the American Government as an excuse for the Patriot Act and the Iraq War. I am not alone in this belief. As the months and years go by the number of people believing the 'official' story about the attack diminishes. In many parts of the world only conspiracy theorists now believe that what happened in America on 11th September 2001 was the responsibility of Al Qaeda. Only nutters believe that Muslim extremists attacked America. Sane, sensible people believe that the twin towers attack was the work of the Americans or the Israelis. Even in New York, where, not surprisingly, they don't really like to think such things, 49% of the public believe that their Government had advance knowledge of the attacks and let them happen. Almost as many believe that the attack on their city was the work not of foreign terrorists but of their own Government.

The alternative theory, favoured by some, is that Mossad – Israeli intelligence – arranged the attack in order to boost support for pro-Israeli policies in the Middle East. Whenever this theory is put forward it is usually opposed and dismissed on the grounds not that it is 'impossible' or 'unlikely' but that it is 'anti-semitic' to say such a thing.

It is easy to stick with the original, convenient story that Muslim extremists hijacked aeroplanes in order to attack America and that the American security services blundered both in letting 19 Islamic fanatics into the country and in ignoring warnings that an attack by aeroplanes on buildings was possible. And it's difficult to accept that an American Government would have wilfully and knowingly killed so many of its own people. Some of those who defend the Government (usually people paid to defend it) claim that even to criticise the American Government, and to suggest that it is capable of such a terrible deception, is to give comfort to terrorists. But then, in the immortal words of Mandy Rice-Davies, they would say that wouldn't they?

The evidence against the American Government is overwhelming and, as much as I would prefer to suppress the idea of some awful conspiracy, I really cannot.

Here are just a few of the facts which have convinced me that the evil man the Americans should be hunting for is living not in a cave in Afghanistan but in the White House.

The twin towers of the World Trade Centre in New York had been built to survive the impact of a Boeing 707 (a plane the same size, and carrying as much fuel, as the planes which actually hit the towers). The fact that both buildings collapsed in just seconds astonished architects and engineers. Bush's pals claim that the steel supports which should have held the building in place melted in the fireball and caused the floors of both buildings to crash. But this is nonsense. The heat from the explosion simply wasn't great enough to melt all that steel. The pictures show that most of the fire exploded outwards.

And the original estimates by fire-fighters who reached the building confirms that the blaze should have been containable. Two firemen reached the crash site on the 78th floor and a tape exists of them radioing down to their base to confirm that just two hoses would be enough to get the fire under control. This tape has been kept secret and when relatives were finally allowed to listen to it, they had to sign strict confidentiality agreements.

Why, then, did the whole building suddenly collapse?

'The buildings should have easily withstood the thermal stress caused by burning jet fuel,' claimed the laboratory director at an American underwriting firm which specialises in product safety, in questioning the official explanation. 'If steel did soften or melt, this was certainly not due to jet fuel fires of any kind, let alone the briefly burning fires in those towers. That fact should be of great concern to all Americans.' The laboratory director also claimed that his firm had checked and approved the steel that was used in the twin towers when they were built. (You should know that the laboratory director was subsequently sacked for questioning the official explanation of what happened and that the bosses who sacked him denied his claims.)

So, if the steel didn't melt, what brought down the towers?

Another official explanation is that the towers were brought down by the impact of the planes hitting them.

But this theory doesn't stand up either.

The initial hit on the North Tower destroyed only supporting columns in the building's north face. The damage was asymmetrical. If the damage to the tower caused the collapse then the building would have collapsed to one side – and not straight down. The film of the building collapsing shows that it fell vertically. You can see the aerial on top of the building disappearing downwards quite neatly.

So, what did bring down the buildings?

Well, immediately after the event, some firemen told reporters that they thought that there had been bombs in the building. (Later these firemen were silenced by their chiefs. There's been a lot of silencing going on.)

And the damage in the basement of the building supports them.

A 50 ton hydraulic press in the basement was reduced to rubble. And a steel and concrete fire door was totally demolished. Witnesses said that there was an explosion as if from a bomb.

So, if there was a bomb, who planted it?

Did Al Qaeda operatives also manage to put explosives into the building?

Or were explosives put there by American operatives in order to make sure that the towers fell dramatically but neatly – and did so without damaging the rest of Manhattan?

It is certainly a fact that experts who saw the buildings collapse believe that the fall of the buildings looked like a classic controlled demolition.

Van Romero, vice-president for research at the New Mexico Institute of Mining and Technology studied videos of the disaster and concluded that explosive devices inside the buildings caused them to collapse.

Guess what? Without explanation Mr Romero withdrew that opinion just ten days after going public.

And then there is the mysterious collapse of a third building on the World Trade Centre site.

The smaller 47 storey block known as WTC7 was not hit by a plane but it mysteriously fell down some hours after the twin towers had collapsed. The official explanation was that fuel stores had caught fire and made the building unsafe so that it had to be brought down. This is odd because no steel framed building has ever before (or since) collapsed as a result of a fire. And photographs of the building before it collapsed show that it was almost untouched by fire.

So what really happened?

The landlord of the site, Larry Silverstein, suggested at one point that the building had been deliberately demolished. He told an American television documentary that a decision was taken to 'pull' the building.

You'll never guess what happened next.

You will?

You did?

Yes. You're right. This claim was later denied.

The WTC7 building took just seven seconds to collapse and was as text-book demolition tidy as the collapse of the twin towers.

Then there is the problem of what happened to the black box flight data recorders and the cockpit voice recorders from the two planes which hit the twin towers. These boxes, which would have revealed exactly what happened before the planes hit the towers, are virtually indestructible. Black boxes on aeroplanes (which aren't actually black but are boxy) are designed to withstand extremely high temperatures and huge impacts. It is very rare for them not to be recovered in good condition after an aeroplane accident – even when a plane has fallen from a considerable height and exploded on impact.

But, surprise surprise, the black boxes which would have told us all so much about what happened on those planes were never recovered. (Nor, incidentally, did the authorities manage to find the four six ton aeroplane engines which should have been discovered in the wreckage.)

The authorities allegedly went through the wreckage of the collapse with a tooth comb. But they couldn't find either black box or any of the engines.

This is odd because after the attack the site of the twin tower collapse was well protected. Apart from the human remains, there was more than $1 billion of gold from bank vaults in the building. All this had to be looked after. It seems fair to assume that no one stole anything from that site.

Actually, there's another odd thing.

The black boxes and the steel girders and the huge engines may have all been melted into dust but one of the hijackers passports (presumably made of the usual stuff that passports are made of) survived the inferno and was found intact – thereby enabling the authorities to identify those 'responsible' for the attack.

(Maybe they should in future make black boxes out of whatever they use to make Saudi Arabian passports.)

And here's another odd thing. The passport was immediately identified as belonging to a hijacker. How did the authorities 'know' this? Couldn't the passport have belonged to a passenger or even to someone working in one of the twin towers? The sort of high-powered businessmen who worked in the twin towers often had their passports in their pockets or office drawers. But, no, the authorities just 'found' the passport and knew instinctively that it belonged to one of the hijackers.

And then there is the question of the plane that flew into the Pentagon.

After taking off from Dulles Airport in Washington, American Airlines Flight 77 disappeared from radar screens for 36 minutes. It then reappeared. No one has bothered to explain this apparent mystery. The official story is that when the radar blip reappeared the air traffic controllers couldn't work out what it was at first. Perhaps they thought it was a submarine or one of those hats the Queen wears when she goes to the races. Anyway, when they'd got over their shock of seeing a blip on their radar screens, they eventually concluded that from its speed and manoeuvrability it must be a military plane.

This blip was, allegedly, Flight 77 which crashed into the Pentagon.

And as you will know, Flight 77 was allegedly not a military plane.

Now, here's some more funny stuff.

The photographs of the Pentagon which were taken immediately after the plane was alleged to have hit it, show a hole which was impossibly small for an airliner but perfectly shaped for some sort of missile. Witnesses who saw what happened claim that the plane didn't have the roar of an airline but whined like a fighter plane.

One witness is convinced he saw a missile hit the Pentagon.

Normally it would be possible to decide exactly what happened by looking at the CCTV footage from the cameras surrounding the Pentagon.

But guess what?

Video film from all the CCTV cameras which were trained on the Pentagon was taken away by Government agents and has never been released. There were three CCTV cameras which took pictures of the crash: one from a petrol station, one from a hotel and a traffic surveillance camera. The FBI seized all three videos.

It is reasonable to assume that if the video footage which was confiscated really showed an airline crashing into the Pentagon it would have been released to refute the allegations of a conspiracy by the American Government. The fact that the video footage has not been released is strong support for the theory that whatever crashed into the Pentagon was not an airliner.

And if the American Government was lying about that, what else have they lied about? And here's another thing. Where was the wreckage of the airliner which supposedly crashed into the Pentagon? It was never found. The airline just disappeared. Poof. Gone. It presumably either vaporised or was removed by tidy aliens.

Without the videos which the FBI took away we have two choices: either what hit the Pentagon was a huge airliner which somehow managed to squeeze itself into a tiny hole and leave no wreckage behind, or the Pentagon was hit by a smaller military drone which fired a missile just before it crashed.

This second theory explains the small hole in the Pentagon and the lack of any debris but it isn't a theory that Mr Bush likes much.

Finally, it is important to remember that the plane or missile that hit the Pentagon (and the one thing Mr Bush and I agree on is that something clearly did hit the Pentagon) was seen to swerve at the last moment and to hit an area of the building which was largely empty and which had been recently rebuilt with reinforced blast resistant walls. If the plane or missile had hit another part of the Pentagon the death toll would have been thousands rather than 125.

Lucky, eh?

7

'Coming of age in a fascist police state will not be a barrel of fun for anybody, much less for people like me, who are not inclined to suffer Nazis gladly and feel only contempt for the cowardly flag-suckers who would gladly give up their outdated freedom to live for the mess of pottage they have been conned into believing will be freedom from fear. Ho ho ho. Let's not get carried away here. Freedom was yesterday in this country.'

HUNTER S. THOMPSON

8

We have to remember that the Americans have, as all the best policemen say, got 'previous'. What happened on September 11th 2001 wasn't the first time that the American Government has been prepared to destroy American property in order to achieve a political aim.

Back in 1962 the American Government had a secret plan which was code named Operation Northwoods (and which was revealed recently when official archives were opened). The aim of the plan was to fabricate an alleged outrage which would give the Americans an excuse to start a war.

The plot was outrageously simple but fiendishly evil.

Two airliners would take off at precisely the same moment. They would both be painted and numbered in exactly the same way. One plane would take off from a civil airport and the other would take off from a secret military airbase nearby.

The plane which took off from the civil airport would be filled with passengers who looked ordinary but who were, in fact, military personnel flying under false names and dressed in civilian clothes. The plane which took off from the military airport would be empty. It would be a remote-controlled unmanned aircraft.

(I'm not making this up. This was the official American Government plan. It was proposed by America's Joint Chiefs of Staffs in a memo to the Secretary of Defence. It was vetoed by Attorney General Robert Kennedy, brother of the American President.)

The two planes would follow similar flight paths but at some point the passenger carrying plane would drop below radar level and would disappear. It would fly back to the military airbase where the passengers would disembark. The drone aircraft would then take up the other plane's designated flight path. High over Cuba a fake 'pilot' would broadcast an international distress call claiming that his plane was being attacked by enemy fighters. The plane would then be exploded by remote control high over Cuba.

The world would then be told that a plane full of innocent American holidaymakers had been shot down by Fidel Castro and that the American Government had no alternative but to declare war to protect its people.

It's possible to find such deliberate dishonesty even further back in American history. For example, it is now believed that President Roosevelt knew that the Japanese were planning to attack Pearl Harbour in 1941. Roosevelt let the attack happen because he wanted an excuse to take America into World War II. In that raid 2,400 Americans lost their lives.

9

There are more facts about the September 11th attacks which are difficult to explain.

1. Just like the plane which allegedly crashed into the Pentagon, the two airliners which allegedly crashed into the twin towers disappeared from radar screens for some time just before they crashed. Why? Why would hijackers bother to do this? Is it at all possible that the real planes disappeared from the radar when they landed at the handily placed American Air Force Base? This is a Pentagon command centre which houses research laboratories where scientists study computers and radar. Were the planes then replaced by remote-controlled substitutes? Were the 'passengers' who were on the planes real? Are they dead? Were they ever on the plane at all? Are they still alive and living under different identities? Did the hijackers ever really exist? Or was their involvement invented so that Al Qaeda could be blamed?

    It will be of some modest interest to you to know that of the 19 named hijackers who were killed in the attacks on the twin towers, at least eight are still alive and have been seen and identified since the attack. Presumably they parachuted out of the planes, floated down to earth and caught the subway home. Or maybe they were spirited away by small green aliens flying invisible space craft.

2. Why was the building known as WTC7 destroyed after the collapse of the twin towers? Could it possibly be that this was the place from which the remote controlled planes were guided into the twin towers? And was the building destroyed to hide the evidence?

3. Why were four separate sets of air traffic controllers so slow to report the alleged suspected hijackings to the military that fighter planes arrived too late to intercept the allegedly hijacked planes? Was this simply a breach of standard procedures? Or something more sinister? And why, when fighter planes were finally scrambled to intercept the airliners, were they taken from an airbase 150 miles away rather than from the much closer airbase in New Jersey? The television companies got their eye-in-the-sky helicopters to the site of the crashes before the military managed to get there with fighter planes. America, remember, boasts of having the world's most sophisticated armed forces. It costs $350 billion a year to run the American military machine. And yet television companies beat a $350 billion a year organisation to the emergency with camera-toting helicopters. Wow. You'd think all those generals would at least be embarrassed, wouldn't you?

   The military have given a variety of different (and unconvincing) explanations for what happened. The fact remains that air traffic controllers are supposed to call the military if a plane disappears from radar, if they lose radio contact or if a plane goes off course. On this occasion all four sets of air traffic controllers waited before calling the military. Why? And why, when they finally did call the military, couldn't they get through? All through the year there are false hijack warnings, and the military always responds quickly and effectively. On this occasion – when action was really needed – no one did what they were supposed to do. And one has been investigated or punished.

4. It is worth remembering that the twin towers collapsed (oh so neatly) after most of the 50,000 inhabitants had been evacuated. If the towers had collapsed earlier the death toll would have

been much higher than 2,600. Just enough deaths to cause outrage. But not too many.

5. How did so many alleged hijackers manage to get past airport security while carrying weapons? The American Government claims that the hijackers used plastic knives. How do they know? Doesn't plastic melt in the sort of heat that destroys whole buildings and black boxes? Or were the plastic knives made out of the same magical material as the hijacker's resilient passport? Would three plane loads of passengers really give in so easily to hijackers armed only with little plastic picnic knives?

6. The Government claims that it knows what went on aboard the hijacked planes because of mobile phone calls made by passengers on the jets. But it is impossible to make ordinary mobile phone calls from the height at which the planes were flying. Could those calls have been fabricated? The Government could release the tapes of those calls if it wanted to but it hasn't done so. And the Government has even refused to produce billing evidence from phone companies to support its claim that the calls took place.

7. Then there is Flight 93 – the fourth plane which never reached its destination because passengers apparently seized the plane back from the hijackers. The American Government claims that brave passengers stormed the cockpit shouting 'Let's Roll!'. But those alleged tapes have never been released or authenticated either. We have only the word of the American Government that the tapes exist and that brave passengers shouted anything at all.

8. Experienced pilots claim that it would have been impossible for the relatively inexperienced hijackers who are supposed to have been flying the planes which crashed into the twin towers to have performed such precise and intricate manoeuvres. Many pilots have admitted that they couldn't have done it and that the only way to fly planes into the towers with such accuracy would have been by remote control.

9. And what was President Bush doing during the alleged attack on America? He was sitting in a classroom when the attack took place, listening to kids reading a story about goats. Or goats

reading a story about kids. He then flew around for a while before disappearing for several hours and going into hiding somewhere.

10. If the alleged hijackers were devout Muslims, so devoted to their religion that they were prepared to die for it, why did they spend their days before their suicide drinking alcohol, eating pork chops and cavorting with lap dancers? Does that sound real? The man who was the alleged lead hijacker was allegedly seen snorting cocaine in a nightclub on September 10th 2001.

11. The fourth plane which was brought down in Pennsylvania was supposed to have crashed after the passengers fought with the hijackers. But bits and pieces of this plane were found over an eight mile wide area proving that this theory is untenable. The only realistic explanation is that the plane was blown up or shot down. But by whom? And why?

10

So, if the twin towers weren't brought down by planes flown by suicide hijackers who did it? And why?

Were the events of 11th September allowed to happen? Or were they made to happen? Did the neo-conservative controlled American Government ignore evidence of the impending terrorist attack (and then help make things worse) in order to justify the start of a religious war which would give them control of the world's rapidly diminishing oil supplies?

Did the American Government think that they needed an excuse to take control of their own country?

The Patriot Act (which removed traditional freedoms from millions of Americans and which gave the Government astonishing new powers) was brought in within days of the attack and without the politicians who voted for it even having chance to read it.

But, of course, the Patriot Act had been prepared long before the attack ever took place.

Similarly restrictive new legislation brought in by the British Government, allegedly as a result of September 11th, had been conveniently prepared long before 11th September 2001.

11

'The most terrifying words in the English language are: 'I'm from the Government and I'm here to help.''
RONALD REAGAN, FORMER PRESIDENT OF THE USA

12

In the end, there is really one question worth asking: Did the American Government simply close an eye and allow the attack to take place (perhaps deliberately making things a little easier for the hijackers) or was the attack arranged and orchestrated by the American Government?

13

'When I tell the truth it is not for the sake of convincing those who do not know it, but for the sake of defending those that do.'
WILLIAM BLAKE

14

While we struggle to answer this question we must remember that the American Government has consistently and repeatedly lied to its own people and to the world.

We were taken to war because they lied and said that Saddam Hussein had weapons of mass destruction. The American Government lied when it claimed that Hussein was responsible for the September 11th attack.

We should remember the way that the Oasama bin Laden family were escorted out of America after September 11th. We should remember that the Bush family and the bin Ladens did a lot of business together. We should remember, too, that someone made a lot of money shorting the stock of companies which were likely to do badly after the attacks.

Not so much food for thought as food for nightmares.

15

Who poses the biggest threat to your personal freedom and safety?

The Arabs or the Americans.

Think about it carefully.

Who has started more wars and been responsible for more deaths: Osama bin Laden or Tony Blair?

Just asking.

16

Americans who still believe that Osama bin Laden or Saddam Hussein were responsible for what happened on 11/9 frequently claim, when defending the Iraq war, that 'we didn't start it'.

But we did start it.

Just when we started it depends on how far back you want to go.

There was the invasion of Iraq under George Bush senior. And the ruthless massacre of the retreating, surrendering Iraqi army at the end of that war.

There were the sanctions (promoted by the Americans and the British) which resulted in the deaths of 1,000,000 Iraqi women and children.

And what about the bombing of Iraq in 1998 organised by Clinton to coincide with the enquiry into the Monica Lewinsky affair? (That was the one when the American President seemed to deliberately kill innocent Iraqis in order to distract attention from his affair with an employee.)

The list is endless.

17

And then remember, there was the anthrax attack on America just three weeks after 11th September 2001. Just as questions were being asked about the attack on the twin towers, Americans had something else to worry about and the questions about September 11th were put aside.

Five recipients of contaminated letters died of anthrax. Office buildings were closed – including Congress where some of the livelier politicians were just beginning to ask embarrassing questions.

The anthrax attack was, we were told, the work of Saddam Hussein.

Then, mysteriously, the letters stopped and someone

inconveniently identified the anthrax spores as having come from the Government's own laboratories in Maryland.

Who was responsible? Another mystery.

It is my considered opinion that anyone who does not believe that something funny is going on here shouldn't be let out of the house without being under constant supervision. Only the naive or prejudiced could possibly believe that the American Government wasn't involved in what happened on September 11th. The real conspiracy theory now is that Osama bin Laden, Al Qaeda and Saddam Hussein were involved in the September 11th attack.

18

I believe the truth is that Osama bin Laden was a bogey man to distract attention from the real target: the need to invade Iraq and grab the oil. The whole sorry disaster of 11.9.01 was designed to provide an excuse to change the balance of power between the American people and their Government and to provide an excuse to start a war no one outside that Government really wanted or would have otherwise supported. When the Americans went after Saddam Hussein it seemed to some as though they had chosen him as the second best baddy – after attempts to find Osama bin Laden had failed. But Iraq was always the main target.

19

Once you accept that politicians will allow innocent people to die, so that they can achieve their personal and corporate aims, the rules change. Everything changes. And we have to start asking more questions; questions that we would have never dreamt of asking before.

Were the July 2005 London bombings organised by the British Government to terrify us into accepting yet more oppressive legislation? Or did the Government just allow them to go ahead? Sceptics have pointed out almost as many inconsistencies in the story of a militant Muslim attack in London on the 7th of July 2005 as there are inconsistencies in the story of what happened in the USA on 11th September 2001.

There is no doubt that the London bombings must have been

welcomed by the Labour Government which was desperately looking for evidence to support its claim that the country was threatened by terrorists. Blair's Government knew that the London bombings would ensure that its fascist, anti-freedom legislation received strong support from a compliant media and a house full of rubbery MPs.

It is difficult not to appear paranoid in a world where rancid politicians are ruthless (and often crude and brazen) in their attempts to manipulate us through fear.

20

In a way the minor details don't really matter.

It doesn't really matter whether the American Government knew about the proposed attack on New York and the Pentagon and let it happen, or whether they were entirely responsible for the attack.

Maybe they planned the whole thing.

Maybe they just waited for an attack, took as much control as they wanted and needed, and then let it go ahead.

What really matters now are the reasons behind what happened. And the effect the pre-planned responses are having on our lives.

21

'The only ones left with any confidence at all are the New Dumb. It is the beginning of the end of our world as we knew it.'
Hunter S. Thompson

22

The tactical reason for what happened on September 11th was to provide an excuse to invade Iraq.

But the strategic reason for what happened can be summed up in three simple words that even George W. Bush can probably spell: oil, money and power.

23

We started a war against Iraq for four main reasons.

First, because George W. Bush's friends wanted the Iraqi oil.

Second, because American arms companies closely connected

to the American Government (think Haliburton) needed a war zone where they could use up the stockpiles of arms that the American and British Governments had bought but not used. (It wasn't that the sell-by dates on their stockpiles of weapons of mass destruction were dangerously close to their limits but if you don't use up what you have bought you won't buy replacements.)

Third, to show support for Israel and to please all the Jews who had voted for Bush and paid money to his campaign.

Fourth, and possibly most important of all, to sustain the climate of fear deliberately created after the September 11th 'attack' on America. The American Government needed the fear in order to pass oppressive new laws giving politicians and their backers stronger, permanent powers which would take away our freedom. The Americans knew that invading Iraq would heat up the race war they had started against the Muslims.

24

I do not believe for a moment that Blair and the other New Labour Ministers are part of the American conspiracy.

Blair and his corrupt chums are no more than groupies; harlots at the court of neo-conservatism.

Chapter Eight

Identity Cards, Under-The-Skin Chips And The End Of Our Freedom And Liberty

1

The British Government has stated that when ID cards are introduced citizens will be expected to carry them at all times.

'I have no problem with that,' said someone I know. 'What's wrong with being expected to carry an ID card?'

Well, apart from the fact that there is something intrinsically fascist and oppressive about being expected to carry identification with you at all times, one problem is that if it is illegal to leave your house without an ID card then there has to be a punishment for not carrying an ID card.

To begin with the punishment will probably be a search, an arrest, an appearance in court and a fine. But, historically, all the evidence (from Nazi Germany and the USSR) shows that the punishments will become increasingly severe. The fines will provide easy pickings for a Government which is obsessed with gouging money out of already stretched taxpayers.

People who lose or forget their ID card will become lawbreakers with criminal records. This was exactly what happened in Nazi Germany and in the Soviet Union.

2

The Government's plans for ID cards may well break Human Rights legislation on privacy and discrimination. The Government intends to demand and collect so much personal information that they will breach our right to privacy.

A joint House of Commons and House of Lords committee on human rights said that the amount of information due to be held on ID cards amounted to a 'significant intrusion into private life'. The committee also said that they were 'concerned at the range of information that may be held on an individual's record and its apparent lack of relation to the statutory aims (of the Bill)'.

The information on ID cards can, of course, be recorded and used without the knowledge or consent of the individual concerned. Information on ID cards will be made widely available to civil servants and Government employees. And information will be sold to private companies.

3

Information the Government intends to put on ID cards includes: previous residential status, address of main home and any second homes, details of how often information has been accessed, date and place of birth, physical characteristics, fingerprints, nationality, medical details, financial details, criminal record and anything else they think they might be able to sell to data processing companies.

4

Politicians have stopped referring to identity cards. They now prefer to describe them as 'entitlement cards'. I presume that by this they mean that if you have one you will be entitled to stay out of prison but if you haven't you won't. The phrase 'entitlement card' is, of course, just another addition to Labour's newspeak dictionary and fits well with such standards as 'collateral damage' and 'friendly fire'.

5

ID cards are being sold to us on the grounds that they will help the

Government keep terrorists out of the country and make our country safer for us. I used the word 'sold' in the sense of being promoted to us, but in reality of course the word works in the more normal way too. We will have to pay around £100 each for our ID cards. The Government – the same Government which originally said that we would have to pay just £30 for each card – has said that it will pay anything over £100 per card. No one has bothered to explain why it will cost so much or just why we should all have to hand over £100 for a piece of plastic we don't want. But if the Government's ability to control costs is working as well as usual the final fee will probably be considerably higher. One set of independent researchers has already suggested that the bill per person will be more like £220. That's £880 for a family of four. And, presumably, another £220 per person every time you move house, change jobs, find you've got another disease or buy a new car.

Now I'm beginning to see why our corrupt bunch of Ministers are so keen to introduce ID cards. Who will be the first Minister to leave office to spend more time with his family and end up sitting on the board of whichever company gets the job of making and distributing our ID cards?

Disgraced former Home Secretary David Blunkett was wildly enthusiastic about ID cards and seemed to regard them as a cure for everything from athlete's foot to blocked drains. It doesn't take much imagination to see him sitting on the board of a company making ID cards.

6

The claim that ID cards will help protect us from terrorism is such a silly lie (and so easy to disprove) that the only surprising thing about it is not that people believe it (most people will believe anything the mass media tells them as long as they are left to get on with getting drunk and watching *EastEnders*), but that the Government actually had the nerve to suggest it.

The truth (and I'm glad you're interested because no one in the Government or the media is) is that just about everything the Government does to fight terrorism (including ID cards) makes it easier for terrorists to succeed.

7

Unless they are very, very stupid politicians must know that ID cards will do nothing to protect us. They want ID cards because ID cards will help them control us. When you accept an ID card you lose power, independence and freedom and you give all those things to the authority which has issued the card.

8

Many ID cards will be out-of-date within hours of being issued. Are the politicians who advocate ID cards really not aware of the speed and enthusiasm with which many people move house and change jobs? Could the Government's opposition to marriage be partly based on the fact that whenever women marry they change their surname?

9

After the IRA pub bombings in Birmingham in 1974 Harold Wilson's (Labour) Government dismissed the outcry for ID cards. Home Secretary Roy Jenkins studied the idea and concluded that ID cards would be 'hugely expensive and ineffective.' After concluding that ID cards would 'create difficulties for ordinary people' and 'infringe civil liberties', Jenkins warned against responding to terrorist attacks by adopting ever more draconian laws which are 'unwarranted infringements of personal liberty.'

10

Spain had ID cards before the Madrid bombings and the alleged September 11th hijackers all travelled on legitimate papers. The alleged September 11th terrorists in America allegedly showed security guards their identity cards before allegedly boarding the aircraft they allegedly hijacked.

Even if terrorists can't get hold of legal identity cards (a task which won't be any more difficult than getting hold of gas bills, passports or credit cards – in other words ridiculously easy) they will make their own. 'Make their own?' you gasp. 'How on earth could they do that?' Easy. One major firm (a front runner for providing Britain's ID cards and one which has sponsored several meetings at which Government ministers have spoken on the subject of ID cards) had a multi-million dollar deal to make cards for Panama until the contract was cancelled after the company admitted that it had 30,000 blank ID cards in its possession and a Colombian national was found with 500 blank cards in his possession. What, I wonder, would 30,000 blank ID cards be worth on the open market? Is there anyone working for our Government (let alone whichever company gets the contract) dishonest enough, and desperate enough for cash, to get involved? (Put it another way. Can you think of any member of the Labour Party who *wouldn't* get involved for a suitcase full of tax-free lolly?).

11

The only way ID cards will help prevent terrorism will be if terrorists get ID cards with the word 'terrorist' embossed on them.

12

Independent researchers at the London School of Economics have pointed out that the Government's ID card scheme could be a 'one stop shop for fraudsters'. They pointed out something I've been warning about ever since the scheme was first mooted, which is that if thieves manage to steal your fingerprints or iris scan you will lose these very personal bits of biometric data for ever. Unlike your bank details you can't change your iris scan every time it gets nicked. But fraudsters will, of course, be able to fake iris scans and fingerprints.

13

'Instead of wasting hundreds of millions of pounds on compulsory ID cards...let that money provide thousands more police officers.'
TONY BLAIR, SPEAKING IN 1995, BEFORE HE MET GEORGE W. BUSH
AND BOUGHT A HOUSE WORTH SEVERAL MILLION POUNDS.

14

The proponents of ID cards ignore the fact that in order to obtain an ID card (and prove our identity) we will be asked to produce some identification. What will we be told to produce? Passport or driving licence. Two easily forgeable pieces of identification.

15

There are so many flaws in the current system that it is laughable.

When you fill in an application form for a driving licence you have to send in a photograph of yourself. I could send in a photograph of Marilyn Monroe and her picture would appear on my driving licence.

To get your name on the electoral roll is the easiest thing in the world. In less than one hour one national newspaper reporter used fake ID to register to vote in 31 marginal constituencies in the United Kingdom. You need to produce a gas bill to rent a video but to vote all you have to do is fill in a form. You can download the forms online. The reporter gave the addresses of abandoned commercial premises, council blocks and student residences where mail can be picked up easily by outsiders. He found obtaining a vote (and an electoral identification) so easy that in one marginal constituency he obtained a total of ten bogus votes.

16

Numerous organisations are using the ID bandwagon as an excuse to collect information about their members. It seems to me that in many cases the demands for information are absurdly invasive and more likely to lead to identity theft than to prevent it.

When I recently decided that I would put my name back on the General Medical Council's list of registered doctors (I had taken it off a few decades ago) I was told that I had to post a copy of my passport to the GMC as a protection against identity theft. I was then posted a PIN number and a secret password and instructed to visit the GMC's website. On the website I was told to change my secret password and make an appointment to see a GMC official in London. I was told to take my passport with me to the appointment.

All this was, it seemed, the GMC's idea of avoiding the problems of identity theft. In practice, as I pointed out to the GMC, if anyone had a fake copy of my passport they would be able to practice medicine in my name. And by asking me to post a copy of my passport (I declined) the GMC had put my identity at risk. The GMC's rather pathetic attempt to prevent identity fraud seemed to me to be designed more to inconvenience the innocent and honest than to catch or inhibit the crooked.

Two days after I was told about this, my dentist told me that he had received a letter from the General Dental Council asking him to fill in a form requiring him to tell them his religion and his sexual orientation.

Just what religion and sexual orientation have to do with a practitioner's ability to practise dentistry I cannot imagine.

17

Any Labour Party minister who believes that ID cards will protect us from anything (let alone terrorism) is certifiably stupid. I doubt if even the empty-headed Prescott (most of whose thought processes seem to have been borrowed from an educationally subnormal slug) really believes it.

Actually, not all Labour Party ministers even claim that ID cards will keep us all safe from Tony Blair's many enemies. Tony McNulty, a Home Officer Minister in charge of the ID card scheme, (and no, I'd never heard of him either) was reported to have apologised to the nation in August 2005, admitting that Labour had gone too far in claiming that ID cards would be a remedy for terrorism, fraud and the abuse of public services.

Mr McNulty said that ministers should have focused on the benefits to the individual rather than the State, though as far as I am aware he didn't actually say what those might be.

18

Most bizarrely of all, Home Secretary Charles Clarke has claimed that identity cards are 'a means of attacking the Big Brother society'. Anyone who can work that one out might like to write to me and explain it. On second thoughts don't bother: I don't think I would understand the explanation.

Mr Clarke went on to say that 'the ID card system is in fact a bulwark against the surveillance society.'

I am delighted to say when Clarke said that in the Commons he raised laughter from MPs.

They don't get many laughs in the Commons these days (Prescott has become sad rather than just funny) and so I suppose they deserve a little light comedy occasionally.

19

Dame Stella Rimington, former head of MI5, has attacked Labour's plans to introduce ID cards. She has stated that identity cards will not make Britain any safer from terrorists and that nobody in the intelligence services is pressing for ID cards to be introduced.

Dame Rimington said that ID cards might be of some use, but only if they could be made impossible to forge. 'All our other documentation is quite easy to forge,' she said. 'If we have ID cards at vast expense and people are able to go into back rooms and forge them, they will be absolutely useless.'

ID cards will, of course, be easy to forge.

20

As the Labour Party became more desperate to 'sell' ID cards to the public their ramblings became reminiscent of their attempts to explain the war against Iraq. The words 'desperation' and 'surreal' refuse to go away.

'ID cards will help you get into America faster,' said one Government Minister, implying that the cards would in some way help tourists by-pass long queues at American airports.

Anyone who believed that one would probably also find comfort in the suggestion that ID cards would help us check our criminal records more speedily. Maybe Labour wants to turn us all into criminals (it is certainly doing its best) so that we will all be able to realise the benefits of having ID cards.

21

Oh, did they remember to tell you that the new ID cards will contain a chip which will tell them where you are every minute of every day of your life? Since it will be illegal to go out of your home without your ID card (and its implanted chip) the Government (and anyone to whom they sell the information) will always know exactly where you are.

22

And here's another thought that should make you go cold inside. The proponents of ID cards are already suggesting that we have identity chips implanted under our skin. 'This would have made it easier to identify bodies after the Tsunami,' they announced, with breathtaking bad taste.

'Embedding chips under skin is much better than a tattoo,' said an enthusiast. 'We can get more information on an embedded chip than can be put on a tattoo.'

Would you be happy for the Government to tattoo you with a number?

23

The Government also wants to control store cards. They want to know how much money you've got, what you buy and where you buy it. They want to have a monopoly over information about you.

24

You think this is all science fiction?

Read on.

A nightclub in Barcelona called the Baja Beach Club has members who carry implanted microchips the size of a grain of rice in their arms. When the members with the implanted microchips arrive at the club a doorman runs a scanner over their arms, checks their names and photographs and lets them in. Inside the club waitresses run another scanner over each member's arm every time he orders a drink.

It isn't new, of course. I've been writing about implanted microchips for years. The technology was first used in the early 1980s when small transmitters were put into the backs of roaming farm animals so that farmers could keep track of them. Just about a decade later office workers were using radio frequency identification device technology to enter company buildings and to access high security areas. And, of course, many pets have useful tracking devices implanted under their skin so that they can be identified and returned home if they stray, get lost or are stolen.

In 2001 an American company started developing the idea of chips which could be implanted in humans – both to help track people who had got lost or who weren't where they should be, and to provide identification material together with medical records. Fundamental Christians pointed out that this was the 'end of days' since the Bible prophesies that there will come a time when people will have numbers under their flesh. (It's in the Book of Revelations.)

The American Food & Drug Administration (FDA) initially warned that there could be problems with these implantable chips. The chips might migrate and end up elsewhere in the body and, in the worst possible scenario, a chip might produce an adverse reaction and be difficult to locate and remove.

And there are two other problems, one big and one massive. The big problem is that hackers could steal your identification number from under your skin and then hack into the computer company's database. Those who promote this scheme say this risk is slight. But maybe they don't know that hackers seem to have successfully penetrated every computer system in the world – including those operated by the American military which does, so I'm told, make something of an effort to stop this happening.

The massive problem is that your government or employer or bank might one day insist that you wear an implantable device so that they can keep an eye on where you are and what you are doing. They will, of course, sell it as an advantage to you – in the same way that speed cameras are called safety cameras.

The implantable chip isn't science fiction: it's real.

The world's first implantable radio frequency identification microchip for human use (RFID) has now been cleared by the FDA.

The chip system consists of an implantable microtransponder, an inserter, a hand-held scanner and a database containing information about the person in whom the chip is inserted.

The chip can't be seen by the human eye but contains a 16 digit verification number that is picked up when the scanner is passed over the site. The number leads the scanner operator to a database on the Internet. The operator can then get access to whatever information is stored on the Internet site.

Implantable, constantly broadcasting microchips, inserted under the skin, are being used so that the American Government can keep track of its employees and soldiers. The plan is to use them to keep track of visitors to America. You have been warned.

25

New Labour has promised that everyone in Britain will soon wear an electronic tag.

The reason?

To protect us from terrorists, of course.

26

We should all fear the introduction of identity cards and we should all refuse to have anything to do with them. If ID cards are introduced it will be the crooks and the fraudsters who will benefit most and the honest citizens who will lose. Terrorists and criminals will find that fraudulent ID cards (easily obtained) will provide them with a veneer of respectability. The feelings of distrust which will rise among the honest public as officials abuse their power will mean that co-operation with the authorities will deteriorate still further. Petty officiousness and heavy-handed behaviour by thugs with authority will destroy any remaining trust and faith in the police. All this has happened every time ID cards have been introduced. And if you doubt my claim that people with power will abuse it, just remember what happened to Walter Wolfgang at the Labour Party Conference in 2005. Resentment and anger will thrive.

ID cards bring with them the assumption of guilt (rather than the presumption of innocence); they bring state interference and take away individual freedom; they bring coercion and remove consent.

Decent, upstanding citizens may believe that they have nothing to fear from ID cards. But they are wrong. And when they discover that they are wrong it will be too late to do anything about it. If he has never protested or been a member of any protest group, the honest citizen may not have experienced the way policing is managed already and he may not fear that he will be harassed by the police simply for going about his lawful business. But when the state is run by and for villains and extremists it is only the villains and the extremists who will thrive. When the police are hated rather than supported, when harassment is commonplace, then it will be the law-abiding who will have most to fear.

And the bottom line is scary: identity cards will make your identity easier to steal.

27

Some protestors are threatening to disrupt the ID card system by crossing their eyes in front of iris scanners. Others intend to claim that they have undergone a religious conversion and will insist on wearing burqas which will hide their faces. Burqas are traditionally worn by women but it would clearly be sexual discrimination not to allow men to wear them too.

Chapter Nine

Why And How Banks And Other Institutions Put Your Privacy And Identity At Risk

1

If you have tried to open a new bank account in recent years you will have been required to hand over or to post bits of paper which prove your identity. The requirements vary from institution to institution since there are no hard and fast rules about what is or is not required.

Some institutions insist that you give or post them your passport and/or driving licence. Some will be satisfied with a photocopy as long as the copy has been certified by a solicitor (at your expense of course). If you don't have a passport or a driving licence then you can't open an account with those institutions.

Other institutions want shotgun licences, gas bills, tax statements, bank statements and so on. Since the official guidelines suggest that customers should produce separate documents to prove their name and their address, the banks and other institutions usually want one document to prove you are who you say you are and one document to prove that you live where you say you live. Some banks use a driving licence as proof of who you are. Other banks use a driving licence as proof that you live where you say you live.

(None of these documents prove any such thing of course. If a thief steals your driving licence and your gas bill he or she can open an account in your name. The constant demands for, and reliance on, paperwork have made life much easier for identity thieves – as is proved by the massive rise in identity theft in recent years.)

But banks and other institutions don't just demand all this proof from their new customers. They are, increasingly, demanding information from their existing customers. One bank manager who had worked for NatWest for 47 years was asked to produce a gas bill and other forms of identity so that the staff of NatWest bank could transfer the proceeds from a share sale conducted by NatWest to another account held by NatWest. Another branch of NatWest refused to let a customer pay a NatWest credit card bill from his NatWest current account until a handwritten form had been signed and countersigned by the manager. One bank I know of demands that customers bring a copy of their passport, signed by a lawyer, before they can change the address on account documents. Numerous readers have told me horror stories of banks refusing to allow them to take their own money out of their accounts until they have gone to the trouble and expense of providing notification signed by a lawyer confirming that they were who they said they were. In most instances the lawyer who had signed the documents had been a complete stranger. People who have moved back to the UK from abroad, and who cannot produce a gas bill from a British company (contrary to the requirements on many forms there are now no such thing as 'public utility bills' since there are no 'public utility companies', are finding it impossible to open bank accounts. Old people who live in nursing homes or hospitals have become non-existent as far as institutions are concerned. Once again, I have received many tragic letters from old people who have had to sell their homes and move into nursing homes but who have then been unable to persuade their bank to accept their change of address. Most have no need for passports, driving licences or shot gun certificates. Not many nursing home residents have gas bills in their own name.

2

'Good morning, Mrs Smith,' said the bank clerk.

'Good morning, Mr Jones,' replied the customer. She explained the nature of the transaction she wished to conduct.

'Do you have any identification?' asked the clerk. 'I need identification before I can do that.'

'What for?'

'To prove you're who you say you are.'

'But you know me. You've known me for twenty years.'

'Yes, I know. But I need to see some form of identification.'

'I've got a gas bill.'

'That will do nicely.'

The customer, of course, could have picked the gas bill up in the street. The clerk was not allowed to identify the customer even though he had known her for nearly a quarter of a century.'

3

An 80-year-old man wrote to tell me that his bank wouldn't let him take his own money out of the bank unless he produced either a passport or a driving licence – neither of which he had.

His entirely justified sense of frustration and outrage leapt from the page.

How long before old people go into banks and hold them up to get their money out?

4

When you want to close an account, or take your own money out of your account, you will be required to send along your passport and other documents. And, of course, when you visit a solicitor or an accountant you will be required to take documentation. One solicitor I know was hauled over the coals by some petty pen pusher because he had failed to obtain sufficient documentation from his own father before helping him complete a house sale. The absurdities grow daily. One Oxford college was asked to produce its original 15th century charter before it was allowed to open a new bank account.

The real tragedy is that so many people working for banks and other institutions genuinely seem to believe that all their demands for this personal and private information are helping to make the nation safer from criminals and terrorists. Very few of them seem to realise that what they are doing is making life easier – not harder – for both terrorists and criminals.

5

The demands made by banks and other institutions vary constantly and are largely the responsibility of one of the most outrageously incompetent Government departments ever created. It was the Financial Services Authority (FSA) which stood by and did nothing while Equitable Life collapsed and millions of pensioners lost their savings. It was the FSA which allowed the Government to steal shares in the company Railtrack from small investors. And it was the ever useless FSA which ran around in circles squawking but doing nothing when investment companies stole vast quantities of money from investors in the great Zero Dividend Investment Trust scam.

The ever incompetent FSA took over the job of preventing money laundering in Britain in 2001 (nothing to do with the attack on the twin towers, of course) but instead of giving banks and other institutions strict guidelines on what they should and need not ask for, it restricted itself to making vague demands requiring banks to satisfy themselves that their customers are who they say they are. It then reinforced these absurdly imprecise instructions with heavy-handed rules, and backed the rules with a system of fines which gave it the power to demand and take vast quantities of money from banks and other institutions which failed to comply with its regulations. The result is that banks now overload their customers with absurd red tape simply in order to protect themselves from being fined. There is absolutely no consistency except that it is all absurd. As one banker commented: 'The amount all the red tape costs the industry far exceeds the cost of money laundering.' The only things which don't seem to vary from bank to bank are the aggressive arrogance of the employees demanding this information.

Why don't the banks stand up to the FSA?

Well, there is a hidden agenda.

The truth is that banks also want this information for themselves. The so-called wars on terrorism and crime are simply an excellent excuse for institutions to demand and collect private information from you.

Banks want every scrap of information they can find because to them, as to everyone else, information is power and money. They can use the information they demand to sell you new products, to cut down their costs and to improve their profits. And, of course, they can sell the information they obtain (because the 'law' demands that you give it to them) to other people.

What other possible reason can there possibly be for banks demanding (as they invariably do) a whole file-full of new information every time an existing customer opens an additional account with the same institution? Rationally this is absurd and utterly indefensible. From a commercial point of view it makes sense because it gives the bank an additional chance to acquire more new information about an existing client.

6

If you invest in National Savings the National Savings people will happily take your money without demanding to see your passport or any gas bills. All they want is a cheque and your name and an address. They do warn that they 'may search data at a credit reference agency' though I strongly suspect that they don't do this very often. They only require documentary evidence of identity and address from people who live outside the UK .

So, if a Government agency is content to trust its customers just why are banks forced to be so distrusting?

7

Don't let your bank bully you into divulging confidential information.

Increasing numbers of bank customers are receiving letters from people purporting to represent their bank. The letters demand to see passports, birth certificates and other forms of identification and warn of dire consequences if these aren't sent.

But beware! Complying with these demands may severely damage your financial health.

The absurd demands now being made by banks of their customers are allegedly done to help fight the war on terrorism and money laundering. This is nonsense. The demands for private, confidential information are unlikely to have any effect on criminals or terrorists – who will invariably be able to supply van-loads of false or well-forged papers. (As far as I am aware not one criminal or terrorist has yet been caught as a result of these absurd identity checks.)

But their demands can cost you your identity and your privacy.

I recently received a letter from someone claiming to represent the Bank of Scotland. I was asked to send an original document, such as a birth certificate, driving licence, rent card or current firearm certificate to prove my identity and was told that this would help the bank fight crime and terrorism. But the letter came from someone I'd never heard from and from an address that was entirely new to me and which didn't appear on normal bank correspondence. The letter ended with a printed signature. I was asked to send the required private document to yet another address I'd never heard of.

I wrote back to the bank pointing out that since identity theft is now a major problem I did not want to release any personal documents until I had received a signed letter from a senior bank officer who undertook to take personal responsibility for the security and safe return of my documents. I also insisted that the bank should confirm that it would make no copies of my documents.

I pointed out that my requirements were designed to protect the security of the bank, the nation and myself, and added that the careless disposal of unwanted documents by financial institutions was doubtless a factor in the spread of identity theft. I explained that the letter purporting to come from the bank had a printed signature, that the address on the letterhead did not match the Bank's address on previous communications and that the address on the ready paid envelope I was sent bore no relationship to either of these addresses.

I heard nothing more from the bank – even though I sent a copy of the letter I received from the bank to my normal contact.

Maybe the letter was a hoax and wasn't from the Bank of Scotland at all. Maybe a terrorist group was collecting birth certificates, driving licences, rent books and firearm certificates.

Who knows? No one at the bank cared enough to reply.

8

'All change is for the worse, so let us have as little change as possible.'
THE THIRD MARQUESS OF SALISBURY

9

When they demand 'proof of identity' banks and other institutions invariably claim that they need the information in order to protect you from fraud and identity theft, to protect themselves from criminals and to protect the nation from terrorists and money launderers.

'As part of the fight against crime and terrorism,' one bank employee wrote (clearly not wanting me to miss her point), 'and in line with other major financial services organisations, we are currently carrying out a review to re-confirm the identity of our existing customers. This initiative has the full backing of the Financial Services Authority and is fully supported by the Government.'

Then came the quiet threat.

'Due to the importance of this initiative, failure to provide this information could result in future difficulties in the normal operation of your account(s).'

Finally, in case I'd missed the point about crime and terrorism, back it came:

'We are sorry for any inconvenience this may cause,' wrote the member of the bank's Know Your Customer Team (Retail Regulatory Risk Department) 'and thank you in advance for your help in assisting us in the fight against crime and terrorism.'

In order to help them fight crime and terrorism they wanted me to send them documents from a long list of possibles.

I avoided these demands by the simple expedient of closing all my accounts.

10

Alleged identity checks are a dangerous, time wasting nonsense.

Thousands of customers of major banks have already been tricked into supplying confidential information via the Internet. Criminals use the information they obtain (such as passwords) to steal money or to hijack the identities of the people they trick. Fraudulent e-mails, tricking customers into parting with personal details, cost American banks and credit card companies $1.2 billion in 2003.

Crooks don't need to know for certain that you have an account with a specific bank. If they pretend to represent a major bank and send off 1,000 letters to 1,000 names taken at random there is a good chance that 10% of the individuals targeted will have an account with the bank that has been selected.

My advice: be very wary about sending information to anyone purporting to represent a bank.

11

I am told (and I believe it) that if you refuse to do as you are told when banks demand information than they are likely to report you to the authorities.

So what?

Just what are the authorities going to do?

Your privacy and security are important. Don't allow yourself to be intimidated by banks and other financial institutions.

12

The FSA's regulations require banks to look at private documents. But the rules don't say that I have to entrust my documents to the post or allow anyone to copy them. I now tell banks and other institutions that they can make an appointment to see me. I assure them that when an accredited representative arrives I will show him or her whatever documents they need to see.

13

Remember that although the FSA has authority over banks and other institutions it has no authority over you (assuming you are not a bank or other institution). The vagueness of the law and the ability of the FSA to fine companies means that the law is constantly being misinterpreted by overzealous, jackbooted officials who care nothing for the principles their actions are allegedly serving but a great deal for their own sense of self-importance.

14

Some institutions craftily allow you to send them a cheque before they demand documents from you. If you then decide to refuse to send the documents they request they will refuse to return your cheque.

15

If you want to refuse to give out information explain that you are protecting your own and the nation's security interests. Point out that it would be unpatriotic of you to dish out information carelessly. No bank can possibly complain about your caution.

16

'Many young people, it is true, do not seem to value freedom. But some of us still believe that, without freedom, human beings cannot become fully human and that freedom is therefore supremely valuable. Perhaps the forces that now menace freedom are too strong to be resisted for very long. It is still our duty to do whatever we can to resist them.'
ALDOUS HUXLEY

17

Here is a genuine letter which I sent to a bank which had demanded information from me:

Thank you for your letter received today, requesting personal and private documents from me. It is my policy not to send copies of confidential documents through the post since to do so exposes me to identity theft and puts the country's security at risk. You may, however, make an appointment to view selected documents. Alternatively, as a gesture of goodwill, I will show them (not provide copies) at my local branch of your bank. If you would like to follow this route please ask the branch to get in touch with me to arrange an appointment. In order to protect security my documents must not be copied but you may make a note in your files that the documents have been seen.

The bank abandoned its demands to see my documents.

18

Banks often demand that customers post their passport to confirm their identity. This you should never, ever do. I would suggest that you close any account you have with a bank which asks you to do this on the grounds that their concern for your security is clearly non-existent.

The Passport Office does not send out passports in the post. They send them by courier and the envelopes, which are delivered by hand, carry a red stamp warning, with a telephone number to call if the package is delivered incorrectly. The red stamp carries the words: 'DO NOT POST IN THE ROYAL MAIL'.

19

The Government has instructed banks that no one in the UK should be denied access to a bank account just because they cannot provide the necessary documentation. (The Government is increasingly keen on collecting money through banks – and, specifically, through the Internet. It cannot possibly collect money from people who don't have bank accounts.)

The result is that all UK banks are required to have an 'exception process' to enable people to open bank accounts without providing the usual forms of proof. As a tax-paying, law-abiding British citizen you may have to jump through endless hoops to open a bank account. Other people don't have to do all that.

Naturally, terrorists and money launderers would regard it as cheating to take advantage of this loophole.

They probably don't need to bother anyway.

20

You might reasonably expect that the banks, insurance companies, stockbrokers, telephone companies, travel agents, stores, pension providers and other organisations which arrogantly and rudely demand so much private and confidential information from you will look after the information they acquire. If they cared about security they would treat the information they obtain with respect.

But they don't.

The companies which demand your private information (ostensibly to protect you and the country) are then often scandalously careless with that information.

21

According to the American Federal Trade Commission, data theft resulted in $50 billion worth of losses in the USA 2004. Much of the theft and most of the losses resulted as a direct result not of the guile of data thieves or the gullibility of individual citizens but the carelessness of large corporations who had demanded, and been entrusted with, private and confidential personal information.

Financial details, health records and social security numbers are demanded and then discarded with an astonishing lack of care. Many companies which have enormous responsibilities handle confidential data with great recklessness. They fail to instal adequate security software and then, when they have finished with information they discard it without making much of an attempt to ensure that it doesn't fall into the hands of crooks.

And it isn't small, disreputable companies which are careless. Some of the biggest and most notable names in the world of business have been careless with their customers' details. In June 2005, Citigroup, the world's biggest financial firm admitted that it had 'lost' information on 3.9 million current and former customers when some unencrypted computer tapes went astray. The tapes had been shipped by United Parcel Service, a parcel service, apparently without any special safeguards being requested. Other corporations guilty of allowing massive leakages of customer (and employee) data include Time Warner and the University of California, Berkeley. Computer companies and defence contractors seem just as likely as anyone else to be careless. Companies which have been reported to have been in trouble for 'sloppy data management' include Eli Lilly, Tower Records and Microsoft.

The problem is not one which affects only America, of course. Despite the Data Protection Act, it is clear that firms collect too much data, they keep it too long, they don't bother to encrypt it, they don't bother with adequate password protection, they don't check their staff properly, they leave wireless networks open and, when they have finished with information, they discard it carelessly. More than three quarters of the computers disposed of by companies have not been properly cleansed of the data they contain. So, if your bank throws out some old computers the chances are that your personal financial information (the sort needed by thieves who want to steal your identity) will be readily available. Of 350 leading companies which were interviewed 75% had recently sold or given away computers but only 23% of these had bothered to wipe the memories to stop data being recovered. The companies which were interviewed for this study included leading financial organisations holding sensitive customer information. Companies seem not to care that they have a legal responsibility to ensure that information remains confidential. (Some of the companies did reformat hard drives. But this isn't enough. Multiple overwriting or reformatting is required to destroy data and the only really safe way to ensure that data isn't available is to destroy the hard drive completely.) This research shows that crooks don't have to rummage in black rubbish bags in order to steal your identity. All they have to do is stand outside your bank and offer to take away second-hand computers when the bank is upgrading its hardware.

And, of course, government departments everywhere are often wildly reckless with the information they have demanded and stored.

Add to all these the occasions when information has been 'acquired' by crooks (rather than simply lost by banks) and the size of the problem becomes staggering. In one incident alone around 40 million credit card account details were stolen.

22

Banks don't bother to look after your information because it's too much trouble – and they don't care. They know that thieves will steal some money from them. But it isn't their money that is stolen. The card-carrying consumer is the one who pays all the costs for the theft. Interest rates go up to cover it.

Banks and other institutions lose secure information in three ways:

1. Hackers steal it. New software and storage devices have made life very easy for identity thieves – about 4 out of 10 American companies have reported thieves trying to steal information from them. Wireless systems have made it unbelievably simple for crooks to use phones and scanners to suck information out of private networks and systems. Crooks now can simply sit in a car outside your home and collect all the information they want from your computer. Some crooks use 'keylogging' programmes which lodge themselves onto your computer and record exactly

what you type on the keyboard. *Exactly* what you type. So the crook can, from afar, pick up all your passwords for online bank accounts. Anyone who manages any sort of bank account online is asking to have their money stolen. Maintaining up-to-date anti-virus software provides some protection but you must also keep installing the 'patches' which are produced whenever companies discover a vulnerability in their software. Just staying 'safe' can be a pretty much full time job. Other crooks use even simpler methods. So, for example, crooks may send out random e-mails purporting to come from a bank and asking for confidential information (including passwords) to be sent to an address which sounds correct. A number of the recipients will have accounts with that bank and some will dutifully and obediently send off what is requested. The constant demanding of private information has made many people far too willing to hand over confidential information. For example, one e-mail was sent out claiming to be from Citibank. The e-mail asked the recipients to verify their e-mail addresses by visiting a webpage (which was, of course, very official looking) and entering their account and PIN details. It only took Citibank a matter of hours to have this illegal web page removed from the Internet. But in the world of the Internet a few hours is long enough for a huge amount of damage to be done.

2. Employees sell it. Whenever you give your account number, national insurance number or address to an employee you are trusting that employee to be honest. As soon as you give a password to an employee your security is compromised. Many banks and insurance companies have moved much of their confidential administration work to other countries where they may be less in control of what happens. India's call centre industry is now earning £8 billion a year. It employs 350,000 people. Making background checks on all those employees is expensive and time consuming. A number of cases have now been reported in which employees in India have taken advantage of information obtained through working for a bank to defraud customers.

3. Companies lose your private information through incompetence, or throw it away carelessly. A subsidiary of HSBC (Britain's

biggest bank) revealed personal details of thousands of its customers in e-mails. The bank had planned to send individual e-mails to customers saying it was imperative that they get in touch with the bank in the next 24 hours. (Why do people who use e-mail always assume that everyone checks their e-mails at least daily? If I am busy or away I often go a month without checking my e-mails) . However, an operator error resulted in the e-mail addresses of everyone on the distribution list being disclosed in each e-mail. In further e-mails additional information (including details of holiday absences and telephone numbers were revealed). Even more worrying is the fact that when they have finished with the documents which they have demanded from you, banks and other institutions will simply throw them away. They will castigate you if you fail to shred your gas bill (and consider you liable for your own losses if you write your PIN number anywhere). But although banks demand all sorts of confidential information from you (and claim that it is to protect them from fraud and the nation from terrorism) they do not treat the information they demand with any respect. Two journalists recently picked through rubbish bags put out by major banks. They found unexpired debit cards, unused cheque books, customer account details, account numbers, security codes and transaction details. Nothing had been shredded or disguised. When you send a photocopy of your passport to your bank you have a right to expect them to look after it. They probably won't. When the bank has finished with the countersigned photocopy of your passport, your national insurance details, the copy of your tax bill and the original bank statements they have demanded from you, they will probably just stuff them all in a black plastic bag and toss them out in the trash for an identity thief to find – and use. In black bags. Unshredded. And there is little point in asking them to return documents to you when they have finished with them. They won't. Even originals may get thrown out with the rubbish.

23

Thanks to a Californian law which forces firms to tell people when their confidential, non-encrypted information has been lost, the amount of careless and incompetence in the USA is now becoming clear. British companies are under no such requirement to come clean. But it's a safe bet that, bad as things are in the USA, they are worse in the UK.

Early in 2005 a 'data aggregator' called ChoicePoint admitted that identity thieves had stolen vital information on 145,000 people. Soon afterwards the Bank of America admitted that it had lost backup tapes that held the account information on 1,200,000 credit card holders – all of whom happened to be employees of the American Government. Then a shoe retailer called DSW revealed that it had lost data on 1,400,000 customers. Then LexisNexis revealed that 'unauthorised users' had compromised 310,000 identities. The San Jose Medical Group announced that someone had stolen one of its computers and potentially gained access to 185,000 patient records. Then customers of Polo Ralph Lauren heard that a hacker had gained access to 180,000 credit cards at its stores. Then Ameritrade blamed someone else for losing a back-up tape containing personal information on 200,000 clients.

In all these cases valuable personal details have been lost, mislaid or stolen. And once your personal information has been lost or stolen you are, of course, compromised for ever. You can't just change your date and place of birth, parents' names and so on. After their loss, the Bank of America said that it would offer new account numbers to any government employee who wanted them. Great.

24

If your personal information has been stolen how do you prove who you are to the satisfaction of a third party? And how do you know that the person who has stolen your personal information hasn't already rung up and changed your account number? How do you know that after you have changed your account number a thief (your illegal other self) won't ring up and change it again? When your bank was on the local high street and everyone there knew you these problems didn't exist. You could walk into the bank, see someone you knew, and make whatever changes you wanted to make without anyone having any doubts at all about your identity. Of course you wouldn't have needed to make any changes then because your identity wouldn't have been stolen.

25

In 2004, Lloyds TSB Bank sent text messages to some of their customers asking them to call the bank on a number they were given. Customers who did as requested were then asked for their name and credit card number. Potentially, this was an appalling breach of security and is yet another example of banks not taking as much care of their customers' security as they should. If banks start sending text messages to their customers why shouldn't criminals do the same? If a bank wants customers to ring, it should only give the telephone number that is printed on the back of its credit cards.

26

Many banks now send out forms for pre-accepted credit cards. These are outrageously dangerous. If one gets lost it is easy for a crook to obtain a credit card in your name. Everything he needs to 'become' you is printed on the form. All he has to do is sign it, change the address and send it back.

27

In the bad old days, if you visited a strange bank branch a member of staff would ring up your branch and ask for a description of you. A clerk at your own branch would describe you or even speak to you on the telephone.

These days the chances are that no one at your bank knows what you look like. And banks can't even ring one another.

28

There are many simple and relatively inexpensive things banks and other institutions could do to protect their customers' money and identity. But they don't bother. Banks don't yet regard the effort of protecting their customers as worthwhile and unless pushed hard they often insist that the customer bear any losses caused by fraud. And the Government, which could insist that banks do more to protect customers, does nothing. If the Government really wanted to stop terrorists and money launderers there is a great deal it could do to protect our financial integrity and personal identity. The fact that the Government takes none of the simple, practical measures that would actually stop crime proves that it really doesn't care two hoots about protecting us or the country. The system which insists that we provide our passports, gas bills and driving licences before we can open accounts has been designed to satisfy the banks' thirst for more information about their customers (to give them control and enable them to sell us new products more effectively) and to give the Government (which has access to all that information) more control not over the lawless but over the law-abiding.

Chapter Ten

How A Government Of Cheap Crooks Has Destroyed Britain's Infrastructure And Turned It Into A Money-Making Conglomerate

1

When Gordon Brown (surely the worst and least prudent Chancellor the country has ever had) took over as Labour's Chancellor of the Exchequer he had a surplus of £20 billion. He has transformed this into a deficit of £30 billion. (It would be considerably worse if it were not for Labour's creative accounting.) The list of crass mistakes Brown has made would cause a more sensitive man such embarrassment that he would slide into a hole and never peep out. It was Brown whose pension raid helped destroy British pensions. It was Brown whose policies have helped push up oil prices. It was Brown who sold the nation's gold at rock bottom prices. It was Brown who forced means testing onto the nation (thereby destroying incentive for millions). It was Brown who stifled industry and the entrepreneurial spirit with an endless storm of red tape and new tax laws. It was Brown who increased the size of the Government's payroll to an unsupportable level.

Brown will bequeath an effectively bankrupt economy, massive and unsustainable national debts, an enormous national bureaucracy (the cost of NHS bureaucracy alone rose by £1.3 billion between the year 2000 and the year 2004), a broken private pension scheme, an unsupportable bill for social security payments of various kinds and a completely unsupportable wage and pension bill for national and local civil servants. The annual cost of public sector pensions now takes up an enormously high percentage of the total public sector wage bill. For example, 85% of the cost of paying for female police officers goes towards paying the pensions of *former* female police officers; 76% of the cost of paying for male police officers is spent on paying pensions for *former* policemen. (It isn't difficult to see why the police need the money taken from speed camera fines. If it wasn't for that input there would be virtually no policemen on our streets at all.) The figures for the army, the NHS, teachers and civil servants are similarly absurd. And, of course, the figures are rising every year.

In November 2005, the Government admitted that the crisis over public sector pensions was twice as bad as it had previously claimed. It confessed that the bill for paying pensions to civil servants now works out at £30,000 for every household in the country. (This is the figure I forecast it would cost in my book *The Truth They Won't Tell You (And Don't Want You To Know) About The EU* which I wrote six months before the Government's admission.)

The state has stopped being a provider of a tax paid infrastructure (its sole task) and has become a profit making conglomerate which has to make money because the income from taxpayers is no longer enough to pay the salaries and pensions of all the state employees. According to figures I have seen, taxpayers have to support around 6 million civil servants, at least as many people registered as long-term sick, unemployed or on some sort of fake scheme designed to minimise the unemployment figures and many millions of retired civil servants receiving pensions. Non-state employees have to work until they are 65 before they can hope to get any sort of pension (this figure is likely to rise to 70 or even higher before long) but in the autumn of 2005 the representatives of several million public sector workers 'persuaded' the Labour Government, our agents as their employers, to allow them to continue to retire at 60 at the latest. These public-sector workers, many of whom retire on inflation-proofed pension schemes, have cumulative pension rights of somewhere between £550 billion and £1,000 billion. (The vagueness is not mine but the Government's). Public sector workers make up less than 10 % of all employees but their pension rights represent a third to a half of all pension rights of all British employees. The long-term economic problems posed by this fiscal responsibility are so vast as to be almost unimaginable. Local council rate bills are likely to have to rise by at least 10% a year indefinitely in order to cover the pension costs of past and present council employees alone. As the number of retired employees goes up (faster than existing pensioners die off) so the burden on rate payers will rise still further. If rate bills do not rise by at least 10% a year then services will have to be cut in order to find the money. The one thing councils will not (and cannot) do is cut back on pension payments. Ambulance services, fire services, police services, schools, road repairs and so on will all deteriorate far into the foreseeable future. No one in central or local government will admit this – or dare admit the cause.

2

The Labour Government has repeatedly promised to cut back the number of civil servants. But they have, just as repeatedly, reneged on this promise. Instead of cutting the number of state employees they have hired more. During 2005 the Government took on an additional 95,000 employees. This lifted the Government payroll to 5.8 million. And the culture in which these millions work is now one of self-preservation rather than public service. The main aim of their existence is to exist, rather than to serve or to make the nation a better place. It isn't difficult to find examples of this. A few flakes of snow are enough to close schools and council departments while businesses which will not survive if they fail to provide the service they are paid for carry on despite the difficulties.

3

In the old days it was not uncommon for men and women in their fifties and sixties to inherit a house, and perhaps a little money from their parents. They would use this windfall to help supplement their own pensions; spending it to make their later years more comfortable. In turn they would expect to leave some money, and perhaps a house, to their children.

Today, older citizens need to spend everything they can on looking after themselves. As the NHS deteriorates and as local authorities find themselves increasingly unwilling and unable to pay anything towards nursing home care so old people will have to spend every penny they have on looking after themselves. As NHS waiting lists stay long, and NHS dentistry retains a mythical presence, so pensioners will have to spend their savings on buying private health and dental care. (Some people may still remember Tony Blair's constant promises that everyone would be entitled to an NHS dentist.)

The result will be that there will be no more inheritances. Fewer and fewer people will inherit money from their parents. (And although the Labour Party probably haven't worked this out yet, one result will be a massive reduction in the amount citizens pay in inheritance tax.)

Indeed, many people in their fifties and sixties will find themselves having to help their parents pay their heating bills. As pensions shrink, local services decline and taxes rise, so the demands on the pensioner's purse will rocket. The result will be that pensioners may have to sell their homes and move in with their children. Far from having financial expectations, men and women in their fifties will find themselves having to spend their savings on their parents. Their own financial future will be even gloomier. Each generation will find its own problems worse than that of the previous generation.

4

'Blessed are the young, for they shall inherit the national debt.'
HERBERT HOOVER, FORMER PRESIDENT OF THE USA

5

The British economy, which is heading for real trouble, is already failing. The Government lies and tells us that inflation is controlled at around 2 to 3% per annum. That's a downright lie. They keep inflation at that level simply by excluding vital factors such as the rapidly rising cost of fuel, rates and mortgage interest from the official figures. The real figure is closer to 10-15% per annum. Those who rely on their savings to survive are being battered into penury by low interest rates and high inflation rates.

In a fascist country it is the sick, the weak and the needy who suffer most. We are seeing, at first hand, the institutionalised, economic oppression of the masses by the state. Remember: fascism means that the state comes first and the people come a long way second. The state's employees exist to defend the state rather than to care for the people. Their loyalties are to the state.

6

'Politicians have proved that the people can be made to believe absolutely anything.'
RICHARD CONDON (WRITING IN *PRIZZI'S MONEY*)

7

The economy is failing because the Labour Government consists of men and women who have far too much faith in themselves, who can't stop themselves interfering even (or should that be especially) when they don't know what they are doing, who think they can manage when they patently can't, who think they always know best even when they never do, who are far too willing to do what America and the EU demand regardless of the consequences for the country they are being paid to 'lead', and whose motives are fundamentally selfish when they should be selfless.

'All you need in life is ignorance and confidence. Then success is sure,' said Mark Twain. Oh, how well he knew Blair, Straw, Blunkett, Byers, Hain, Prescott *et al.*

8

'In general, the art of Government consists in taking as much money as possible from one group of citizens to give it to another.'
VOLTAIRE (1764)

9

The British economy will continue to fail for several quite simple, quite basic reasons.

LIVING IN A FASCIST COUNTRY

First, small businesses everywhere are either struggling or failing. Since most people in Britain are employed by small businesses this inevitably means that the amount of money available for spending is declining rapidly. For most businesses the last few customers provide all the profit. Take away 10% of the customers (because they can't afford to spend) and you remove all the profit.

Small companies aren't suddenly going bankrupt because the people running them have all caught a bad case of Prescott-style incompetence. They are going out of business because the EU and the British Government want to destroy small companies. That is the only conceivable explanation for what is happening. Why else do they introduce so much paperwork, so many unbelievably complex new rules which have a disproportionately disruptive effect on small companies, and so many new taxes? There is no other possible explanation. The bureaucratic, fascist, totalitarian state (as favoured by the EU and Britain's three unrepresentative main political parties) is vehemently opposed to small companies because small companies tend to be run by independent, rebellious people and independent, rebellious people are usually unsympathetic to the statist, fascist cause.

What neither the bureaucrats of the EU nor our politicians seem to understand, of course (and here it is easy to assume that this is partly because they are intrinsically stupid and partly because most of them have absolutely no experience of life in the real world), is that if you destroy all the small companies then you will never have any big ones. It is, I suspect, their utter ignorance of business life which means that they simply don't appreciate that big companies don't start off that way but grow, over time, because a hard-working entrepreneur has put his heart and soul into what he does. It is worthwhile remembering that the communist regimes took complete control of production and distribution through the simple but effective technique of destroying commerce with a surfeit of rules and taxation. The EU and the Labour Government are doing exactly the same thing.

Conspiracy theorists will have noticed, by the way, that secret and secretive organisations such as the Bilderbergers, which have an inordinate amount of power over all our lives, are comprised of an entirely unhealthy mixture of politicians and representatives of large companies. Faced with such a genuine conspiracy (and when groups of rich and powerful people regularly meet in secret to discuss the future of the world it is fair to assume that they don't have the ordinary family's interests at heart) democracy has no chance.

Second, Brown's extraordinary faith in means testing has resulted in a world where most citizens understand that saving money is pointless. The man who saves will be punished. The man who spends will be rewarded. This bizarre philosophy helped to keep the economy going through the first few years of Brown's tenure but it is now leading directly to trouble. Indebtedness is rising dramatically. The number of people getting rid of their debts by going bankrupt is rocketing. And this will only mean that thousands more small businesses which are struggling to survive will fail because their debts have not been met.

Third, Brown has raised taxes dramatically and has put Britons amongst the highest taxpayers in the world. Many of the new taxes ('stealth taxes') have been introduced sneakily so as to avoid comment and complaint. Income tax, first introduced to finance the war against Napoleon, has been paid in Britain for more than two centuries. But the amount of tax legislation has roughly doubled in the eight years since Gordon Brown became Chancellor. In other words the Labour Government has produced as much tax legislation in eight years as all the previous Chancellors produced in 200 years. Brown has created a nightmare mixture of tax laws and a plethora of incomprehensible tax forms which no one (not even the professionals) understands. Labour taxes are unfair, unjust and horrendously complicated. Taxes on companies have risen so fast during Labour's years in Government that it isn't just small companies which are hurting; many large firms are now moving their headquarters abroad. 'The UK is not as fiscally secure and stable as it used to be,' said the head of tax policy for Ernst and Young. He added that blue-chip companies are considering moving their headquarters overseas because of Gordon Brown's tax policy.

Fourth, and surprisingly you probably won't have read this anywhere else, 300,000 self-reliant, relatively well-off Britons are leaving the country every year. Instead of spending their savings, their earnings and their pensions in London, Birmingham and Manchester they are spending their savings, their earnings and (what New Labour has left of) their pensions in Lyon, Marbella and Cape Town.

10

Unelected employees of the EU allow themselves to retire at the age of 50 on a 65% pension. In other words, if they receive £100,000 when they are working at 49 they will receive £65,000 a year when they retire at 50. This will, of course, be paid for by taxpayers. EU employees pay no national taxes and receive generous bonuses and allowances for everything from housing to school fees.

In 2005, for the 11th successive year, auditors refused to approve the European Union accounts because of fraud and mismanagement.

11

'As the machinery of mass production is made more efficient it tends to become more complex and more expensive – and so less available to the enterpriser of limited means. Moreover, mass production cannot work without mass distribution; but mass distribution raises problems which only the largest producers can satisfactorily solve. In a world of mass production and mass distribution the Little Man, with his inadequate stock of working capital, is at a grave disadvantage. In competition with the Big Man, he loses his money and finally his very existence as an independent producer; the Big Man has gobbled him up. As the Little Men disappear, more and more economic power comes to be wielded by fewer and fewer people. Under a dictatorship the Big Business, made possible by advancing technology and the consequent ruin of Little Business, is controlled by the State – that is to say, by a small group of party leaders and the soldiers, policemen and civil servants who carry out their orders. In a capitalist democracy, such as the United States, it is controlled by what Professor C. Wright Mills has called the Power Elite. This Power Elite directly employs several million of the country's working force in its factories, offices and stores, controls many millions more by lending them the money to buy its products, and, through its ownership of the media of mass communications, influences the thoughts, the feelings and the actions of virtually everybody. To parody the words of Winston Churchill, never have so many been manipulated so much by so few.'

ALDOUS HUXLEY (*BRAVE NEW WORLD REVISITED*)

12

Millions of people believe that every aspect of British life has deteriorated in the last decade. Here are ten reasons why hard working tax payers are leaving the UK and don't intend to come back:

1. Health care has deteriorated so much that even private hospitals no longer provide an acceptable level of care. The incidence of MRSA infections in British hospital is far higher than anywhere else in the world. The quality of service provided by GPs is appalling.

2. National tax levels have risen dramatically under the Labour Government. But the quality of the infrastructure provided has collapsed.

3. In many urban areas of the country it is not safe to go out of the house after dark. Gangs of hoodies now rule the streets. In country areas home owners live in fear of burglars; knowing that at night there is no chance of persuading a policeman to call. Instead of protecting life and property (the task for which they are paid for) the police now spend their days installing and operating money-gathering speed cameras.

4. Our traditional freedoms are disappearing fast. So many new laws are being introduced that it is becoming increasingly difficult even for lawyers to keep up. The Labour Government seems determined to stamp out every last vestige of freedom enjoyed by British citizens. Political correctness has become a real problem in Britain and has had a devastating effect on our cultural life. It is hardly surprising that those who can leave are leaving.

5. Local taxes have risen to absurdly high levels as councils struggle to pay pensions to former employees. Employees in the private sector, and the self-employed, know that although they will be lucky to be able to retire at age 65 they must pay for index-linked pensions to be paid to former council employees who retired five, ten or even fifteen years earlier than that.

6. Thanks to the Labour Government's incessant warmongering, many citizens who were proud of their country are now ashamed of it.

7. House prices in Britain are now so high that it is possible for many home owners who have paid off their mortgages to sell their UK home, buy a home abroad and live on the difference.

8. British justice has disappeared. Muggers, thugs and robbers are rewarded with free holidays and CDs. Victims who dare to protect themselves and their families end up in prison. The importation of the 'no win, no fee' system from the USA means that insurance premiums have rocketed and many people running small businesses can no longer afford to pay them.

9. The quality of the food available in our shops has dropped to appallingly low levels. Supermarkets have been allowed to drive small shops out of business with the result that choice is now just a memory. Our town centres have been taken over by charity shops and estate agents. The small, traditional shops which gave our town centres flavour, and added so much to variety and choice, are disappearing rapidly. To give one example: the number of second-hand bookshops in Britain has halved in the last five years. Competition from the Internet may have played a part in this tragic and probably irreversible loss. But the increase in council rates – raised to pay the growing pensions bill – and the dramatic increase in red tape, have done even more damage.

10. Britain's transport infrastructure has deteriorated remarkably. Our roads are constantly being repaired. Our railways are dirty, unreliable and not even safe any more.

13

The Government never concerns itself with the people who are leaving. The Government never asks people why they are emigrating and if they ever intend to come back.

And yet these are crucial questions.

The people who are quitting (in vast numbers) are, on the whole, people who have made a success of their lives in Britain. They tend to be middle-aged and middle-class. They usually own their own homes, often run their own businesses, and invariably have some savings. They often have skills which are now in short supply. The people leaving in huge numbers are doctors, dentists, plumbers and builders. They are tax payers; net contributors to the national budget.

Their loss is a serious problem.

But no one in the Government cares enough even to make any basic enquiries about where they are going, why they are going, what they are looking for and what has caused their disillusionment. And, make no mistake about it, these people are disillusioned.

When you are settled and should be comfortable, you don't sell everything, leave all your friends and relatives and go to live in a foreign country just because the weather is better. (Actually, many people are not leaving their friends at all. My wife and I now know more people who live in France and Spain than we know who live in Britain.)

The significance of all this is, of course, that the very nature of the country is changing. A country is a living thing; constantly growing, forever changing. It is alive and therefore it can die. And nothing is changing Britain more than the nature of the population. Every year the number of Britons who leave Britain far exceeds the number who return. Inevitably, this means that the very nature of the country must change. Emigration is changing Britain just as much as immigration. The people who are going out are changing things just as much as the people who are coming in.

Look at any graph showing immigration and emigration figures and you can immediately tell when Blair and New Labour came into power. The graph showing the net immigration figures went up almost vertically when Blair took over in 1997. (And the immigration figures are certain to be much, much higher than the official estimates.) At the same time the number of Britons leaving – and not coming back – started to rise. And the number of Britons leaving has continued to rise ever since.

14

'Must the citizen ever for a moment, or in the least degree, resign his conscience to the legislator? Why has every man a conscience then? I think that we should be men first, and subjects afterwards. It is not desirable to cultivate a respect for the law, so much as for the right. The only obligation which I have the right to assume, is to do at any time what I think right. Law never made men a whit more just; and by means of their respect for it, even the well disposed are daily made the agents of injustice.'
HENRY DAVID THOREAU

15

Government statistics show that every year over 6,000 unaccompanied children arrive in Britain claiming asylum. Children. By themselves. No parents. No aunts or uncles. Just children, arriving by themselves, sent to Britain by their families. The cost of caring for these children is phenomenally high. And the children are likely to be a burden for many years. The official estimate is that each child will cost £50,000 a year for the first 20 years of his or her life. If you feel like depressing yourself you can easily work out the cost to the nation. Don't forget that there are another 6,000 children coming in every year.

16

Immigrant work permits have been increased by 350% under the Labour Government. The total number of new workers moving into Britain is officially running at 145,000 a year. Dependents are additional to this total. After four years all these immigrants can apply for permanent settlement and 95% are approved. This total does not, of course, include asylum seekers and unofficial immigrants who arrive in Britain illegally. These figures are much, much higher. The Government wants the immigrants because it believes (wrongly) that having a lot of young immigrants moving into the country means that the average age in the country will be lower and that, therefore, the nation's worsening pensions crisis will worsen more slowly. The Government is wrong because many immigrants who work send their earnings back 'home' and may even go back home themselves when they have acquired some capital. The Government has also greatly underestimated the cost to the nation's infrastructure. One of the reasons why waiting lists for NHS diagnostic procedures and for treatment are so long is that there are now millions of recently arrived immigrants needing treatment for long standing health problems. Anyone who objects to this is dismissed as a racist by the politically correct (most of whom don't have to wait because they have private health care insurance or because their positions enable them to jump the queues). The education system is being destroyed by foreign students arriving at British universities and being subsidised to varying extents by the institutions and by taxpayers.

Big companies want immigrants, of course, because generally speaking they work harder, longer and cheaper and help to keep wages costs down.

17

Attempts to draw attention to institutional incompetences are invariably blocked by people who have a vested interest in maintaining the status quo. A few years ago, when I wrote a weekly column for a tabloid newspaper called *Daily Star,* a reader sent me computer print-outs showing that when the NHS purchased such staples as toilet rolls, pens, envelopes, soap, washing powder and so on, it paid more for them (even though it was buying in huge quantities) than you or I would have paid if we had shopped at our local supermarket. I compared the prices the NHS was paying with the prices I would pay locally and showed that the NHS was wasting billions by paying more than if it had done its shopping at local stores. The story was published on the front page of the paper and on the day of publication the Prime Minister, Margaret Thatcher, gave instructions that copies were to be distributed to every member of the Cabinet. There was uproar within the NHS. Within days important Government employees had swung into action and it was announced that there would be an enquiry. But the enquiry was not into the fact that the NHS was wasting billions of pounds of our money. The enquiry was into just how I had obtained the information which had caused so much embarrassment.

18

The UK economy is now almost totally dependent for its survival and apparent growth upon the British Government. Without the money the Labour Government spends so freely the country would by now be in a deep recession. In 2004 the British Government spent £484 billion – a massive 6.6% rise on the previous year. A report from the Organisation for Economic Cooperation and Development (OECD) shows that public spending in the UK has risen as a share of gross domestic product (GDP) from 41% in 2001 to more than 45% in 2004. It is still rising. This sort of profligacy is unsustainable and irresponsible. The nation's hospitals are filthy and incompetently run, the country's infrastructure is still dependent on Victorian engineering, the transport system is gridlocked, schools are a disgrace (with an increasing number of students finishing their education laden with worthless diplomas but semi-literate and semi-numerate.)

No other country measured by the OECD comes close to matching the Labour Government's rate of spending. Brown (the self-styled prudent chancellor) has overseen a swing from a massive budget surplus to an equally massive budget deficit.

The Government claims that the nation's economy is growing. What a deplorable piece of spin this is. Nearly 40% of the UK Treasury's forecast of 3.25% GDP growth in 2005 will come from government expenditure! Capital investment by the private sector is lower than it has been for decades. Personal and corporate bankruptcies are rising at a rate of knots and are now higher than they have ever been. Consumer expenditure is falling equally rapidly. The only source of income for many companies is now Government spending. Investment advisers now frequently direct investors towards companies involved in public sector spending. It is recognised as one of the few ways to make a profit these days.

19

Our fascist state has become so distracted by Blair's Wars (an expensive business) and its own needs that it is now failing to fulfil its real obligations to its taxpaying citizens. The state's employees are using our money and their delegated power to do things we never asked them to do and don't want them to do. They have forgotten that we, as taxpayers, have any rights at all. In a fascist state the taxpayer only has responsibilities – not rights.

In a way, it is possible to argue that the whole nation is being used to keep the Labour Party in power. The state is now more important than the citizens. And that's pure, unadulterated fascism.

20

The state exists to provide infrastructure and to pay for this is allowed to tax the electorate. But this Government now uses the taxes it raises for other things (funding wars designed to boost Blair's employment possibilities, hiring civil servants to vote Labour and hiring expensive spin doctors to make the lies ever more convincing) so that there is virtually nothing left for the essential infrastructure. The British Government now spends a massive 45% of the nation's Gross Domestic Product but it spends most of the money on the wrong things and so the country is falling apart.

All this is pure fascism.

21

As our country's essential services crumble, and the Government scrabbles for money to keep even rudimentary services alive, our so-called leaders have adopted the final insult: they are trying to make money out of the services we pay for.

The state as transformed by Blair and New Labour no longer exists to look after us (its sole real purpose) but to use us to ensure its own survival. We now exist to serve the Government and its officials. The nation's infrastructure exists to support a fascist state which itself exists to protect Blair and his chums from the penury and obscurity they so richly deserve.

In a fascist state taxes get higher and higher and services get lower and lower. The arrogance of the Government when dealing with the electorate has dribbled down and soaked into all its functionaries and uncivil servants: local authority drudges, policemen, health care workers and others no longer remember to treat the public with the respect due to employers.

The increasing cost of paying for deteriorating public services means that our quality of life is falling at a dramatic rate.

22

'You may not transfer or try to transfer any of your rights and responsibilities under this agreement. We may transfer any of ours without your permission...,'
FROM CONDITIONS OF USE PRINTED ON A T-MOBILE ELECTRONIC TOP-UP CARD PROMOTIONAL LEAFLET.

23

British middle-class married families have the biggest tax burden in the world. A traditional family, consisting of a married couple (one working, one staying at home) and two children pays an effective tax rate of 70% on every £1 earned above average earnings.

This high tax rate is a result of the Labour Government's nasty tax credits system. The Government is obsessed with the philosophy of 'means testing' which means that as individuals earn more so they pay more tax and more national insurance but lose tax credits. It is this system which has proved to be such a huge disincentive.

24

Thanks to New Labour (and their plethora of crafty stealth taxes) Britain now has the highest tax rates in the world. Many Britons pay 70% tax. In the USA the top rate of tax is 45%. In Switzerland the top rate is 24%. In Luxembourg it is 14%. The second worst country is Australia with 52%. Even in France, a country with an excellent infrastructure which is traditionally known as a high tax nation, the tax taken by the Government is considerably less than it is in Britain.

25

In Britain a hard-working couple earning a combined £24,000 a year are, after tax, £4 a week better off than a single mother living entirely on State benefits.

26

The result of the Labour Government's invidious means testing system is that workmen don't want to work long hours because if they do they lose benefits and pay more tax. Millions of people now manage and limit their working lives according to tax rules. (This, of course, is just one of the reasons why it is impossible to find a plumber or any other workman.)

And it is means testing which discourages people from saving for their old age.

But the Government doesn't see the damage it is doing. (Or perhaps it does.) Labour is bringing in plans to introduce means testing into the legal system. Magistrates will be able to charge higher fines when offenders have a higher income. The harder you work the bigger the fine you'll pay. If you choose to live off the state you'll pay a modest fine. If you work long hours to look after your family you'll pay a much bigger fine. Labour Ministers claim that means testing in our courts will rebuild public trust in a system which is regularly flouted by offenders. That, of course, is a downright lie. Introducing means testing into our courts is merely a cynical attempt to gouge more money out of the middle-classes.

27

A recent survey showed that only 6% of British taxpayers think they get value for money out of their Government. The other 94% feel that they are paying too much tax for the services they receive. There is no doubt that the quality of public services has been in decline for years but has deteriorated rapidly since Labour took office. It isn't difficult to see why. The dramatic increase in the number of civil servants, bureaucrats, spin doctors and Blair's former flat mates on the national payroll has added billions to the outlay (and will add billions more in future pension payments). And the Ministry of Defence has confirmed that it spends around £30 billion a year on Blair's hobby of starting wars.

28

The people who organise public services no longer seem interested in improving those services. Their concern now is only in making public services as profitable as possible.

29

If slaves are people who have little freedom and few rights, but who are expected to pay for the excesses and pleasures of their rulers by paying punitive taxes, then we have become slaves.

30

The fascist principles espoused by New Labour have spread, with astonishing speed, amongst state employees, who now regard service to the state (and the Labour Party) as taking priority over service to the citizens.

LIVING IN A FASCIST COUNTRY

Labour's Britain is full of departments which describe themselves as 'services that benefit the community' but which have helped destroy the real people who truly benefit the community. Invariably the people who work in these departments are well paid (many civil servants have received pay rises averaging 8% a year recently – much, much higher than the rises in the private sector). Civil servants (whose pay cheques and pensions are guaranteed however much or however little work they do) fail to understand the value of time. Queues on motorways and long waits in hospital out-patient departments don't mean anything to policemen and NHS employees whose only obligation is to turn up and to leave. If they understand that the pointless closing of vast stretches of motorway (where there are no signs of any work being done) makes driving hard work and increases stress and accidents, they patently don't care. New EU employment regulations mean that it is almost impossible to admonish (let alone fire) anyone employed as a civil servant. It is for this reason that the NHS is awash with incompetent and dishonest employees who cannot be sacked.

There was a time when the British people could rely on the impartiality and integrity of civil servants and the judiciary. No more. Since New Labour came to power judges and civil servants have simply done what they've been told to do. The disgraceful Hutton enquiry into the background to the illegal invasion of Iraq was an example of the way enquiries into Government action end up in predictable exoneration for the criminals. The, in my view, equally disgraceful verdict in which Mr Justice Lindsay failed to order the crooked Labour Government to return the £6 billion which the Government had stolen from Railtrack investors is, I fear, an example of a judge apparently bending over forwards in what seemed to many to be a desperate yearning to accommodate the requirements of his political masters.

In one case after another judges have allowed the bad guys (the Government and their advisors) to get away with murder. (Literally, in the case of the Hutton enquiry). The public, the law and justice are the perennial losers.

Civil servants, long proud of their independence used to guard the interests of the public against the greed, vanity, conceit and other various sins of politicians. No more. As numerous incidents have shown, our civil servants now align themselves and their interests not with the public (who pay their salaries and index-linked pensions) but with the politicians whose favours and endorsements they crave.

'You can't do that!' cried one commentator, appalled at one of the Labour Government's plots.

'We can do anything we like,' replied a senior civil servant. 'We're the Government.'

'We' you will note.

The appalling behaviour of civil servants and spin doctors in the run up to the theft of Railtrack from its shareholders illustrated only too well the way in which the Government's employees have now chosen to stand shoulder to shoulder with politicians. One civil servant wrote about 'grannies' losing 'their blouses' if the Government stole Railtrack. Civil servants seemed more concerned about American investors than about British taxpayers and investors.

31

In the dark, old days the police were there to protect you and your family. No more. Today, the police are there to make money. They have their own pension problems to deal with and today's police forces exist to make money not to provide a service. Hospitals are an essential part of the nation's infrastructure but they too are encouraged to find ways to make money. Every piece of our nation's infrastructure is now being expected to bring in money.

32

The Government will fine you £1,000 for not paying your car tax. But you only have 15 days in which to pay the tax. So, if you dare go away for more than 15 days at the time when your tax is due you will be fined. Effectively, it is now illegal for car owners to go away from home for more than two weeks around the time when their car tax is due to be paid.

33

The Government has announced that analogue television signals will be switched off by 2012. (In some parts of the country they will be switched off long before then.) Viewers who want to continue to be able to watch television will have to purchase digital television sets or other special equipment to enable them to continue to watch their favourite programmes. Many viewers will have to spend money having new aerials put up because digital transmitters run at one fiftieth the power of analogue transmitters. Some parts of the country which currently have poor analogue reception will get no reception at all when the analogue signal is switched off. There will be little or no improvement in the quality of the picture we see on our screens. Millions of existing television sets will have to be replaced. Small, hand-held TV sets won't work. The television sets in the bedroom, the kitchen and the children's bedroom will all have to be replaced or separately adapted. One Freeview box will not suffice. Every television recorder will have to be replaced or converted too. What, then are the benefits of this? The Government claims that digital television will give viewers more choice. But has the explosion in the number of channels available really given us more programmes that we really want to watch? Viewers who wanted 200 channels could get them by subscribing to cable or satellite services. So, what's it really all about?

It is, of course, about money. The Government wants to licence a raft of new services and release the old frequencies so that it can sell them. The last time the Government auctioned frequencies to the mobile telephone companies they made billions.

34

The Post Office announced that the second delivery was going to stop. This, they said, was so that they could improve their service to customers. But what they actually did was abandon the first delivery with the result that many businesses now receive their day's mail late in the morning – sometimes nearer to lunchtime. This change makes life intolerably difficult for businesses. Back in the days of the penny black you could post a letter just about anywhere in Britain and expect it to get to its destination on the following day at the latest. It was not uncommon for mail to arrive at its destination on the same day that it was posted.

Mail delivery isn't the only service provided by the Post Office which has changed for the worse. In early 2005 around 400 local post offices closed in a period of weeks. The Post Office announced that it wanted to close hundreds more of its main branches to make money by selling off the valuable real estate. The Post Office also announced that thousands of loss-making rural post offices would close. Most of these rural post offices were, of course, also the village shop.

This piece of 'progress' will make Post Office queues even longer. (In many towns, the queues in Post Offices already twist and turn inside a snaking system of barriers and not infrequently stretch out onto the pavement.) And, many more villages will die and turn into dormitories as elderly people who are cut off from yet another essential service have to sell their homes and move into blocks of flats in nearby towns. Many old people rely on their local village Post Office as a place to collect their pension and stock up on essential supplies. Losing the Post Office work will, when added to the price competition from supermarkets, the rising insurance bills, the red tape and the higher staff costs mean the end for countless small shops.

Local councils could help by reducing business rates. But they won't. They need every penny they can raise to pay their own massive pension bills.

35

Instead of being society's punishment for bad behaviour, fines have become legal extortion; a tax on mobility; protection money charged to those who work; punishment for being independent. Only politicians and policemen are exempt. (I remember living close to a policeman and a fire officer. I always knew when they were coming home for lunch. Both would turn on their sirens so they could speed through the traffic and, presumably, let their wives know that they were on their way home.) Many towns have become speed trap towns; like those old American mid west towns which survived on the fines they charged the tourists travelling through.

36

The roof of Publishing House (where this book was published) was damaged a year ago. Thieves tore a chunk of it off and tried to get into the building. When we found the damage we called the police who repeatedly promised to send someone round. Nine months later we were still waiting for someone to potter along. But if they ever do appear there will be nothing for them to see. We had to get the roof repaired. Our experience is by no means unusual. Fewer than five per cent of break-ins and less than three per cent of vehicle crimes are solved in some police force areas. Most of the time the police get nowhere near identifying a suspect let alone catching one. In areas where crime figures appear to be improving it is only because people have given up bothering to report thefts, break-ins and assaults. What's the point? Most people who do bother to report a crime to the police do so only so that they will have an incident number to pass on to their insurance company. (Though an increasing number of people no longer bother to make insurance claims since insurance companies have a reputation for putting up a claimant's premium by the value of the claim.)

This disinterest in real crime compares badly with the enthusiasm for making money out of motorists. If I dare to park my car outside Publishing House I will be given a parking ticket. Even after I explained that there was no other way to get books and other material into the building other than by parking outside the authorities still refused to allow me to park there. If I take a chance I get a parking ticket within minutes.

37

Actually, the police don't take much interest in parking these days. There isn't much money in it unless you're a private car clamper. There is far more money to be made out of fining speeding motorists. That's the new growth industry. And that's where police resources are now being directed.

The rash of speed cameras spreading like ugly roadside warts are an excellent example of the state abandoning its responsibilities and trying to turn an essential service (the police) into a profit-making opportunity.

The vast majority of voters want policemen patrolling their streets. The evidence shows clearly that when there are policeman to be seen, walking or cycling through neighbourhoods, the incidence of crime falls dramatically. The vast majority of voters do not want policemen sitting in cars parked on motorway bridges. The evidence shows clearly that speed cameras do not reduce accidents on the road. (On the contrary, speed cameras actually increase accidents.)

But our cash-strapped Government has realised that whereas there is no profit to be made out of preventing crime there is plenty of money to be made out of motorists. Crooks are a difficult target. They are tricky to catch and they often resist arrest. Preventing crime is an expensive business. Catching motorists, on the other hand, is very easy and is an enormously profitable business. These days the authorities instal cameras and cones months before motorway roadworks are even started – presumably in the hope that the fines they collect will pay for the work that needs doing. (The only people I have ever seen working on motorways have been the workmen putting out the cones.) Cameras are made 'live' long before a single workmen has drunk his first cup of tea.

Speed cameras are now so profitable that huge stretches of motorway are coned off for no discernible reason – other than to create false speed limits to feed the cameras. Put in the right position, and neatly hidden behind a bridge or road sign, a camera can cover its purchase cost within days. One speed trap raised £4.5 million in five years. A camera in Essex caught 2,000 motorists in 24 hours. That's an income of £120,000 a day from one camera. Speed cameras are the proverbial licence to print money.

38

In the last decade or so motorists have paid more than £700 million in penalties as a result of being caught by speed cameras. There is no evidence whatsoever that even a single life has been saved, and our roads certainly haven't got any safer. A report produced by independent researchers for the Highways Agency showed that speed cameras make 'no significant difference' to road safety. The Transport Research Laboratory monitored 29 motorway roadworks sites between November 2001 and July 2003 and concluded: 'No significant difference was observed in the personal injury accident rate for sites with and without speed cameras.'

The Government kept this inconvenient information hidden for 18 months until campaigners forced the Department of Transport to publish it under Freedom of Information Act.

39

A review of 6,000 speed cameras in England and Wales revealed that 743 speed cameras had resulted in an increase in accidents and casualties. (I suspect that a study of the areas preceding and following speed cameras would show an even greater increase in accidents and casualties.)

Another study, conducted by publication *Motorcycle News*, also showed that fatal road accidents have risen dramatically in areas where the use of speed cameras has increased. In Hertfordshire the number of cameras went up by 24% and the number of road deaths went up by 34.2%, while in County Durham, which has just one mobile camera unit, the number of deaths fell by 24%.

The West Midlands Police force dismantled ten speed cameras and removed film from another 50 after admitting that speed cameras could make roads more dangerous. Two of the cameras were obscured by a bridge. One was hidden behind a road sign. The West Midlands Casualty Reduction Partnership (who thinks up these names?) admitted that motorists had been braking suddenly after spotting the cameras at the last minute and that there was 'a potential safety hazard'.

Other research has suggested that speed cameras create more accidents because motorists and motorcyclists accelerate away from the cameras too quickly. There have also been suggestions that motorists avoid fixed camera sites by taking other (often more congested, potentially more dangerous, routes). And throughout the country in recent years, despite the spread of speed cameras, the figures show that the number of road deaths has increased steadily.

A Department of Transport audit in 2004, found that the number of people killed or seriously injured had gone up at one in seven camera sites. At many camera locations the number of deaths or serious casualties had increased by up to 9%. Naturally, Labour Party politicians ignored the facts and claimed that accidents were going down and speed cameras were saving lives.

The repeated suppression of the truth about speed cameras shows that both the politicians and the police are ruthlessly committed to making money rather than saving lives. The people who are paid to look after us are exploiting us. The Government and the police have deliberately and knowingly created an unsafe environment for motorists. And if that's not criminal behaviour I don't know what is.

40

There is also considerable doubt about the *accuracy* of speed cameras.

One research group has shown that police speed guns routinely give false readings. Tests on a hand-held device used by policemen standing at the roadside found that an incorrect reading was given for nearly one in three vehicles travelling at just 30 mph. Errors of 20 mph occurred. A lorry travelling at exactly 30 mph was recorded at 53 mph and a parked vehicle was clocked at 6 mph. On a truck travelling at 30 mph a false result was obtained seven out of 22 times. Any movement the officer makes can create an error. A second survey, conducted by the *Daily Mail,* raised serious doubts about the accuracy of laser guns which are used to catch over a million motorists a year and which bring in £100,000,000 in fines. In the *Daily Mail* investigation the laser gun officially approved by the Home Office and used in nearly 3,500 mobile speed units hidden in police vans, police cars or on police motorbikes, recorded a parked car as doing 22 mph, a slow moving bicycle at 66 mph, an empty road at 33 mph and a wall at 44 mph. In one test the equipment was found to be measuring the speed of overtaking cars rather than the car being targeted. Dr Michael Clark, described as Europe's leading expert on laser technology, says that the gun is defective because its wide beam can easily pick up the wrong vehicle. A NASA laser scientist has said that over just 300 metres there is only a 60% chance of a human operator hitting a 12 foot wide target with a laser gun. Not many cars are 12 foot wide so the chances of hitting something other than the targeted car are very large. In addition, if the device is not held firmly on the target it can produce an erroneous result by 'slippage'. Moving just the thickness of a human hair can be enough to produce an error. Reflections from road signs and other cars can also add to confusion and bad results. Unsurprisingly, the Home Office, with a financial interest in speed guns and the policemen who handle them, continues to give them their unqualified support. The main expert witness used by the Crown Prosecution Service to convict motorists in laser gun speeding cases is a millionaire retired police officer who imports the device into Britain from America.

Only when results are patently absurd are the courts allowed to take any notice. (One driver was acquitted after a speed gun recorded him as doing 25 mph above his car's top speed.) But on at least ten occasions the Crown Prosecution Service has suddenly dropped cases against motorists when ordered by a judge to hand over video film taken at the time of the alleged offence.

41

Maybe one hidden reason for the enthusiasm for speed cameras is that by disqualifying drivers the Government hopes that it will ease road wear (and therefore save money) and disguise the coming oil shortage. Certainly the Government believes that drivers who are forced off the road will car-share.

42

Police chiefs have for some time been puzzled why, although the number of speeding tickets is rising dramatically, the number of people being disqualified from driving for acquiring a fourth three point speeding penalty is now falling. In 1999, around 500,000 people got speeding tickets. By 2003 the figure was up to 1,800,000.

In 1999 the number of motorists disqualified for acquiring 12 points on their licences was 34,000. By 2003 the total was down to 33,000.

Some political advocates of speed cameras have suggested that this is because speed cameras are working and that once a motorist has been caught he will drive more slowly.

This is simply not true.

The truth is that the Government's dishonest obsession with speed cameras has produced another unpleasant side effect: it has encouraged dishonesty among people who would have never previously dreamt of lying to the courts.

A survey by Churchill Insurance produced results which suggest that over 700,000 drivers have now avoided points on their licences by persuading a partner to admit to a speeding offence. 'Point swapping' is being used to save thousands of motorists from a driving ban.

One in seven of those who have 'donated' speeding points to a partner (usually a wife or girlfriend) say that they would lose their job if they lost their driving licence.

Some drivers have confused the police and the courts (and have escaped prosecution) by claiming that they could not remember who was driving on the day when the speeding offence occurred. Under these circumstances the police have to provide evidence proving which driver was driving. Unless the offence was picked up by the sort of camera which takes pictures from the front (and the picture is a clear one) the police will have no idea whom to prosecute. And so they can't prosecute anyone.

43

Is there an inverse relationship between the effort a police force puts into combating motorists and the level of serious crime in an area?

There could be. In some areas famous for their speed cameras, local citizens have complained that burglars there aren't being arrested at an acceptable rate. (Though, I suppose the burglars do run a high risk of being caught if they speed away from a crime.)

44

Speed cameras encourage bad driving.

Now that the police have installed motorway speed cameras which measure the speed a driver takes to travel between two fixed points, an increasing number of motorists are lane-hopping so as to confuse the cameras. This is a tricky business because, in addition to looking out for speed cameras hidden behind trees, and youths armed with bricks on top of bridges, the driver must constantly struggle to remember which lane he was in when he last went under a camera. (Lane swapping is in itself an immensely dangerous practice because every time you change lanes you increase the risk of having an accident. Despite this, the frequently offered instruction to motorists not to change lanes is, I suspect, designed to boost revenue rather than reduce accidents.)

Some motorists now drive with their headlights on full beam in the hope that this will 'blind' the cameras. Some straddle two lanes in order to avoid cameras above particular lanes.

New long distance speed cameras have to prove the identity of the driver and so tinted windscreens are coming into fashion. And motorists slow down suddenly and without warning when they spot vans parked on bridges. (Actually, it is often wise to change speed on motorways. On three separate occasions bricks and other items have been dropped from motorway bridges directly in front of our car. On none of these occasions have the police ever taken any action or shown any interest whatsoever in the danger. So when we see someone on a motorway bridge I tend to change speed as much as it is safe to do so.)

45

A reader of mine claims he rings the police whenever he sees a police van parked on a bridge. 'At speed,' he says, 'it's impossible to differentiate between a speed camera and a rifle. I tell the police there's a sniper on the bridge about to start mowing down cars. It gives them a little excitement.'

46

Crime is now so commonplace (and the police are so disinterested in helping to prevent it) that signs have started to appear at motorway service stations telling motorists not to 'leave loot in your boot'.

So, what are holidaymakers supposed to do? Take all their suitcases, buckets and spades with them when they pop into the restaurant or call to use the toilets?

If the police think that thieves are targeting motorway service stations why don't they have policemen patrolling there?

47

Many people now use radar detectors in their cars. The police want these gadgets banned. But even the dimmest politicians can see the problem. If speed cameras are really there to warn motorists of danger spots, and to save lives, then radar detectors which pick up the cameras early must save lives. To make radar detectors illegal would make as much sense as making speedometers illegal. If the police ban radar detectors then they will be admitting that the cameras are just there to make money – and not to save lives.

Taking away radar detectors (and we have one in our car) would, I suspect, also be a breach of the Human Rights Act. If speed cameras are set up at accident black spots – as the authorities claim they are – it is clearly sensible to have a detector to warn when approaching a black spot. And it would clearly be contrary to human rights to prevent motorists from protecting themselves and their families. If speed cameras are not at accident black spots then the Government and the police are both lying.

Finally, the extra warning provided by a radar detector means a motorist can be prepared for motorists ahead suddenly braking.

48

If the police were accountable, and subject to the usual rules and regulations as the rest of us, they would, I suspect, be in serious trouble for describing 'speed cameras' as 'safety cameras'. The police should start being honest. They should call them 'money cameras'.

49

In areas where the police don't have enough cameras to put in all their speed cameras housings they fit a working flash. Essex police said 'The flashes alert speeders that they have broken the law and leaves them guessing as to whether they will get a fine.' Great. Let's increase the stress on motorists.

50

While strolling around Paris recently I saw, within a single hour, policemen patrolling in cars, on motorbikes, on mountain bikes, in vans, on roller blades, on foot and on horseback. Some were in twos, some were in threes and some were in little clusters. Quite a few were smiling. Several gave advice to tourists who were lost. The day before and the date after were much the same.

My wife and I sat in a café reading about marauding, murdering gangs of feral youths in England. We tried to decide when we had last seen policemen in England who weren't sitting in a car on a motorway bridge.

I said I thought I'd seen two policemen in a car six months earlier.

My wife remembered them but says they were parked in a side road waiting for speeding motorists so they didn't really count. Neither of us could remember when we had last seen a policeman's legs.

51

Hospitals have to make money too. That's why so many of them are moving into the private medicine business. Hospitals deliberately maintain long NHS waiting lists so that they can sell private X-rays and scans to desperate patients who know that if they have to wait a year for an essential test they may well be dead before they get any treatment. It's a ruthless way to turn a service into a profit-making opportunity.

And most hospitals now charge sick people to park their cars when attending for treatment. Visitors who turn up to feed dying patients and to clean the floor around a relative's bed must also pay to park their cars.

52

Even libraries are now expected to become profitable centres. My local library is constantly selling off books by classic authors. On one recent visit I bought good condition reading copies of books by Joseph Conrad, P.G. Wodehouse and Evelyn Waugh for 10 pence each. I frequently find first editions on their 'dumping' shelves. Books are dumped to make more room for CDs by Robbie Williams and such educationally valuable DVDs as *Meet the Fockers*. Naturally, these products are rented out. What a long way libraries have come from the idea of providing somewhere for people to educate themselves; joining together thought-provoking authors and interested readers. The modern library has become little more than a rental shop, offering only that which seems potentially profitable. This is not why libraries were founded, nor is it why they exist. Readers often tell me that they have great difficulty in finding copies of Publishing House books in public libraries, and in persuading librarians to order copies. The reasons usually given are that Publishing House is a small publisher and that I am rather too controversial an author. Sadly, making people think is, it seems, not acceptable these days. It is much safer, politically, to order another Robbie Williams CD.

And more profitable too to spend money buying CDs and DVDs (which can be rented out for a fee) rather than books (which have to be loaned for nothing).

53

If you want to sing in a pub or hold a charity event you have to pay for the privilege. This is just another form of taxation. Carnival organisers in Somerset were told that they would have to pay £64,000 for a licence in order to put on a carnival and collect money for charity.

54

New Labour has decided to introduce 'board and lodging' charges for citizens who have been wrongfully imprisoned and who have been awarded compensation for wrongful conviction. It is difficult to believe but this means that innocent people who have been locked up for years, who have subsequently been found to be innocent and who are given money by the state in modest compensation, have a big chunk of their compensation taken back off them to pay for the cost of the cell they have occupied and the food they have consumed while in prison.

For example, a citizen who served 11 years for a murder it was later recognised that he had not committed was charged £37,158 for food and lodging. Former prisoners who have tried to question this charge in the courts have been warned that if they do so they risk losing much of the rest of their compensation payment in legal fees. Indeed, they might even find that the legal costs exceed their compensation in which case they would, of course, end up back in prison for failing to pay their lawyers.

55

In some seaside and rural areas local businessmen suspect that the authorities want to stop tourists visiting – even though businesses rely on tourists to survive. They point to the fact that local authorities deliberately use speed cameras, parking restrictions and road works set up in mid-summer to reduce the number of tourists. In many towns public conveniences have been closed. The council's income comes from local taxes and does not rise if there are more tourists. But the council's costs do rise when tourists arrive. (Roads need mending and extra rubbish has to be collected). The council no longer sees its own financial interests as being aligned with those of local people. And so the council puts itself first. That's local fascism in action. All this explains why so many towns are unwelcoming to visitors.

Chapter Eleven

Sending Tanks To Heathrow: How And Why Politicians Learned To Use Fear As A Weapon

1

The American and British Governments realised some years ago that fear can be used as a potent weapon. In the 1920s it was claimed that *The Times* reporters had habitually acted as agents for the British arms manufacturer Vickers Armstrong and had submitted news reports designed to increase the fear of war so that the company's share price would rise. In commenting on the allegation, *The Times*, then still widely regarded as the nation's journal of record, admitted that the claim was true but stated, in mitigation, that only two reporters had been involved. They had, however, been reporting from capitals in the Balkans, where the assassination of Archduke Ferdinand of Sarajevo triggered the First World War.

2

Our fear leads to their power. The more we fear, the more powerful they become. And the fear doesn't necessarily have to be rooted in reality. The fear can be worse than the reality – just as hope is often better than fulfilment.

Living In A Fascist Country

Today, our Government deliberately creates fear, and we live with a background level of so much 'toxic stress' that we are all constantly on edge. Fear makes millions turn to television for comfort, support and friendship, and the television has become a `family' for many who cannot bear the realities of the world and who do not understand their constant sense of fear and of not belonging. Programmes such as *MASH, Cheers* and *Friends* provide the companionship and sense of belonging that so many crave. It is not difficult to argue that the Government is directly responsible for the modern epidemic of stress-related diseases.

By making us afraid they make us welcome their new strong laws. When we are frightened we like the idea of having a strong government to protect us and so we are prepared to sacrifice our rights and our freedom. Riddled with fears we are prepared to forget that once we sacrifice our rights and our freedoms we will never get them back.

3

'As Dr William Sargant has pointed out...John Wesley's enormous success as a preacher was based upon an intuitive understanding of the central nervous system. He would open his sermon with a long and detailed description of the torments to which, unless they underwent conversion, his hearers would undoubtedly be condemned for all eternity. Then, when terror and an agonising sense of guilt had brought his audience to the verge, or in some cases over the verge, of a complete cerebral breakdown, he would change his tone and promise salvation to those who believed and repented.
By this kind of preaching, Wesley converted thousands of men, women and children. Intense, prolonged fear broke them down and produced a state of greatly intensified suggestibility. In this state they were able to accept the preacher's theological pronouncements without question. After which they were re-integrated by words of comfort, and emerged from their ordeal with new and generally better behaviour patterns ineradicably implanted in their minds and nervous systems.'
ALDOUS HUXLEY (*BRAVE NEW WORLD REVISITED*)

4

For the Americans and the British, the politics of fear really started with the Cold War – between the West and the Soviet Union.

Surprisingly, there was never any real sound foundation for the Cold War. It was all based on a deliberate misinterpretation of a series of telegrams sent back to America by an American diplomat based in Russia. George Kennan's observations in the late 1940s set the tone for American foreign policies which led to the foundation of NATO, the post war arms race in conventional and nuclear weapons, the growth of the CIA and the disaster that was Vietnam.

Kennan started all this with a series of telegrams sent in early 1946 from the American embassy in Moscow. In his telegrams Kennan explained that the Soviet regime was implacably opposed to America and that its designs on the world included 'violent destabilisation'. He softened this reading of the situation by arguing that Russia and the Soviet Union could be contained by a mixture of political bargaining, cultural pressure and diplomacy.

However, back home in the USA, the arms industry, and the generals at the Pentagon (who have often had close links with one another) used Kennan's words as an excuse for starting a very profitable arms race.

When it finally became clear in the early 1980s that the Soviet Union was no longer much of a real threat to anyone except gymnasts trying to win Olympic medals, the American neo-conservatives started the rumour that the Soviet Union was co-ordinating and controlling terrorist campaigns all around the world.

It was, said the neo-conservatives, the Russians who were responsible for everything from the IRA in Ireland to the Bader Meinhof gang in Germany. This bizarre and totally mendacious theory (in fact, of course, it was the Americans themselves who were financing the IRA) was based on a book which was itself based on disinformation which had been purposely distributed by the CIA to discredit the Russians.

Astonishingly and almost unbelievably the neo-conservatives actually argued that since it was impossible to prove that the Russians had secret weapons 'or were behind international terrorism' the very absence of proof actually proved that they had the weapons and were planning all the terrorism campaigns. The fact that no one could substantiate a link merely showed that they were just being very clever about it.

5

'We look forward to a world founded upon four essential human freedoms. The first is freedom of speech and expression – everywhere in the world. The second is freedom of every person to worship God in his own way – everywhere in the world. The third is freedom from want. The fourth is freedom from fear.'
FRANKLIN D ROOSEVELT 1941

6

Today, this absurd alleged link between Russia and terrorism has been replaced by the argument (fondly repeated endlessly by Bush and Blair) that the world is threatened by an international terrorism movement. This, of course, is even more absurd and is a theory which is so plain silly that even a spy fiction author wouldn't use it.

The truth is that there are lots of small, isolated terrorist groups but there is no global terrorism movement. Only idiots such as Bush and Blair pretend that there is.

7

'In Chinese camps the young Western captives were systematically subjected to stress... To intensify their guilt, prisoners were made to write and rewrite, in ever more intimate detail, long autobiographical accounts of their shortcomings. And after having confessed their own sins, they were required to confess the sins of their companions. The aim was to create within the camp a nightmarish society, in which everybody was spying on, and informing against, everyone else.'
ALDOUS HUXLEY, WRITING ABOUT THE TREATMENT
OF PRISONERS IN THE KOREAN WAR

8

If you exclude the conspiracy between the USA and the UK, there is no global terrorist movement. The concept of 'global terrorism' was deliberately conceived and is sustained by the British and American Governments as a way of oppressing their respective populations, of forcing through anti-libertarian legislation and of excusing their aggressive international policies and, above all, as an excuse for taking control of the world's oil.

9

Though there is no global terrorism movement there are, of course, quite a number of individual terrorist groups around the world which are fighting for their own individual causes. They are not united and they are not working together. There are no more of them now than there were at any other time in history. And their enthusiasms and size have, without doubt, been given support by the actions of the Bush-Blair axis of terror. Their status and size have been exaggerated by American Zionist neo-conservatives for their own purposes. The idea of an international or global terrorism movement is a trick used by politicians to distract us from the truth and to give them more spurious authority.

Terrorists don't want to destroy the world, they want to attack and replace particular regimes. For example, Israel's enemy is Palestine. America's enemy is the Muslim world. Russia's enemy are the Chechens who want independence.

The political leaders of these countries talk about international terrorism because it distracts attention from the fact that *they* are the real bad guys who have created the problem.

10

The first (and last) modern, democratic English revolution took place in the 17th century when a group of citizens led by Oliver Cromwell rejected rule by King Charles and his lapdog parliament and called for rule by 'countrymen like ourselves' not by 'knights and gentlemen that make us laws, that are chosen for fear and do but oppress us, and do not know the people's sores'.

11

American and Britain are giving support to oppressive, totalitarian regimes all around the world because it suits them to be able to claim that terrorism is now a world wide problem. They claim (apparently without even a smirk) that the Chechens, the Palestinians, the Iraqi freedom fighters and the Taliban are all part of some global terrorist movement. Bush, Putin and others all identify their national problems as global problems. Blair simply nods and agrees with them all.

Incidentally, it is worth remembering that when the American colonists rebelled against King George III, they thought of themselves as separatists.

England called them terrorists.

12

'If you want a picture of the future imagine a boot stamping on a human face.'
GEORGE ORWELL

13

As I write this there are separatist groups in around 25 different countries. It suits the American and British Governments (and Putin's Russian Government) to lump all these groups together because it enables them to pretend that we are fighting a global terrorist movement. It is much easier for them to frighten us if we can be persuaded that the terrorists are a bigger danger than they are. In reality it is a political and military nonsense to do so.

The Chechens, fighting in Russia, have been lumped together with Al Qaeda by American and British politicians. This is laughable nonsense. The Chechens are fighting for freedom for their own homeland. Many independent observers believe they have a good case. When Chechen separatists held hundreds of people captive in a Moscow theatre in 2002 Putin sent in the troops and simply gassed everyone – hostages and separatists. He didn't care how many people died because he knows that deaths create fear and fear gives power. Half the hostages were killed by the Government gas. Afterwards Bush sent Putin a message congratulating him. The British Labour Government was similarly supportive. Since they want Putin to support their own outrages they could hardly do otherwise.

As an aside it is worth taking a look at what the Chechens did next – and where they got the idea from for what they did.

14

Two years after the Moscow theatre debacle, Chechen rebels (most of whom were widows of men killed by Putin's army) targeted a Russian school, where children were taken hostage.

Strategically it seems a crazy thing to do. Theoretically, the Chechens have a pretty good case. On a moral basis they have just as much right to global support as, say, the people of Kosovo who were 'liberated' by the British and Americans. But in practice, the Chechens have had little public support for their fight for independence. Their battle against oppression and ethnic cleansing has been widely ignored by a media obsessed by the activities of the Beckhams and Big Brother contestants. However, surely killing children meant that they were even less likely to win public support? Where on earth could the Chechens have got such a crazy notion? What on earth could have possessed them to behave in such an evil way?

You've got three guesses.

And the three answers are: America, Britain and Israel.

America, Britain and Israel have, for some time now, been deliberately targeting children.

America and Israel use landmines, cluster bombs and other explosive devices deliberately designed to kill or maim children. Britain, as America's best friend and partner in crime, must share the responsibility and the shame.

♦ The Americans and British have deliberately fired cluster bombs into civilian areas. The hundreds of individual bomblets contained in a cluster bomb are scattered over a wide area. They have shiny casings to attract children, and each 1,000 pound cluster bomb contains up to 300 little bombs which look like small toys. Many don't explode when they are dropped – exploding only when they are picked up by small children. Experts believe that cluster bombs violate the rules of war.

♦ Blair's American allies deliberately bombed Iraq's water supplies in the First Gulf War and then, for years afterwards, refused permission for water purification equipment to be installed in Iraq. The result of this (and other sanctions) was that, according to the United Nations, around one million Iraqi citizens –

including 500,000 children – died slow and painful deaths.

♦ Three children (one aged 13) were among the 680 innocent people held at America's illegal prison camp at Guantanamo Bay. Blair did nothing to stop this war crime.

♦ The Israelis fired internationally banned flechette shells (which explode into thousands of razor sharp darts) at a children's soccer field in Gaza. Boys were playing on the field at the time.

The evil idea behind all this is that if you maim and kill children you demoralise the adult population and make them easier to control.

The Chechens, having learnt from Bush, Blair and the Israelis, clearly believed that if they upset the Russians and created anger and outrage within Russia then Putin would lose power. And, if Putin lost power then his replacement might give the Chechens the independence and freedom they want.

What the Chechens did in Russia was unforgivably wrong.

But they were following the example set by Bush and Blair.

Bush and Blair should adopt the slogan 'Kill Children And Win Wars'.

It's what they do. And it's what they are teaching the rest of the world.

15

'The society described in Orwell's fable ('1984') is a society permanently at war, and the aim of its rulers is first, of course, to exercise power for its own delightful sake and, second, to keep their subjects in that state of constant tension which a state of constant war demands of those who wage it.'
ALDOUS HUXLEY

16

If bombing and killing innocent civilians is terrorism then Britain and America are the world's most potent terrorist nations and Bush and Blair are the world's worst terrorist leaders. Two men who claim to be Christian and who have built their reputation on their Christianity, are both war criminals who have made immorality acceptable.

17

In February 2005, Ian Blair, the Metropolitan police commissioner (described by some as 'Britain's most senior police officer'), warned of the risk of a terrorist attack in the UK in the run up to the 2005 General Election.

Encouraging a sense of fear which could only help the sitting Government, Ian Blair claimed that Britain was at risk because of our presidency of the G8 group of countries and the EU.

This seemed to me to be total nonsense. Presidency of these two organisations did not seem particularly likely to attract terrorist action. Conveniently for the Government, Ian Blair, didn't mention the invasion of Iraq as a possible cause of terrorism in Britain.

This, it seemed to me, either suggested that Britain's senior police officer was making an overtly political statement or was exhibiting a strategic incompetence which should disqualify from him any job requiring a functioning brain.

18

It is (just about) possible to argue that there are more terrorist sympathisers in the world today than there were five years ago. If this is so then it is undoubtedly because Bush and Blair have created the new terrorists. Bush and Blair need terrorists like rock stars need dark glasses and groupies. Without terrorists and their supporters Bush could not push through his plan.

19

'Societies are composed of individuals and are good only in so far as they help individuals to realise their potentialities and to lead a happy and fruitful life.'
ALDOUS HUXLEY

20

The creation of new terrorists can take place in the UK as well as anywhere else in the world. Within the UK the more power the Government takes for itself, and the more it prevents people protesting and demonstrating for the causes in which they believe, the more support terrorists will receive. And the more oppressive the Government becomes, so the greater the terrorist threat becomes.

Politicians either understand this (in which case they are quite deliberately exposing us to ever-greater danger) or else they are very, very stupid.

21

Life can be regarded as a series of negotiations, and there was a time when Governments and people regarded negotiation as an art.

No more.

Today, governments regard negotiation as a sign of weakness. 'We will not negotiate with terrorists,' they state baldly, as though this was something to be proud of. Countries (such as Italy) which are suspected of having negotiated the release of kidnapped terrorists are regarded with disdain by those who haven't.

There was a time when the art of negotiation was regarded as an essential part of life. History shows that for two thousand years Governments and police have negotiated (often with success) with kidnappers, lunatics, robbers and hostage takers. Refusing to negotiate was always regarded as extreme, foolish and stubborn.

(Now even large companies have adopted this policy too. Time and time again I come across corporate employees who state baldly (and with a certain amount of strange pride) that whatever they are offering is non-negotiable. Every business deal has become a kidnapping. Everywhere, and to everyone, negotiating seems to be regarded as a sign of weakness.)

Why have governments become so stubborn?

The answer, as usual, is simple.

Governments (and this is particularly true of the British Government) refuse to negotiate (or make any genuine effort to release victims) because it helps them to keep the voters frightened. Every time terrorists kill a kidnapped British citizen the Government's job of scaring the public is made easier.

Politicians and their families are, of course, very well protected.

22

23

The Americans have deliberately ratcheted up the threat of serious
nuclear conflict in order to create yet more fear. One Russian General
recently pointed out that the Americans are now making nuclear
weapons an instrument for solving military tasks, and are, therefore,
lowering the threshold for nuclear weapon use. He pointed out, not
entirely unreasonably, that his country has to react to that and is
doing so.

It's difficult to avoid the conclusion that the Americans probably
regret the fall of the Soviet Union and the collapse of the Cold
War.

24

America's current war on terrorism is simply the latest of a whole
series of absurd 'wars'. In almost every case the American
Government's silliness has been followed with equal enthusiasm by
the British Government. The war on terrorism is likely to run and
run because it has proved far more effective than its predecessors:
the war on poverty, the war on drugs and the war on cancer.

These three previous wars have, of course, been a complete
failure for the simple reason that in every case the war was waged
on the symptoms, rather than on the problems themselves, because
in order to tackle the problems it would have been necessary to
fight large profitable corporations. And no modern government will
do that.

25

The American and British Governments claim that we must fight a
war against terrorism because there is a global terrorist movement
which threatens our freedom and our future. This is a pretence.
They know it is not true. Terrorism is the manufactured excuse for

everything bad that happens to us. We are not at war with anyone. We are being deliberately frightened out of our skins by people who know that fear is the most potent force of all; the most effective way of oppressing the population and suppressing dissent.

Chapter Twelve

Governments Lie All The Time: How The Media Helps Them Deceive The Voters

1

The politicians have changed our language and have, as George Orwell predicted so accurately in *1984*, adopted the principles of 'new-speak' and 'double-think'.

While the broadsheet newspapers and our broadcasters worry about punctuation, and put all their energies into evaluating the damage done to our society by splitting an infinitive, the politicians are distorting our language to hide the truth and deceive us.

It began decades ago when the Ministry of War suddenly became the Ministry of Defence. And so, 'war' becomes 'peace' and we are told that we must give up our freedom in order to protect it.

When the American army displays its incompetence yet again the results are not the murder of its allies but death by 'friendly fire'.

When the Americans bomb the wrong village, or find some other way to murder several hundred thousand entirely innocent women and children, the results are airily dismissed as 'collateral damage'.

When Labour Party politicians talk about ID cards they call them 'entitlement cards' (a wonderful piece of Orwellian newspeak). When they talk about speed cameras (a crude and dishonest attempt to take more money from us) they call them 'safety cameras', assuming that this will trick people into thinking that speed cameras are there to save lives.

The lying and the spinning and the deceit are, it seems, second nature now. Politicians and their aides do it without thinking.

When Sir Christopher Meyer, a former British Ambassador to the USA said that 'there is plenty of evidence home-grown terrorism was partly radicalised and fuelled by Iraq' a Downing Street spokesman told the BBC that 'events in Iraq could never justify a resort to terrorism'.

Now, where did that come from?

Meyer had simply pointed out what every other sane person in the UK already knew.

But the Prime Minister's office twisted this by saying that the war on Iraq didn't 'justify a resort to terrorism'.

Where did that word 'justify' come from?

No one had claimed that the terrorism was justified.

It was, as usual, just an over-slick piece of attempted deceit from the Prime Minister's office; designed, presumably, to mislead the public and to distract attention away from the truth.

2

Blair claims that the London bombings in July 2005 were caused by Muslim extremists misunderstanding the teachings in the Koran. If he really believes this then he must surely be the only person in the world who does. Every independent observer knows that if London was bombed by Muslims it happened because we invaded Iraq in 1991 and, more recently and more specifically, in 2003. The Muslim extremists themselves say that is why they are bombing us and it is reasonable to assume that they know their own motives better than Blair does.

Anyone who puts forward the view that the bombings were caused by the war is dismissed by Blair as an apologist for the bombers, a supporter of the terrorists. Labour even want to make it illegal to say there is a link.

3

The spin and the manipulation gets everywhere these days. And it's far more important than most people realise. It isn't just a question of the Government burying bad news (as they so notably did on September 11th 2001) and hoping no one will notice.

Here's a small, subtle example of media manipulation.

On discussion programmes about the Middle East, television interviewers often identify guests who are Muslim – so that the viewers will know that the speaker has a vested interest in the subject under discussion. Quite right and proper. But they never identify Jewish speakers as Jewish or Zionist.

Don't Jews (and particularly Zionists) have just as great a vested interest in what happens in the Middle East as Muslims?

Of course they do.

So, what is happening here?

I suspect that it suits the Government's purpose to have Muslims identified (and their arguments regarded as biased) but not to have Jews identified.

4

'Hitler's dictatorship differed in one fundamental point from all its predecessors in history. It was the first dictatorship in the present period of modern technical development, a dictatorship which made complete use of all technical means for the domination of its own country. Through technical devices like the radio and the loud-speaker, eighty million people were deprived of independent thought. It was thereby possible to subject them to the will of one man.'
ALBERT SPEER, HITLER'S MINISTER FOR ARMAMENTS

5

The media reinforces existing prejudices, creates prejudices of its own and imposes its own prejudices on the public.

Some years ago I used to help judge the Bride of the Year competition organised by the *Daily Mirror*. The whole event was largely masterminded by the late Marje Proops, the paper's agony aunt and she, I and one or two 'celebrities' would turn up at some smart London location and inspect the finalists. I was never quite sure what I was doing there, for although I was then a fairly regular contributor to the paper I had no official status. But it was a fairly 'fun' day and everyone (even the losing finalists) seemed to treat it all rather well. The brides all got their picture in the paper.

I remember well that one year the finalists included a very lovely bride who stood out from the other contestants. She was black. I thought that she seemed an excellent choice and was arguing her case when Marje took me aside.

'We can't choose her,' Marje told me quietly.

'Why not?' I asked, innocently.

'She's black,' said Marje.

I was stunned and didn't quite know what to say. After a moment I murmured something about having noticed this. 'Does it matter?' I asked.

'Oh yes,' replied Marje sternly. 'We couldn't possibly pick a black girl.' She frowned. 'The readers wouldn't like it.'

'Then what is she doing here?' I asked.

'It looks good,' replied Marje, soothingly. 'Makes it clear to everyone that we aren't being prejudiced.'

However much the newspaper's policy may have changed since then, this was certainly the *Daily Mirror's* policy as understood and practised by a woman who was to many people the face and voice of the paper at the time.

6

'Freedom of the press in Britain means freedom to print such of the proprietor's prejudices as the advertisers don't object to.'
HANNEN SWAFFER (1879-1962)

7

Since 1999 just eight giant global corporations have owned over 70% of the world's media including: television, newspapers, magazines, radio, satellite systems, cable, book publishing, film production and distribution, movie theatre chains, the Internet, billboards and theme parks.

8

'In the totalitarian East there is political censorship, and the media of mass communication are controlled by the State. In the democratic West there is economic censorship and the media of mass communication are controlled by members of the Power Elite.'
ALDOUS HUXLEY

9

It is sometimes difficult to avoid the feeling that parts of the media are determined to encourage terrorism. The genetic codes for dangerous pathogens, including smallpox, poliomyelitis and Ebola are all available on the Internet. And the American media has reported exactly where and how to buy the DNA base pairs with which to construct these killers. Mail order DNA can be purchased in the USA for as little as 40 cents a base and it wouldn't take much money (or much know how) for a terrorist group to prepare its own biological weapons of mass destruction. But then, perhaps that's all part of the plan.

10

'There are laws to protect the freedom of the press's speech, but none that are worth anything to protect the people from the press.'
MARK TWAIN (LICENSE OF THE PRESS, (1873))

11

There used to be a firm line between editorial and advertising. This line no longer exists. Films, television and radio programmes and magazine and newspaper articles may now all contain what is called 'product placement'. In films this usually means simply that the hero will drive past a poster advertising a product. But in newspapers and magazines the failure to differentiate between advertising and editorial is more dangerous. Press releases are often printed verbatim and columnists and feature writers may be sponsored to promote particular items. It is now not uncommon for a writer to be paid not by the magazine publisher but by the advertiser whose product he promotes. Even articles about celebrities are 'placed' as promotional items; designed to sell a new album or film and approved beforehand by the 'star' and his or her publicity agents. As a result it is becoming increasingly difficult to trust anything you read, hear or see.

12

'Can it be maintained that a person of any education can learn anything worth knowing from a penny paper? It may be said that people may learn what is said in Parliament. Well, will that contribute to their education?'
The Third Marquess of Salisbury

13

One of the primary reasons for the formation of the European Union was to promote free travel between the member countries. But when a suspect, wanted for questioning about the July 2005 London bombings, was found to have travelled to Rome, apparently without having to show a passport, there was uproar. Just about every national newspaper demanded to know how such a thing could happen. Commentators on the radio and on television were outraged. And yet these are the same newspapers which campaign for the European Union and the same commentators who tell us how a United States of Europe will benefit us all.

14

Politicians don't just spin. They also lie outright. They have done it for years. And because most of us tell the truth most of the time we never quite realise just how much they do it. The Americans lie so much that all American politicians should have noses the length of the Amazon.

For example, go back over half a century.

It has now been revealed that the American Government knew that the Japanese attack on Pearl Harbour was coming but they allowed it to take place because it was politically convenient. The people who died were sacrificed by their Government because the USA was heading into a recession and a long, expensive war was considered to be the only way out of it. (Wars stimulate the economy

– partly but not solely by providing work for the arms industry.)

It's generally accepted by many Americans that they weren't told the truth about the Oklahoma bombing. Timothy McVie was executed as a convenient scapegoat but there are many unanswered questions about the Government's possible involvement in the atrocity. Many Americans believe that the bombing was carried out by their Government in order to prepare the nation for the introduction of tougher laws. (This, of course, is precisely what Hitler did when he burnt the Reichstag in Berlin. The burning, used as an excuse for Hitler's clampdown on terrorism, was arranged in order to give Hitler's National Socialist Party more control over the population.)

And there are serious doubts about what happened to the TWA plane which crashed in July 1996. The official explanation is that a malfunction caused the crash. But a vast number of experts have given evidence that they saw missile trails heading for the plane. And photographs of the plane's wreckage show huge holes in the fuselage. It is inconceivable that these holes could have been made by anything other than missiles.

More recently, look what happened when the Americans blew up the Chinese Embassy in Belgrade in 1999. The Americans were busy bombing as much of Serbia as they could at the time, though no one was terribly sure why, other than the fact that it was perhaps the turn of the Serbs to be attacked. It was suggested by politicians that the bombing of the Chinese Embassy was just another American accident. The media in the UK and the USA never questioned this claim.

In a way, the gullibility of the media can be excused. After all, although the American military had claimed that their missiles were so accurate that they could be fired through a small window from a thousand miles away, practical experience had prove that this was just another American lie. Journalists had become so accustomed to American military incompetence, and the fact that American sharpshooters couldn't hit a barn door from six feet, that when the Americans launched a missile the only people who didn't take cover were the people who were the targets. So the claim that the Chinese Embassy had been hit by mistake was accepted and journalists, who had grown accustomed to counting the number of wedding party guests killed by American bombing raids, accepted the extraordinary claim from the Americans that this was just another example of their incompetence.

It wasn't until six months later that the truth leaked out: the Americans had deliberately blown up the Chinese Embassy because they had believed it to be full of electronic intelligence gathering equipment. (The Americans don't like other countries having bombs, oil, seeds, money or information and they will kill and destroy in order to prevent that happening.) The significant thing here, of course, is that the American Government was allowed to get away with its lies because editors and journalists let them.

15

How can you tell a Politician is lying?
His mouth is open and words are coming out.

16

The Americans don't much like foreign journalists. In 1999 they succeeded in blowing up the Serbian television station and managed to kill two make-up girls. They blew up the Kabul bureau of television station al-Jazeera in 2002 and they bombed its Baghdad bureau in April 2003. There have been reports that, dissatisfied with destroying its offices, Bush wanted to completely destroy the Qatar based TV station al-Jazeera, presumably on the grounds that he didn't like what they were broadcasting.

17

'There is no such thing, at this date of the world's history, in America as an independent press. You know it and I know it. There is not one of you who dares to write your honest opinions, and if you did, you know beforehand that it would never appear in print. I am paid weekly for keeping my honest opinions out of the paper I am connected with. Others of you are paid similar salaries for similar things, and any of you who would be so foolish as to write honest opinions would be out on the streets looking for another job. If I allowed my honest opinions to appear in one issue of my paper, before twenty-four hours my occupation would be gone. The business of the journalists is to destroy the truth, to lie outright, to pervert, to vilify, to fawn at the feet of mammon, and to sell his country and his race for his daily bread. You know it

and I know it, and what folly is this toasting an independent press? We are the
tools and vassals of rich men behind the scenes. We are the jumping jacks, they
pull the strings and we dance. Our talents, our possibilities and our lives are
all the property of other men. We are intellectual prostitutes.'
JOHN SWINTON, EMINENT NEW YORK JOURNALIST SPEAKING IN 1880
AS GUEST OF HONOUR AT A BANQUET GIVE FOR HIM BY OTHER
LEADING JOURNALISTS. A GUEST WHO KNEW NOTHING ABOUT
JOURNALISM HAD PROPOSED A TOAST TO 'THE INDEPENDENT PRESS'
AND THIS WAS SWINTON'S REPLY.

18

Dr David Kelly was a Government scientist. An expert on Iraq. He had a considerable amount of experience working both in Iraq and Russia. He is alleged to have killed himself after the pressure of being interrogated by a bunch of moronic MPs. (I have been quizzed by committees in both the House of Commons and the House of Lords and my enduring memory is that these are not bright people.)

Dr David Kelly knew that Blair had deceived Parliament and the nation over the alleged existence of weapons of mass destruction in Iraq. Even though he was clearly a loyal servant of the establishment, Kelly was equally clearly a danger to the Government. His evidence would have been of enormous help to those who believe that Blair is more of a bare-faced liar than an incompetent dissembler and 'over-enthusiastic interpreter of rather dodgy intelligence'. From what I've seen of the published evidence the death of Government expert Dr David Kelly (which was officially described as 'suicide') was most certainly not suicide. In my professional opinion, as an ex-police surgeon with ten years experience, Dr Kelly did not commit suicide. And if he didn't commit suicide, he was murdered. The obvious question to be asked is: who stood to gain by Dr David Kelly's death? There aren't too many suspects.

19

And then there was Robin Cook.

The suspicions over the death of Dr Kelly have led credence to suspicions about the almost equally convenient death of Robin Cook, a healthy man of 59 with no history of heart disease and no conspicuous risk factors, who suddenly dropped dead of a heart attack.

How convenient that the Labour Party's most powerful anti-war campaigner (who, as a former Foreign Secretary must have known where lots of rotting bodies were kept) should suddenly drop dead just as Bush and Blair are planning to invade Iran. Cook would have been a fearsome embarrassment. He was a busy writer of newspaper articles and, it is fair to assume, not entirely popular in Washington.

20

'If a nation expects to be ignorant and free, it expects what never was and never will be. The people cannot be safe without information. Where the press is free, and every man able to read, all is safe.'
THOMAS JEFFERSON

21

'Nothing can now be believed which is seen in a newspaper.'
THOMAS JEFFERSON (A LITTLE LATER IN HIS CAREER)

22

In the months and years after the invasions and bombings of Afghanistan and Iraq both Bush and Blair (and their supporting players) have frequently lied to their respective voters; claiming that the world is now a safer place (when any moderately intelligent observer can see that it isn't) and that they have given these countries freedom and democracy (when it is only too painfully obvious that they haven't). Blair and Bush know that if they lie often enough and loudly enough then their lies will become perceived truths. Blair and Bush are the modern day Hitler and Goebels. It was, after all, Tony Blair's mentor Adolf Hitler who, in *Mein Kampf*, wrote :'(People) more readily fall victims to the big lie than the small lie, since it would never come into their heads to fabricate colossal untruths, and they would not believe that others could have the impudence to distort the truth so infamously.' And it was Hitler who, in addition to his view about the size of a lie being important, believed that if a lie was repeated often enough it would, eventually, be confused with the truth by the greater part of the population.

315

Hermann Goering, Hitler's No 2, speaking before being sentenced to death at the Nuremberg trials, also gave advice obviously used by George W. Bush and Tony Blair.

'Naturally, the common people don't want war,' Goering said. 'Neither in Russia, nor in England, nor for that matter in Germany. That is understood. But, after all, it is the leaders of the country who determine the policy and it is always a simple matter to drag the people along, whether it is a democracy or a fascist dictatorship, or a parliament, or a communist dictatorship. Voice or no voice the people can always be brought to the bidding of the leaders. That is easy. All you have to do is tell them they are being attacked and denounce the peacemakers for lack of patriotism and exposing the country to danger; it works the same in any country.'

23

What is particularly worrying about all this, is not just the fact that modern politicians lie almost as often as they open their mouths but the fact that the mainstream media is prepared to suppress the truth and support the lies we are told. The media has become part of the lie, rewriting history to suit the demands of the politicians and their paymasters. The Government puts out information and radio and TV stations and newspapers simply print what they are told to print. They are unbelievably compliant. The Government and the media and large international corporations now share aims and have combined their resources to achieve those aims. And remember, it is in their interests that we remain constantly afraid, invariably misinformed and concerned about our health and our wealth.

When Blair went on holiday to the Caribbean in August 2005 the press was told not to report where he'd gone. (Blair presumably didn't want the voters to know that he was on yet another of his freebies). Obediently, the press complied. At the Government's behest the media tell us what they want us to know, and what to think about it.

It is to the media's disgrace that they do this. It is to our disgrace that we allow them to get away with it. Most people are simply too concerned with what is happening in the soaps and the reality programmes on TV to care about what is being done in their name in Afghanistan or Iraq. Liberty and democracy have been drowned in a sewage filled sea of irrelevant television and bent newspaper reporting.

Actually, although we like to think that we have a free press we haven't had a free press for a long time. For decades, American corporate interests have been buying up newspapers, magazines, TV stations, and radio stations. Arms companies and oil companies, which need to control public opinion do it easily by simply buying up great chunks of the media. It started back in 1917 when American corporations, headed by banker J.P. Morgan, bought the top 25 American newspapers in order to control the news content. And it's still going on today.

24

'Freedom of the press is guaranteed only to those who own one.'
A.J.LIEBLING

25

It was long ago realised that coercion alone was neither an effective nor a productive way of running the country (for one thing it was not economically wise to tie up men and resources in constant battles). By the time of Woodrow Wilson's Presidency it was recognised that the best way to control people was not by beating them or killing them but by controlling attitudes and opinions. The arrival of the mass media made this easy. Today's Governments control the news, and control public opinion, just as carefully as do despots and military juntas. Because they are reluctant to show their hand by using violence on their own people, they control the way we think and respond with propaganda. The word 'propaganda' first entered the *Encyclopaedia Britannica* back in 1922. Britain was probably the first nation to recognise the value and importance of propaganda and Nazi Germany, the USSR and the South African Government were followers not leaders. Britain, remember, actually used to have a Ministry of Information which was directed to control and direct the way people thought. That was its sole purpose. These days governments are not quite so obvious. Instead of having a single, rather clumsy and obvious Minister of Information, the Labour Party has planted spin doctors in every Ministry to make sure not that the Ministries follow party policy (they will do that anyway) but that the news which is put out suits the party's purpose. It was, remember, one of these spin doctors who decided that 11th September 2001 was a good day to bury bad news. The media cooperate because it suits them. Before the Labour Party came to power in 1997 they toured the owners of the national press to arrange deals. I was told, for example, that one national newspaper group promised to support the Labour Party in return for the freedom to takeover a television station and to sidestep monopoly rules. The BBC always supports the Government for the simple reason that it owes its franchise and its licence fee and its very existence to the Government. It pretends not to be but it is a Government-owned and run broadcasting subsidiary.

26

'Used in one way, the press, the radio and the cinema are indispensable to the survival of democracy. Used in another way, they are among the most powerful weapons in the dictator's armoury. In the field of mass communications as in almost every other field of enterprise, technological progress has hurt the Little Man and helped the Big Man. As lately as fifty years ago, every democratic country could boast of a great number of small journals and local ewspapers. Thousands of country editors expressed thousands of independent opinions. Somewhere or other almost anybody could get almost anything printed. Today the press is still legally free; but most of the little papers have disappeared.'
ALDOUS HUXLEY (*BRAVE NEW WORLD REVISITED*, 1959)

27

Today we have a society where all decisions which affect us are made, in theory, by Parliament but in practice by institutions which practise authoritarian control and which are themselves controlled and led by whoever backed whoever won the last election. It has been said that power remains strongest when it is kept in the dark, and that if exposed to scrutiny, it will lose its potency and quickly evaporate. Blair and his colleagues know this. That's why they are so keen to make sure that the truth remains hidden. A representational democracy only works when the men and women who do the representing are benevolent and enlightened and prepared to put self-interest second and their responsibilities to their constituents first.

Thousands of Non Governmental Organisations and Quangos exist mostly to exist and to some extent to represent the interests of lobby groups. They certainly don't exist to represent the people. The participation of the public in public life is severely limited. Decision making is everywhere made by tyrants with nice smiles.

Controlling the way people think has become something politicians do routinely, particularly when they want to do something which they know or suspect might not be popular with the people who are supposed to be in charge – the general public. In the USA the Reagan administration founded an Office of Public Diplomacy which organised Operation Truth to persuade the public to agree to its offensive and murderous policies in Central America. Both in the USA and in the UK Governments routinely and consistently conduct precisely the sort of psychological operations which used to be used to subdue populations in captured enemy territory.

The Government now regards us as the enemy. The corollary, of course, is that we must, if we are to survive, regard the Government as the enemy.

28

'Of course it is possible for any citizen with time to spare, and a canny eye, to work out what is actually going on, but for the many, there is not time, and the network news is the only news for most even though it may not be news at all but only a series of flashing fictions.'
GORE VIDAL

29

You won't see me on TV these days. You won't hear me on your radio. You are unlikely to read about me or my books in national newspapers or magazines.

I used to appear on national TV and radio several times a week. There was a time when my articles and columns regularly appeared in countless publications.

No more.

I still receive invitations to appear on TV or radio. But the invitations are invariably cancelled when the inexperienced researcher who has made the phone call or sent the e-mail is advised of their mistake.

These days I don't even bother talking to anyone representing a media organisation. I know I'll be cancelled before the broadcast takes place or the article is published. In the dark and distant past, when I was just starting out as an author, each new book publication would be greeted with a long and exhausting tour of the nation's radio and television stations. These days, now that I've sold a lot of books, producers no longer dare invite me into their studio.

Coldly, clinically and efficiently I have been banned from radio, TV and print media.

I have even, on many occasions, been banned from making public appearances.

On one occasion, when I was due to speak at an open air animal rights rally opposing vivisection, the Home Secretary and the police effectively shut me up by introducing a temporary law preventing me, or anyone else, travelling to the site of the rally. (When the rally was rearranged and the Home Secretary and police failed to ban my second attempt to speak they used a less subtle approach. A helicopter hovered right above the stage where I was speaking so that the noise would drown what I was saying.)

On another occasion the Oxford Union invited me to speak in a debate on vivisection. They then withdrew the invitation. They said that they had to do this because no one would speak against me. I offered to do both sides of the debate. The Oxford Union refused. They didn't want me there at any price.

In South Africa I was booked to take part in a debate at the University in Johannesburg. But at the last moment all the speakers who had been booked to oppose me pulled out. No one would agree to debate with me. Eventually a speaker had to be flown up from Cape Town.

Why all the bans?

Simple, really.

I've annoyed too many powerful people. The Government doesn't like the fact that I tell the truth. The medical establishment doesn't like the truth being aired. Nor does the drug industry, the food industry or the chemical industry. Policemen and judges don't like the truth being aired and nor do civil servants. The list goes on and on.

Most editors (whether of broadcast programmes or print media) are too scared of losing their jobs to risk upsetting the people in power. I'm regarded as too dangerous to be allowed on air. I'm renowned for telling the truth about delicate issues. And the truth is something the establishment – and the media – usually prefer to keep tucked away in filing cabinets.

I've grown accustomed to this.

But there have always been one or two avenues left open.

I could, for example, lecture at meetings or symposia.

Could.

Past tense.

If you still believe that Britain is a land of free speech read on. And be prepared to be startled.

30

In July 2004 I was invited to speak at a new conference in London. The conference was, I was told, intended to tackle the subject of medication errors and adverse reactions to prescribed drugs. The company organising the conference was called PasTest. 'For over thirty years PasTest has been providing medical education to professionals within the NHS,' they told me. 'Building on our commitment to quality in medical and healthcare education, PasTest is creating a range of healthcare events which focus on the professional development of clinicians and managers who are working together to deliver healthcare services for the UK. Our aim is to provide a means for those who are in a position to improve services on both national and regional levels. The topics covered by our conferences are embraced within policy, best practice, case study, clinical management and evidence based practice. PasTest endeavours to source the best speakers who will engage audiences with balanced, relevant and thought-provoking programmes. PasTest has proven in the past that by using thorough investigative research and keeping up-to-date with advances in healthcare and medical practice, a premium educational event can be achieved.'

Goody, I thought.

Iatrogenesis (doctor-induced disease) is something of a speciality of mine. I have written numerous books and articles on the subject. My campaigns have resulted in more drugs being banned or controlled than anyone else's. A previous Government admitted that it had taken action because of my articles.

The conference organisers offered to pay me £1,500 plus £500 in expenses for two hours of my time. In addition to speaking at the conference they wanted me to help them decide on the final programme.

I thought the conference was an important one and would give me a good opportunity to tell NHS staff the truth about why drug side effects are such a big problem, why one in six patients in hospital is there because he has been made ill by a doctor and why doctors are now one of the three most important causes of illness and death in British hospitals. I signed a contract.

PasTest wrote to confirm my appointment as a consultant and speaker for the PasTest Conference Division.

And then there was silence. My office repeatedly asked for details of when and where the conference was being held.

Silence.

Eventually a programme for the event appeared on the Internet. Curiously, my name was not on the list of speakers.

Here is part of the blurb promoting the conference:

'Against a background of increasing media coverage into the number of UK patients who are either becoming ill or dying due to adverse reactions to medication our conference aims to explain the current strategies to avoid Adverse Drug reactions and what can be done to educate patients.'

Putting the blame on patients for problems caused by prescription drugs is brilliant. Most drug related problems are caused by the stupidity of doctors not the ignorance of patients. If the aim is to educate patients on how best to avoid prescription drug problems the advice would be simple: 'Don't trust doctors.'

The list of speakers included a variety of people I had never heard of including one speaker representing The Association of the British Pharmaceutical Industry and another representing the Medicines and Healthcare Products Regulatory Agency.

Delegates representing the NHS were expected to pay £250 plus VAT (£293.75) to attend the event. Delegates whose NHS Trust would be funding the cost were asked to apply for a Health Authority Approval form. The NHS was paying to send delegates to a conference where someone representing the drug industry would speak to them on drug safety.

We asked PasTest what had happened to my invitation to speak. We were told that: 'certain parties felt that he (Vernon Coleman) was too controversial to speak and as a result would not attend.'

Could that, I wonder, be the drug industry?

Is the drug industry now deciding who they will allow to speak to doctors and NHS staff on the problems caused by prescription drugs? If I was banned at the behest of the drug industry do NHS bosses know that people attending the PasTest conference will only hear speakers approved by the drug industry? And if I was banned at the behest of the medical profession why are doctors frightened of the truth? (If they think my views are wrong they would surely be happy for me to appear so that they could counter my arguments.)

PasTest offered me a fee of £1,500 to speak at their conference. Because I had a contract they have paid me *not* to turn up. I used the money to buy an advertisement for my book *How To Stop Your Doctor Killing You*.

Details of the ban were sent to every national and major local newspaper in Britain. None reported it. Health spokesmen for Britain's three main parties were uninterested in what had happened.

31

'In regard to propaganda, the early advocates of universal literacy and a free press envisaged only two possibilities: the propaganda might be true, or it might be false. They did not foresee what in fact has happened, above all in our Western capitalise democracies – the development of a vast mass communications industry, concerned in the main neither with the true nor the false, but with the unreal, the more or less totally irrelevant.'
ALDOUS HUXLEY (*BRAVE NEW WORLD REVISITED*, 1959)

32

If you want the truth these days you have to go outside the mainstream establishment-dominated media. You can't believe everything you read in the papers. You can't believe anything you see on TV or hear on the radio. And you certainly can't believe anything you hear or see on the BBC.

Epilogue

We Should Become Enemies Of The State Because The State Is The Enemy Of The People

1

'Happiness depends on being free, and freedom depends on being courageous.'
THUCYDIDES C 455-400 BC, *HISTORY OF THE PELOPONNESIAN WAR*

2

Our Government lies and lies again, they spy on us in every conceivable way, they confiscate without evidence, they imprison without trial, they have given away our birthright, they have committed heinous crimes against our will and in our name, they have stolen our rights and our liberties; they have taken away our privacy, they want us numbered and marked, they refuse to tell us the truth about what they are doing, they spin, spin and spin again, they have introduced punitive 'stealth taxes' to pay for their excesses and incompetences and they have, through wickedness and incompetence, ruined our pensions but they have constantly raised and protected their own.

All crime rates are soaring. But the biggest crimes of all are committed by governments. The politicians we pay to look after us are criminal recidivists.

Living In A Fascist Country

We are living in a fascist state. How did it happen? And how do we get out of it?

3

The biggest threat to our freedom, our safety and our lives comes not from terrorists, criminals or bird flu but from our Government. It is our Government which has created wars out of peace and which does virtually nothing to prevent global warming. It is our Government which insists on foisting genetically engineered food on us even though we don't want it. It is our Government which is destroying our history and handing our future to mean-spirited men in Brussels and Washington.

4

'Do not forget those who fought the battles for you, and bought your freedom with their genius and their blood.'
Emile Zola

5

The direction of our lives is being controlled by three entirely separate forces:

1. The neo-conservative Zionist imperialists in the USA who control Bush and American policies (both internal and external) and whose short, medium and long-term aims are power over the entire planet. These are baddies in the style of the baddies in Ian Fleming's James Bond books.

2. The British Labour party politicians who are driven by greed and vanity, whose interests are entirely selfish and who see support for America's neo-conservative Zionist imperialists as their best way to become individually wealthy and to retain power.

3. The bureaucrats, businessmen and politicians who control the EU and who are building a European Federal State (whether we like it or not) for their own purposes. (For more about this see my book *The Truth They Won't Tell You (And Don't Want You to Know) About The EU.*)

325

6

'Liberty means responsibility. That is why most men dread it.'
GEORGE BERNARD SHAW

7

Unless the inflation-proofed pensions for Government employees are reduced, the NHS and other public services are destined to continue to deteriorate. Unless benefit payments to the millions who claim to be sick (but aren't) are stopped, our schools and our roads will crumble. Unless the Government makes serious attempts to cut its own payroll the future looks bleak. Our infrastructure will deteriorate even if taxes are raised and raised again.

A nation can either afford to pay benefits to millions of its citizens, or it can afford to provide a free health service: no nation can possibly afford both.

Unless we do something to change the way we are governed, the future is bad. Everyone honest is going to get poorer. As the NHS continues to collapse, so more and more people will find themselves having to pay for basic and essential medical and dental services. Pensions will shrink and shrink again. Unemployment will rise as red tape and high taxes force more and more companies to move manufacturing to China and to outsource service industries to India. Taxes and rates will rise as the Government (and its successors) struggle to cope with ever-rising wage and pension costs − not to mention benefit payments.

To make things worse heating and fuel costs will rise remorselessly as the shortage of oil and gas pushes up prices.

8

'The end of law is not to abolish or restrain, but to reserve and enlarge freedom.'
JOHN LOCKE 1690 , SECOND
TREATISE OF CIVIL GOVERNMENT

9

New Labour has destroyed the security of the country for generations to come and has involved us in an endless war we cannot possibly ever win. Thanks to the greed and idiocy of a vain and unimaginative set of fools we are now all exposed to a great and everlasting danger. Our liberty and privacy and security are going to be under constant and increasing threat.

10

'No new war; no new taxes; no attempt against the Church; no repeal of the conditions upon which the crown was settled upon the King; no foreigners in employment; no standing army; no Long Parliament; no restraint of the liberty of the press; no insulting the memory of the Queen. Total: no alteration of the Constitution in Church and State.'
POLITICAL MANIFESTO ISSUED IN 1715 ON BEHALF OF THE TORY PARTY (KNOWN THEN AS THE CHURCH PARTY) BY FRANCIS ATTERBURY, BISHOP OF ROCHESTER

11

Everything is getting worse. The trains are bad. The roads are bad. The mail is bad. The hospitals are bad. The streets are strewn with litter and drunks. You can no longer rely on finding a GP at night. There is no NHS dentistry (despite the Prime Minister's personal promises). Supermarkets are destroying small bakers, small dress shops and small book shops.

12

'There is no need to be honest with organisations which are crooked.'
AYN RAND

13

The days of world travel are nearly over (it will soon be too expensive or too dangerous for Britons to travel around the world) and before long even the moderately wealthy will seek to live in gated communities where guards patrol the perimeter fence and the entrance gate. Visits to the outside world will be rare and regulated.

14

'Silence (when freedom is threatened) is not golden; it is yellow.'
TOM ANDERSON

15

I keep asking myself: Are Blair, Straw, Brown, Prescott et al really this evil?

Or are they terribly, terribly stupid?

Are they, perhaps, a little bit evil and a lot stupid or a lot stupid and a little bit evil? Or are they a lot evil and a lot stupid? The only combination that didn't figure was that they might be a little bit evil and a little bit stupid.

In the end I came to the conclusion that, on the whole, these Masters of our Parliamentary Universe are evil *and* stupid. It doesn't matter how much of which.

Evil and stupid.

All of them.

16

Blair, his proponents say, is well-intentioned; a religious man; a good man; a skilful politician; a great leader.

He is, I tell you with some confidence, none of those things. He is a lying, war mongering whore who has sold his country into slavery and danger so that he and his irredeemably obnoxious wife can live in the style enjoyed by their rich friends.

17

'No free man shall be taken or imprisoned or dispossessed,
or outlawed or exiled, or in any way destroyed, nor will we
go upon him, nor will we send against him except by the lawful
judgement of his peers or by the law of the land.'
CLAUSE 39, THE MAGNA CARTA, 1215

18

'To no man will we sell, or deny, or delay, right or justice.'
CLAUSE 40, THE MAGNA CARTA, 1215

19

We have elections so that we can elect parliamentary representatives. But we have no representation. And our representatives are even taking away our right of protest. The result is that the people of Britain have no voice. What went wrong?

20

'Those who would give up essential liberty to purchase a little temporary safety deserve neither liberty nor safety.'
BENJAMIN FRANKLIN

21

The Government machinery (the civil service) has been seized by power and money-mad politicians who are (whatever they may call themselves) fascists.

Over recent years much has been written about there being a conspiracy among bankers, industrialists and politicians who want to form a world government, and introduce a world tax and a world currency.

I now believe that there *is* a conspiracy.

It's a behind-closed-doors conspiracy which involves American oil and arms companies and neo-conservative Zionists. It's a conspiracy involving American bankers and businessmen and politicians. The Bilderbergers? They're little more than a front to take our eyes off what is really happening.

22

I don't believe that Blair, Prescott, Brown, Straw, et al are part of any conspiracy. They are too stupid. Their greed is small time. They are followers not leaders and I don't think they have any idea what is going on. The Labour Party is headed by men and women who are driven not by a large dream of world power but by small dreams based on greed for power and status and money.

Blunkett would do anything to save his grace and favour central London mansion and the chauffeur driven car and all the other perks. And Blair wants to make enough money to pay for his central London mansion.

23

'The willingness to break rules now and again is what distinguishes free men from robots.'
LEN DEIGHTON (WRITING IN LONDON MATCH)

24

Why hasn't there been a revolution?

Several reasons.

They control the media. So most people don't understand what is going on.

The politicians lie. And the media report the lies as truth.

They use fear to control us.

It is now illegal to protest and to demonstrate. The police have been politicised and instead of being our protectors have become our enemy.

And in true Roman fashion, our leaders keep us occupied with circuses.

25

'Individuals have the duty to violate domestic laws to prevent crimes against peace and humanity from occurring.'
NUREMBERG WAR CRIMES TRIBUNAL 1945-6

26

The people are still looking the other way, watching television. The ones who are beginning to realise that something is wrong still hope that what they think is happening isn't really happening at all. Or that if it is someone else will do something about it.

Most people are too tired, too exhausted by the problems of

getting through the day, to do anything.

And too frightened.

They know that anyone who pokes a head above the parapet, who dares even to heckle, will be arrested.

These are scary, scary times to rebel.

27

'You should never have your best trousers on when you go out to fight for freedom and truth.'
HENRIK IBSEN (AN ENEMY OF THE PEOPLE, 1882)

28

We avoid it. We close our eyes and make our excuses because we know it's happening but we don't want to believe it's happening. We shut the door, close the curtains, tear open a box of chocolates and watch the TV.

Bread and circuses.

29

'There is only one decisive victory: the last.'
KARL VON CLAUSEWITZ

30

How did Tony Blair, a serial liar and a war criminal, manage to find enough voters to put him back into Downing Street? Why don't people seem to care when an innocent man, lawfully travelling in London, is shot seven times in the head? Why do most people think that sort of ultimate police brutality (the sort of behaviour which the British have always condemned when it has taken place in funny little countries where the President has a fleet of Mercedes motor cars and a bank account in Liechtenstein) is acceptable? Why do so many people think that ID cards are a good idea? ('Why would you object if you have nothing to hide?'). Why do millions believe that having our roads and towns festooned with CCTV cameras is a good thing – when there is absolutely no evidence whatsoever to show that the cameras enable the police to catch criminals, or actually help prevent crime?

There are several reasons.

First, most people don't have the foggiest idea what is really going on. Most people get what they call 'news' from their television set, their radio or their newspaper. The really frightening thing is that most teenagers and twenty-somethings are even more woefully ignorant than their elders. Most TV stations, radio stations and newspapers have cut back on genuine reporters and now concentrate on three types of 'news': the stuff they are fed by the Government and which they reprint unquestioningly; the stuff which they are fed by large corporations which they reprint unquestioningly and the stuff which concerns celebrities which they largely make up because making stuff up is easier than having to go out and knock on doors and because celebrities don't complain as long as their names are spelt properly.

That's news 21st century style.

Second, most people are scared witless and their attitudes and actions are driven by their fear.

Third, millions of people are now totally dependent on the Government for the money with which to pay their bills. They are dependent either because they work for the Government or because they receive benefits from it in some way.

Fourth, most people simply don't care what is going on as long as it doesn't affect their standard of living, the price and availability of alcohol and their ability to watch television for six hours on those evenings when they aren't going to a club or a pub. The 'me me me' culture is now ingrained in our society and the selfishness has been varnished into place by a difficult to argue with suspicion that even if we don't like what is going on there isn't anything we can do about it so we might as well have a good time and just put up with things as they are.

31

'Despots themselves do not deny that freedom is excellent; only they desire it for themselves alone, and they maintain that everyone else is altogether unworthy of it.'
ALEXIS DE TOCQUEVILLE , L'ANCIEN RÉGIME 1856

32

We have too many lawyers, too many bureaucrats and too many guards. There are too many people working for national and local government. There are too many quangos. There are too many people who have protected jobs (and pensions).

We would all be better off if 90% of the lawyers became gardeners, 90% of the guards became bakers and 90% of the people with 'protected' jobs just sat around and watched television all day.

33

'The first thing we do, let's kill all the lawyers.'
WILLIAM SHAKESPEARE

34

'When I speak of Fascism in England, I am not necessarily thinking of Mosley and his pimpled followers. English Fascism, when it arrives, is likely to be of a sedate and subtle kind (presumably, at any rate at first, it won't be called Fascism)...Fascisms as it appears in the intellectual is a sort of mirror-image – not actually of Socialism but of a plausible travesty of Socialism.'
GEORGE ORWELL (*THE ROAD TO WIGAN PIER*)

35

We need a revolution.

Historically, there have always been revolutions when a government has abused and used the people too much and for too long.

Eventually, the mass of people, the ones who are normally compliant, and who prefer a quiet life, will rise up, say 'enough is enough' and fight to claw back their lost freedoms and rights.

How much more abuse are we going to take?

36

The French Revolution introduced the notion that individuals could be right and could have rights, and that society could be wrong and have no rights.

The French Revolution was the most fundamentally anti-fascist political movement ever. Primarily a revolution led by and for the middle-classes against the leadership of an overbearing and demanding monarchy, it introduced an era of fierce nationalism, with the French, under the inspired and inspiring leadership of Napoleon Bonaparte taking over much of Europe.

37

'Only the paranoid survive.'
ANDY GROVE (OF INTEL)

38

We can no longer rely on our Government to protect or defend us, or to do any of the things we should reasonably be able to expect it to do. We cannot expect our Ministers to do the things we pay them to do. We can, however, rely on our Government and its paid servants to interfere in all areas where it has no reason to interfere and where its efforts will adversely affect our lives in all the important ways.

Politicians and civil servants have forgotten that the individual must always come before the state and that the state is nothing but a melange of individuals.

39

George Orwell warned the world to be aware of militancy, constant war, over organised bureaucracy, loss of freedom, fanaticism, big brother and thought control.

He was oh so frighteningly right.

Our fascist leaders are being helped by apathy, triviality, aimless violence, alcohol and all the other aspects of a truly decadent society.

40

The Soviet Union collapsed not because of outside pressure from America but because the people inside the Soviet Union no longer believed in or trusted their rotten and corrupt political and administrative system.

The same thing will eventually happen in the West.

Be prepared. Be ready. Be part of it.

41

I object to the fact that my taxes are being used for terrorism (and to encourage terrorist activity against my country). I object to the fact that by paying taxes I am supporting a Government and a Prime Minister who are in breach of the Geneva Convention. I am embarrassed by the fact that our leaders are in breach of guidelines laid down at the Nuremberg Trial. I am ashamed that my Government is conducting an illegal war and that I am paying fat salaries to war criminals who occupy the moral low ground.

Legally and morally I should not be paying taxes. By paying taxes I am encouraging war criminals.

I am ashamed that I do not have the courage to refuse to pay taxes to this corrupt and evil Government.

But I will fight them.

42

We cannot, of course, have a revolution in the old-fashioned sense. They've got all the guns and the tanks.

So, it's time for a peaceful revolution among the sensible, law-abiding, hard-working people who hate what has happened (and is happening) to their country.

When middle-class revolutions occur they are infinitely more robust than anything else.

43

Your country doesn't love you any more. But it needs your love more than ever.

We want our country back. We want our freedom back. We want our rights back.

And we want to be rid of the lying, cheating, self-serving bastards who have taken these things from us.

We must spread the truth to those who are confused and who feel helpless and who do not understand why or how the world is changing. And we must spread the truth to those who do not yet understand that anything is happening.

We must prepare ourselves to refuse to accept identity cards and intrusive visits from cheap-suited invaders who want to photograph inside our homes.

If we are to fight successfully we must stand together, shoulder to shoulder, and protest in our thousands.

But before then we must, above all else, spread the word so that when the time is right it is they, not we, who will be alone.

44

Governments always assume that silence means approval. If people do not vote they assume that it means that their policies are acceptable. If people do not stand up and shout they assume that we are happy to lose our history, our freedom and our dignity. If we say nothing they will assume that we accept their lies and believe that only by losing our freedom can we defend it.

We must be prepared to let them know that we do not approve.

45

The Government is not the country. The Government works for the country.

We are the country.

46

Our Government is our enemy. We should have no patience with bureaucrats, Government employees and people who work for local authorities. They are not our friends. They are the enemy, or representatives of the enemy.

47

Too many people have, like millions of 'good Germans' in Germany in late 30s and early 40s, settled for silence, rationalisation and hypocrisy in exchange for personal safety and being left alone.

48

I would be happy to pay taxes so that people who genuinely need help are provided with it. I would be happy to pay for a good and efficient infrastructure. But there is no political party prepared to offer me this.

I would vote for a party which promised not to start illegal and unnecessary wars. But there is no such party.

I would vote for a party which would take us out of the European Union. But none of the three big parties will promise me this.

I would vote for a party which promised to treat people and animals with respect. But there is no party which I can trust to do this.

There is no party catering for me, or for millions of others who want these things.

And the Government forbids protesting or campaigning against the things of which we disapprove.

We have all been disenfranchised.

Therefore, there can be no democracy.

49

Millions of people feel increasingly resentful because they have been made to feel ashamed of their country.

50

Every society honours live conformists and dead troublemakers, but tends to sneer at dead conformists and live troublemakers. Societies are always controlled by the establishment. Rebels are always hated while conformists (who support and do not threaten the establishment) are revered, praised and feted. After death everything is reversed. The rebels are revered, praised and feted and the conformists are forgotten. The major contributions to society are all made by people who are outsiders. Yesterday's dead troublemakers often seem to us to be men of imagination, passion and foresight.

51

Whenever you move away from the herd, the herd will criticise you, revile you and call you crazy. Then, when they find out that you were right, they will either blame you for what happened (saying that you made it happen), claim that you made a lucky guess or simply ignore you and give the credit to someone else entirely.

It is the way.

52

Don't ever expect justice. And don't expect the police to play fair. Regard your doctor as a potential killer. Remember that your bank manager wants to steal your money. Don't trust anyone who works for the Government. Remember these basic truths and you will avoid much disappointment.

53

'The only thing necessary for the triumph of evil, is for good men to do nothing.'
EDMUND BURKE

54

We should all become enemies of the state because the state (which no longer recognises any rules) is assuredly the enemy of the people. We must fight the evil barbarians who are a menace to our nation, our heritage and our way of life; as well as to the basic principles of truth, integrity and freedom.

55

Our society is in great danger. Bush and Blair have done enormous damage to our privacy and our security. They plan to do more. And now that they have lowered the standard for public life the standard will probably remain low for years to come. In a just world Blair and the rest of his sorry band of incompetent misfits, ne'er do wells and professional deceivers, would be serving very long prison sentences for recklessly endangering the lives of the citizens they are paid to protect. In the world in which we live they will all receive massive index-linked pensions, police protection and remunerative directorships in the oil, armaments and tobacco industries.

The three major political parties in Britain will do absolutely nothing to solve the problems we now face.

Indeed, it is no exaggeration to say that they *are* the problem. Blair, the Great Betrayer, has sold our heritage and our future for the prospect of a few directorships which will enable him to pay the mortgage on the ostentatious house he can't afford and should never have bought. But leading politicians in the Conservative and Liberal parties have done little or nothing to stop him and would, I suspect, do most of the things the Labour party does if they thought they too could get away with them.

So what do we do?

We can protest about the way the Government has taken away our freedom, handed over our freedom to the European Union and to America and ignored centuries of history, culture and civilisation. In the UK, as in America and in many other countries (particularly the English speaking ones) the Government has stolen our civil rights.

The one thing we can do which really will help is to spread the truth about what is happening. If you are alarmed by the truths in this book, and share at least some of my views, then you can help by sharing these truths with your friends, neighbours, relatives and colleagues.

Can we really change things?

I believe so. I certainly think we can, for example, do far, far more than those superficial media-acceptable pseudo-revolutionaries who seem to believe that they can foster change by working with the Blairs and the Bushes of this world, but whose efforts seem to me to give extra credibility to the very people to whom they claim (so very loudly and so very profitably) to be opposed. Their efforts seem to me designed to attract publicity and to sell records, concert tickets, films and so on rather than to pose serious questions or threaten the comfort and security of the establishment.

If I didn't believe that we could pose serious questions, and seriously disrupt the complacency of the fascist establishment which has taken charge of our world, then I would find a beach somewhere with no phone, no newspaper deliveries and no mail. I certainly wouldn't bother writing books like this. I believe that it is the role of an author with humanitarian instincts to make the work of the state more difficult; to discomfort the establishment and constantly to encourage revolt among the citizens.

If we let them get away with suppressing the truth and oppressing the truth tellers what do we have left? Certainly, no freedom. Nothing really worth fighting for.

And so we have to stand up to the myriad parts of the establishment which find the truth embarrassing and the telling of the truth inconvenient. Spend some of your time trying to save the world from the businessmen who want to steal it and the politicians who want to be bribed to give it to them. If we don't protest the Government will assume (and will claim) that we approve of what it is doing. And we will have no right to complain when it's all too late.

56

We must also spend some of our time and energy protecting ourselves and our families against the immediate threat to our personal safety and privacy.

We are all vulnerable today; we are vulnerable in ways that most people don't understand.

57

If you feel shocked or horrified by what you have read, and you would now like to spread the word, please tell your friends about this book. If you care about freedom and privacy please help us reach more people. Nothing helps spread the word more effectively than 'word of mouth'. If you have learnt something from this book, please tell your friends about it. Contact Publishing House for details of the special prices we offer to those who want to help spread the word by purchasing additional copies of this book to give away. Or visit www.vernoncoleman.com where you will be able to find all sorts of useful information.

We may be living in a fascist country. But it doesn't always have to be this way.

The Author

Instinctively anti-authority and recklessly uncompromising, Vernon Coleman is the iconoclastic author of over 90 books which have sold over 2 million copies in the UK, been translated into 23 languages and now sell in over 50 countries. His best-selling non-fiction book *Bodypower* was voted one of the 100 most popular books of the 1980s/90s and was turned into two television series in the UK. The film of his novel *Mrs Caldicot's Cabbage War* was released early in 2003. In the 1980s, although several of his books had been high in the best-seller lists, he got fed up with nervous publishers trying to edit all the good bits out of his books and so he started his own publishing conglomerate which began life in a barn and now employs five people at Publishing House.

Vernon Coleman has written columns for the *Daily Star, The Sun, Sunday Express, Planet on Sunday* and *The People* (resigning from the latter when the editor refused to publish a column questioning the morality and legality of invading Iraq) and has contributed over 5,000 articles, columns and reviews to 100 leading British publications including: *Daily Telegraph, Sunday Telegraph, The Guardian, The Observer, The Sunday Times, Daily Mail, Mail on Sunday, Daily Express, Woman, Woman's Own, Punch* and *Spectator*. His columns and articles have also appeared in hundreds of leading magazines and newspapers throughout the rest of the world. He edited the *British Clinical Journal* for one year until a drug company told the publisher to choose between firing him or getting no more advertising. For twenty years he wrote a column which was syndicated to over 40 leading regional newspapers. Eventually, the column had to be abandoned when Government hired doctors offered to write alternative columns without charge to stop him telling readers the truth. In the UK he was the TV AM doctor on breakfast TV and when he commented that fatty food had killed more people than Hitler he wasn't fired until several weeks after a large food lobbyist had threatened to pull all its advertising. He was the first networked television Agony Aunt. In the past he has presented TV and radio programmes for both BBC and commercial channels though these days no producer who wants to keep his job for long is likely to invite him anywhere near a studio (especially a BBC studio). Many millions have consulted his Telephone Doctor advice lines and his websites and for six years he wrote a monthly newsletter which had subscribers in 17 countries. Vernon Coleman has a medical degree, and an honorary science doctorate. He has worked for the Open University in the UK and is an honorary Professor of Holistic Medical Sciences at the Open International University based in Sri Lanka. He used to give occasional lectures but these days the invitations are usually withdrawn when big companies find out about it.

Vernon Coleman describes himself strategically as a libertarian radical humanitarian anarchist but tactically as a non-violent revolutionary anarchist. He has received lots of really interesting awards from people he likes and respects but would never accept any from people he doesn't like or respect. He is, for example, a Knight Commander of The Ecumenical Royal Medical Humanitarian Order of Saint John of Jerusalem, of the Knights of Malta and a member of the Ancient Royal Order of Physicians dedicated to His Majesty King Buddhadasa. In 2000 he was awarded the Yellow Emperor's Certificate of Excellence as Physician of the Millennium by the Medical Alternativa Institute. He is also Vice Chancellor of the Open International University. You will not be surprised to hear that he has not been offered, and would not accept, any award by the British Government.

He worked as a GP for ten years (resigning from the NHS after being fined for refusing to divulge confidential information about his patients to state bureaucrats) and has organised numerous campaigns both for people and for animals. He collects hobbies and accumulates books and is a long-term member of the MCC. He has been intending to learn to speak French for over half a century but has made very little progress. He can ride a bicycle and swim, though not at the same time. He loves cats, cricket (before they started painting slogans on the grass), cycling, cafes and, most of all, the Welsh Princess.

Vernon Coleman is balding rapidly and is widely disliked by members of the Establishment. He doesn't give a toss about either of these facts. Many attempts have been made to ban his books but he insists he will keep writing them even if he has to write them out in longhand and sell them on street corners (though he hopes it doesn't come to this because he still has a doctor's handwriting). He is married to Donna Antoinette, the totally adorable Welsh Princess, and is very pleased about this. Together they have written two books: *How To Conquer Health Problems Between Ages 50 And 120* and *Health Secrets Doctors Share With Their Families.*

Publishing House

Publishing House (and its imprints: Chilton Designs, the European Medical Journal and Blue Books) doesn't have a massive sales force (actually, it doesn't have a sales force at all). Publishing House doesn't have a board of eminent directors (since it's not a limited company it doesn't have any directors). Publishing House doesn't have offices in a skyscraper (it does have offices but just an upstairs and a downstairs). And there is no PR department full of bright young things called Hyacinth and Jacaranda. (There isn't a PR department at all).

But Publishing House has one enormous advantage over the conglomerates.

Publishing House cares passionately about books.

The big multinational publishers have marketing departments which decide which books will sell. They then commission books that the sales force think they will be able to flog. They won't even consider a book until they've done a marketing feasibility study.

Publishing House publishes books it thinks should be published and then tries to sell them. Naturally, Publishing House tries to make a profit. If it didn't it wouldn't last long. There are printing bills, electricity bills, phone bills, rates, insurance and so on to be paid. And there are no outside sponsors or advertisers and no benevolent backers.

Publishing House has been in business since 1988. Its books have been translated into 23 languages and are sold by other publishers (including some big ones) in over 50 countries. Large print and audio versions of some books are available. One has been made into a film.

The big publishers insist that every book should make a profit.

Publishing House doesn't work like that. Some books make more money than others. But that's fine. As long as the better sellers subsidise the other books. Publishing House doesn't mind if a book is a little slow to sell. Like good parents Publishing House loves all its children equally – however successful, or unsuccessful, they might be.

Despite all the talk about the need for each book to stand on its own two feet many big publishers make an overall loss. They are kept alive – effectively as vanity publishers – by other parts of the conglomerate. So, for example, the TV division or the magazine division may help to subsidise the book publishing division.

Publishing House believes that book publishing can, and should, be allowed to stand alone. Moreover, Publishing House believes that small publishers are now the only *real* publishers in existence.

Big publishers often accept sponsorship from outside companies. Publishing House never does, but prefers to rely on the sale of books to pay the bills. None of the Publishing House books are sponsored or carry any advertising. There is no outside advertising or sponsoring on the website. It is this which enables us to remain truly independent. Publishing House publishes books which international conglomerates wouldn't dare touch.

Big publishers have lost touch with people's needs. They are slow and unwieldy. It can take them two years to turn a typescript into a finished book. (Publishing House can, if pushed, get a book out while the material is still topical.) Big publishers are too market orientated and derivative. They produce more of what other publishers did well with last year. Publishing House looks forwards not backwards. Big publishers pay huge amounts as advances to film stars, politicians and young hot shot authors. Much of the time they don't earn back those advances. They don't care because the books are just seen as 'tools' to help other parts of the empire. For example, a conglomerate will publish a politician's dull biography as a way of putting money into the politician's pocket.

Big publishers worry enormously about upsetting powerful politicians and other corporations. The big conglomerates need to cooperate with the establishment because they are *part* of the establishment. Publishing House stands outside the establishment and doesn't give a fig for what politicians or corporate bosses might (or might not) think. Because there are no worries about upsetting establishment figures, Publishing House can publish books that large, modern commercial publishers would never dare publish. Like this one.

For a catalogue of Vernon Coleman's books
please write to:

Publishing House
Trinity Place
Barnstaple
Devon EX32 9HG
England

Telephone	01271 328892
Fax	01271 328768

Outside the UK:

Telephone	+44 1271 328892
Fax	+44 1271 328768

Or visit our website:

www.vernoncoleman.com

Also by Vernon Coleman

Why Everything Is Going To Get Worse Before It Gets Better

(And What You Can Do About It)

Why Everything Is Going To Get Worse Before It Gets Better explains why things are so bad, why things are going to get worse, how we can rescue ourselves, how we can save our country and what we can do to protect ourselves and our loved ones in the meantime.

Vernon Coleman explains why our health service is so bad that asylum seekers go home for treatment when they fall ill, why our education system is so bad that illiteracy is now commonplace, why millions no longer respect the courts or the police and why virtually no one now trusts our financial institutions. He explains how we've been betrayed by our Government (which has taken away our freedom and our privacy and which deliberately uses fear to promote its policies), why our lives are run not by people but by organisations and why we are now living in a fascist State – where the rights of individuals come second to the demands of the system.

Why Everything Is Going To Get Worse Before It Gets Better is both terrifying and yet, in the end, reassuring. Vernon Coleman shines light into dark corners, explains precisely what has gone wrong (and why) and offers original solutions.

Because he believes that things will get worse before they get better he also offers practical advice designed to help readers survive the painful years ahead.

Paperback £15.99
Published by Blue Books
Order from Publishing House • Trinity Place • Barnstaple •
Devon EX32 9HG • England
Telephone 01271 328892 • Fax 01271 328768
www.vernoncoleman.com

Also by Vernon Coleman

England Our England
Sound reasons to reject the euro and the EU

'The European Union is widely regarded as a rather annoying joke. When people think of the EU they think of butter mountains, wine lakes and daft rules about straight bananas.

There is a nationwide tendency to think that the crooked, laughably incompetent officials in Brussels are somehow irrelevant and insignificant to our daily lives; no more than an expensive, international extension of the civil service.

But the EU is no joke.

There has been squabbling and fighting in Europe for three millennia. Caesar, Charlemagne, Pope Innocent III, Napoleon and Hitler all tried to unite these countries under a single flag. They all failed.

It is no exaggeration to say that the European Union poses the greatest threat to democracy, and to our freedom and privacy, that there has ever been. .

In an attempt to explain the truth – and to warn you of what is happening to your world – I've prepared a summary of some of the things you should know about the European Union; facts which the main political parties certainly won't tell you. Your TV station, radio station and newspaper probably haven't warned you about these things.

As you read this book remember that this is not a piece of science fiction. These are not bizarre, paranoid fantasies.

This may turn out to be the most frightening book you've ever read. But everything in it is true.'

Vernon Coleman

Paperback £8.99
Published by Blue Books
Order from Publishing House • Trinity Place • Barnstaple •
Devon EX32 9HG • England
Telephone 01271 328892 • Fax 01271 328768
www.vernoncoleman.com

Also by Vernon Coleman

Saving England
The Case for Independence

"This book is about England rather than Britain for an excellent reason. If the EU's plans for Britain are carried through to completion it will only be England which will disappear. Scotland and Wales will retain their identity as regions of the new European superstate. England, however, will disappear and will be converted into nine anonymous regions.

Whereas it is widely perceived as a 'good thing' when Scottish and Welsh nationalists fight for the identity and independence of their nations, England nationalists are neither thick on the ground nor well respected.

If we don't do anything to save her, England is doomed. It will be no good saying 'We should have done something' when our nation has become a footnote in the history books. It is up to us to do something. And we must act soon. The main part of this book explains just why we must act. The final part of this book explains what we must do."

From the Foreword to *Saving England* by Vernon Coleman

Paperback £8.99
Published by Blue Books
Order from Publishing House • Trinity Place • Barnstaple •
Devon EX32 9HG • England
Telephone 01271 328892 • Fax 01271 328768
www.vernoncoleman.com

Also by Vernon Coleman

Spiritpower

Discover your spiritual strength

- Find out who you are (and what you want)
- Three words that can change your life
- How to get what you want out of life
- Use your imagination and your subconscious mind
- Why you have more power than you think you have
- How you can control your own health
- Why you shouldn't be afraid to be a rebel
- How to stand up for yourself
- Know your fears and learn how to conquer them

What the papers say about *Spiritpower*:

'The final tome in his trilogy which has produced the best-sellers "Bodypower" and "Mindpower", this is Dr Coleman's assessment of our current spiritual environment, and his prescriptions for change. He advises both awareness and rebellion, recommending ways to regain personal autonomy and fulfilment.'
(The Good Book Guide)

'"Spiritpower" will show you how to find freedom and give meaning to your life.'
(Scunthorpe Evening Telegraph)

'This is a handbook for tomorrow's revolutionaries. Dr Coleman offers an understanding of the society we live in, in order to show where our freedom was lost.'
(Greenock Telegraph)

Paperback £12.99
Published by EMJ Books
Order from Publishing House • Trinity Place • Barnstaple •
Devon EX32 9HG • England
Telephone 01271 328892 • Fax 01271 328768
www.vernoncoleman.com